School-Based Behavioral Assessment

The Guilford Practical Intervention in the Schools Series

Kenneth W. Merrell, Founding Editor
Sandra M. Chafouleas, Series Editor

www.guilford.com/practical

This series presents the most reader-friendly resources available in key areas of evidence-based practice in school settings. Practitioners will find trustworthy guides on effective behavioral, mental health, and academic interventions, and assessment and measurement approaches. Covering all aspects of planning, implementing, and evaluating high-quality services for students, books in the series are carefully crafted for everyday utility. Features include ready-to-use reproducibles, appealing visual elements, and an oversized format. Recent titles have Web pages where purchasers can download and print the reproducible materials.

Recent Volumes

Executive Skills in Children and Adolescents, Third Edition:
A Practical Guide to Assessment and Intervention
Peg Dawson and Richard Guare

Effective Universal Instruction: An Action-Oriented Approach to Improving Tier 1
Kimberly Gibbons, Sarah Brown, and Bradley C. Niebling

Supporting Successful Interventions in Schools:
Tools to Plan, Evaluate, and Sustain Effective Implementation
Lisa M. Hagermoser Sanetti and Melissa A. Collier-Meek

High-Impact Assessment Reports for Children and Adolescents:
A Consumer-Responsive Approach
Robert Lichtenstein and Bruce Ecker

Conducting School-Based Functional Behavioral Assessments, Third Edition:
A Practitioner's Guide
Mark W. Steege, Jamie L. Pratt, Garry Wickerd, Richard Guare, and T. Steuart Watson

Evaluating Educational Interventions, Second Edition:
Single-Case Design for Measuring Response to Intervention
T. Chris Riley-Tillman, Matthew K. Burns, and Stephen P. Kilgus

The Data-Driven School: Collaborating to Improve Student Outcomes
Daniel M. Hyson, Joseph F. Kovaleski, Benjamin Silberglitt, and Jason A. Pedersen

Implementing Classwide PBIS: A Guide to Supporting Teachers
Diane Myers, Brandi Simonsen, and Jennifer Freeman

Social and Emotional Learning in the Classroom, Second Edition:
Promoting Mental Health and Academic Success
Barbara A. Gueldner, Laura L. Feuerborn, and Kenneth W. Merrell

Responding to Problem Behavior in Schools, Third Edition:
The Check-In, Check-Out Intervention
Leanne S. Hawken, Deanne A. Crone, Kaitlin Bundock, and Robert H. Horner

School-Based Behavioral Assessment, Second Edition:
Informing Prevention and Intervention
Sandra M. Chafouleas, Austin H. Johnson, T. Chris Riley-Tillman, and Emily A. Iovino

School-Based Behavioral Assessment

Informing Prevention and Intervention

SECOND EDITION

SANDRA M. CHAFOULEAS
AUSTIN H. JOHNSON
T. CHRIS RILEY-TILLMAN
EMILY A. IOVINO

THE GUILFORD PRESS
New York   London

Library of Congress Cataloging-in-Publication Data

Names: Chafouleas, Sandra M., author. | Johnson, Austin H., author. | Riley-Tillman, T. Chris,
    author. | Iovino, Emily A., author.
Title: School-based behavioral assessment : informing prevention and intervention /
    Sandra M. Chafouleas, Austin H. Johnson, T. Chris Riley-Tillman, Emily A. Iovino.
Description: Second edition. | New York : The Guilford Press, [2021] |
Series: The Guilford practical intervention in the schools series |
    Includes bibliographical references and index.
Identifiers: LCCN 2020040509 | ISBN 9781462545254 (paperback) |
    ISBN 9781462545261 (hardcover)
Subjects: LCSH: Behavioral assessment of children. | Children with disabilities—Education. |
    Learning disabled children—Education. | Educational psychology.
Classification: LCC LB1124 .C43 2021 | DDC 370.15/28—dc23
LC record available at *https://lccn.loc.gov/2020040509*

About the Authors

Sandra M. Chafouleas, PhD, is a Board of Trustees Distinguished Professor in the Neag School of Education at the University of Connecticut. Dr. Chafouleas is the author of more than 150 publications, regularly serves as a national presenter and invited speaker, and is the recipient of multiple national and university awards for her scholarship and mentoring. Prior to becoming a university trainer, she worked as a school psychologist and school administrator in a variety of settings supporting the needs of children exhibiting social, emotional, and behavioral challenges.

Austin H. Johnson, PhD, BCBA, is Assistant Professor of School Psychology in the Graduate School of Education at the University of California, Riverside. Dr. Johnson's research interests focus on the identification and implementation of evidence-based behavioral assessment and intervention practices in order to support teacher success and equitable, positive student outcomes. He is associate editor of the *Journal of School Psychology* and is a licensed psychologist and board certified behavior analyst.

T. Chris Riley-Tillman, PhD, is Associate Provost and Professor of School Psychology at the University of Missouri–Columbia. Dr. Riley-Tillman is a Senior Advisor for the National Center on Intensive Intervention, a Fellow of Division 16 (School Psychology) of the American Psychological Association, and a member of the Society for the Study of School Psychology. He is also the creator and lead developer of the Evidence Based Intervention Network, a nonprofit website developed by researchers that contains intervention and assessment resources for educational professionals.

Emily A. Iovino, PhD, is a postdoctoral scholar at the Collaboratory on School and Child Health at the University of Connecticut. Dr. Iovino has presented nationally and published on topics such as school-based behavior screening, caregiver health and well-being, and supporting district and school implementation of policies and practices related to the Centers for Disease Control and Prevention's Whole School, Whole Community, Whole Child model. Her primary research interests involve social–emotional and behavioral assessment and intervention that supports positive outcomes for children and their caregivers.

Preface

Since the first edition of this book was published, the landscape of school-based behavioral assessment has changed dramatically—not only in the availability of new options, but also in the demand for them. Historically, behavioral assessment was used as a diagnostic tool to confirm risk in specified areas, or was relegated for use in cases presenting with highly intensive support needs. Yet particularly within the past decade, the demand for defensible and usable options across a broad range of behavioral assessment needs has increased substantially. To meet this demand, assessment developers have adapted their work to create and evaluate new options, increasing the availability and diversity of assessments for various purposes. Although there are myriad reasons for this increased demand, we emphasize two primary factors that drive this surge.

The first factor contributing to the increased demand for school-based behavioral assessments relates to the growing acknowledgment of the role that schools play in teaching and reinforcing social, emotional, and behavioral skills. Although there are different perspectives around which skills should be emphasized and how best to teach them in various contexts, there is general agreement that social, emotional, and behavioral skills are critical facilitators of well-being throughout life. As such, schools serve as a primary system of care for supporting a full continuum of student needs across domains of functioning. This expanded role for schools requires assessments that can provide the necessary data to evaluate a broad range of social, emotional, and behavioral skills given the diverse interests and needs that exist across contexts.

The second contributing factor is intertwined with the increased attention to frameworks for integrated multi-tiered systems of support (MTSS). MTSS shift the emphasis from reaction (and potentially exclusionary practices) to prevention and intervention. This shift provides positive and proactive frameworks for meeting the needs of all students; that is, instead of using behavioral assessment in reaction to an identified problem, the focus is on the prevention of the problem through the active teaching of expected skills to all students and the early identification of potential risk. The history of MTSS frameworks began within academic domains—primarily early reading—and then expanded to behavior domains through positive behavioral interventions and supports. However, recent attention has focused on the added value of an integrated MTSS in which all domains of student functioning are addressed within a common framework. This integration necessitates behavioral assessments that can answer varied questions and function beyond the scope of intensive situations involving overt behaviors that could be easily observable.

In summary, the shifts in the role that schools have in providing social, emotional, and behavioral supports have necessitated an increased capacity to use behavioral assessments for broad domains and purposes. In this revised edition, we embrace increased behavioral assessment capacity as a positive development for school-based service delivery. Perhaps the most critical point we make in this edition is that we should expect behavioral assessment tools to continue evolving to meet the ever-changing needs of students, schools, and communities, and that, although the tools will evolve, the process of using data to guide the decisions that are made remains the same. For example, intensive behavior needs will continue to require intensive data-based individuation to determine the most appropriate intervention supports. We continue to support work that addresses the prevention of behavioral challenges and encourage adapting our use of tools as ongoing research continues to better articulate the evidence surrounding defensible, yet efficient, assessment options for early risk identification.

Given the evolving directions in behavioral assessment, the revisions in this edition provide a more cohesive data-based decision-making framework that integrates seamlessly with MTSS. Major themes throughout this edition include (1) the deliberate integration of data-based decision making that is focused on the "for whom" of assessment: populations (whole schools), samples (small groups), and individuals (children with the greatest needs); (2) balancing usable recommendations with critical thinking about evidence; and (3) explicit connections to practice, including more complex case examples that describe how systems are used and work together in the decision-making process.

Chapters 1 and 2 lay the foundations for asking the right questions in school-based behavioral assessment. The language introduced in these chapters is sustained throughout the book to emphasize how data-based decision making is performed at different levels (e.g., whole school, small group, individual student). Chapters 3 through 6 discuss the basics of core assessment methods (extant data, Systematic Direct Observation, Direct Behavior Rating, and behavior rating scales). The presentation of topics follows a similar pattern in each chapter, with the goal of facilitating critical thinking skills and providing the necessary resources to engage in defensible and meaningful behavioral assessment practices. As appropriate, chapter content was revised to reflect the new knowledge and evidence around the defensibility, usability, repeatability, and flexibility of each method. Content revision is most prominent in Chapter 5 on Direct Behavior Rating, given the rapid expansion of research interest in this method and related forms of abbreviated rating scales. Finally, Chapters 7 and 8 close out the book. Chapter 7 presents guidelines on strategies for presenting data, and Chapter 8 offers multiple case studies demonstrating the practical applications of assessment methods within different contexts.

In closing, we emphasize that the guiding purpose of this book is to facilitate sound decision making about behavior supports that promote student success and well-being. Without question, social (e.g., relating and connecting with others), emotional (e.g., affections and feelings), and/or behavioral (e.g., observable actions and conduct) domains are foundational to this positive outcome.

Behaviors matter: for students, for the adults that they become,
for teachers, for parents, for schools, and for communities.

Acknowledgments

A book does not magically write itself, nor does it present entirely novel content. Thus, sincere gratitude must be shared with many who helped to shape this second edition. First, we extend appreciation to all of our colleagues who have contributed their passions in building collective knowledge about behavioral assessment in school settings. Their contributions helped pave the path for our work on this book. In particular, we thank Amy Briesch for her tireless work with us on the first edition of the book, Bhawandeep Bains for her insightful and precise support with copyediting and proofreading, and the many students who served as sounding boards to provide feedback on our ideas. Of course, we also most certainly thank the many practitioners across the nation who have engaged with us on various projects, helping to define the needs in the field and ultimate directions for this book. In addition, we thank our editor at The Guilford Press, Natalie Graham, for her leadership in getting us across the finish line on this second edition, and the late Ken Merrell for championing the initial vision to make this book series a reality, as the ultimate goal for all of our work is to put evidence into practice. And finally, we are grateful for the unfaltering support provided by our families.

Contents

CHAPTER 1

Introduction to School-Based Behavioral Assessment

School personnel engage in two core activities to support student success: **prevention** and **intervention**. By delivering high-quality core services across academic, social, emotional, behavioral, and physical domains, school personnel help students build the skills necessary to succeed and successfully overcome obstacles to success, thereby acting to prevent problems. By being responsive to the needs of children who require additional support in order to succeed through intervention, school personnel attend to the rights of children to a free and appropriate public education in the least restrictive environment possible. Although the foundational tasks of prevention and intervention are likely self-evident to the adults charged with successfully supporting children's well-being, the frameworks that have been used to enact those practices have varied over time.

> **Prevention and intervention are core activities for supporting student success.**

Historically, intervention services in schools have been provided to students through a "refer-test-place" model, with a focus on individual students and their patterns of skills and deficits. For instance, a teacher might identify a student who regularly yells at their peers and refuses to return to class during passing periods, notice a concurrent drop in their grades, and suggest that this student be referred for an alternative class placement or even special education services. After the school support team and the student's parents agree to evaluate the student, the student's data would be collected and discussed to determine whether or not they meet the criteria for a specific designation and/or placement. If the student met the criteria for a behavior disorder, for instance, interventions could be mandated for them within an individualized education program (IEP) and might include a combination of strategies, such as individual time with the school counselor, small-group social skills training, and a behavior contract. The student's goals would be reviewed annually by the team, with the expectation that these interventions will be effective in helping the student to better access the curriculum and eventually succeed in school and beyond.

Viewed in isolation, this process for determining how to intervene with students appears as if it could be effective. If a student exhibits a problem, stakeholders collaborate to determine the specific nature of the problem and brainstorm ways to address it. Unfortunately, this process neglects any consideration of how best to support students; all students are provided with a general education curriculum, and individuals who do not respond to that curriculum are evaluated to determine if they meet the criteria for a disability and are, therefore, eligible for special education services. If the student is not deemed eligible, then they might receive additional support, or they might not. Important concerns, such as how other students are behaving in the hallway, whether students receive high-quality core behavioral instruction that appropriately addresses more challenging situations, or whether students are reinforced for behaving as expected, may or may not be discussed as well during these conversations. When the focus of the intervention and the data collected to evaluate the need for intervention rest entirely upon an individual student or situation, school personnel may miss critical information that informs supports for all students and may bear directly on the environmental and contextual factors influencing that individual student. *A wider view of possible targets of assessment may allow us to engage in proactive or preventive efforts that serve more than a single individual—and even decrease the amount of individual assessment and intervention that we have to do.*

WHY FOCUS ON SCHOOL-BASED BEHAVIORAL ASSESSMENT?

This book is about school-based behavioral assessment. *Behavior* involves social (e.g., relating with others), emotional (e.g., affections, feelings), and behavioral (e.g., observable actions, conduct) domains. *School-based behavioral assessment* refers to those assessment practices that can be applied within school settings to provide information about student functioning in social, emotional, and behavioral domains, with the intention of supporting student success and well-being.

The reasons why behavior is a core issue for prevention and intervention in schools have been made clear throughout the research literature: *Behavior matters for students, for the adults they become, for their parents, for their teachers, for their peers, and for society and the world at large.* Teachers report that classroom management and teaching students with special needs are among their top concerns for additional training (Wei, Darling-Hammond, Andree, Richardson, & Orphanos, 2009), but only 27% of university special education programs include a course on classroom management (Oliver & Reschly, 2010), and only 22% of elementary school teachers report having received adequate classroom management training (Wagner et al., 2006).

> School-based behavioral assessment provides information about student *social, emotional,* and *behavioral* functioning.

Students with behavior problems are more likely than students without behavior problems to experience academic failure (Masten et al., 2005), exhibit "internalizing" problems like depression as adults (Kosterman et al., 2010), encounter the criminal justice system at an earlier age (Patterson, Forgatch, Yoerger, & Stoolmiller, 1998), and be unemployed after high school (Wagner, Newman, Cameto, Garza, & Levine, 2005). Indeed, the outcomes for students with emotional disturbance, a disability category that includes students with significant behavior problems, are very negative for both the short and the long term. Half of all students identified with emotional disturbance drop out of high school, compared with 30% of all students with disabilities (U.S. Department of Health and Human Services, New Freedom Commission on Mental Health, 2003), and less than one-third are employed after leaving school (Wagner et al., 2005).

Evidence-based interventions can prevent and/or remediate the significant and long-term negative outcomes observed for students exhibiting social, emotional, and behavioral challenges. With the knowledge that students *can* be taught to demonstrate positive behavior and that these changes *can* benefit students, educators are faced with the question of *how* best to support positive student behavior in schools. For decades, many of us have thought that effective strategies available in the behavior management toolbox consisted of sending students out of class, giving them an office discipline referral, and possibly suspending or expelling them. This viewpoint is often accompanied by the idea that appropriate behavior should be expected and should not have to be taught in schools—thus, the school's job is to punish a child into behaving appropriately.

Although viewpoints have shifted toward more positive and proactive approaches, punitive and exclusionary practices persist today. More than 106,000 public school students received corporal punishment (physical punishment intended to inflict pain) in 2013–2014 across the 19 states in which such practices are still legal (Office of Civil Rights, 2017). A nationwide survey of state-funded prekindergarten programs suggests that 6.67 of every 1,000 preschoolers were expelled during the 2003 and 2004 academic years (Gilliam, 2005); a significantly higher number of expelled preschoolers were boys and were Black. Critically, although this survey highlighted a number of disturbing trends in our nation's preschools, it also identified one potential factor for mitigating these expulsion rates: preschool teachers who had access to behavioral supports from a mental health professional were significantly less likely to expel a student than those without such support. Although this finding is correlational and not causal, it supports a growing movement to integrate social, emotional, and behavioral support services within a comprehensive student health framework in our nation's education system.

Given the significant negative outcomes associated with unremediated social, emotional, and behavioral problems, and the societal and very human implications of a primarily punitive behavior management approach, we choose to interpret behavior through a different lens. **We believe that behavior is learned, understandable, and serves a purpose for the student**. If Lisa bangs on her desk repeatedly over the course of a school year, and when she does so, her peers look at her angrily and her teacher scolds her, this is a behavior that Lisa has learned: when I bang on my desk, people pay attention to me. Critically, we believe that Lisa was taught this behavior by her teachers and her peers; after all, they are the ones providing the attention! Desk banging is a behavior that works for Lisa; it doesn't take much effort, it is easier than using a full sentence that might be difficult to articulate or than raising a hand that might not be called on, and it's effective because it's really hard to ignore someone banging on their desk.

> **Behavior is learned and understandable and serves a purpose for the student.**

In order to determine why Lisa may be exhibiting this behavior, the extent to which it is typical for other students her age, how often it is currently happening, and whether an intervention we have tried has made a meaningful difference in changing her behavior, we need information that is geared toward answering each of these questions. In other words, we need to collect data. Unfortunately, in an educational landscape in which schools are charged with doing more for their students within traditional academic and expanding social, emotional, and behavioral domains, it is critical to recognize that for some school personnel, the word "data" has joined the more traditional "four-letter words" in the English language. When approached without respect for an educator's time and available resources to follow through with a plan of action, data collection can be just "one more chore" added to educators' already overflowing plates. Thus, at the core of this book lies our premise that *schools should be proactive in identifying and responding to student needs*

School-based behavioral assessment practices must balance defensibility with usability.

with reliable and valid data in order to make defensible decisions. However, this focus on prevention must be balanced with the critical need for efficiency and ease of use of data collection.

WHY ENGAGE IN DATA-BASED DECISION MAKING?

As noted throughout each chapter, the process of data-based decision making informs this book. As described in detail in Chapter 2, we use the Burns and Gibbons (2012) model of data-based decision making, which itself was adapted from a model proposed by Bransford and Stein (1984). We briefly introduce the idea of data-based decision making by asking two major questions when considering how data are going to be collected: *What question am I trying to answer?* and *Which data will best answer that question?* These questions are answered with an additional question about available resources, that is, *What resources are available to collect data?* Although the first two questions may appear simple, it is absolutely critical that we answer them *before* we collect data. All too often, practitioners and researchers alike start with a method and then work backward to determine what questions the data from that method are answering. Many, if not most, school-based practitioners will identify with a scenario in which they are presented with a binder full of data and asked, "What are we going to do with all of this information, and what does it mean?" We too have

Data-based decision making involves asking two major questions: first ask the reason for assessment, and then ask which data are needed given the available resources.

been part of numerous school- and district-level data team meetings in which we are presented with spreadsheets full of student and school outcomes and are asked to figure out what are the next steps to take. If our assessment process starts with the instrument itself rather than with the questions we are trying to answer, we will find ourselves staring at a report and trying to work backward to make sense of it all. If we

instead start by asking *What information do I actually need in order to solve this problem?*, we will collect the data that are relevant to our question and potentially save time and resources, and avoid needless effort.

The type of data that we collect is not just driven by the method used to collect them, but also by the level of inference we are planning on making with the information. For instance, if the intent of an assessment is to identify students who are at risk with regard to a particular behavior (e.g., disruptions in class) or to provide an evaluative statement about the effects of an after-school program to enhance prosocial behavior, the desired level of assessment generalization (or in some cases specificity) should be considered (Riley-Tillman, Kalberer, & Chafouleas, 2005). Is the purpose of the assessment to provide an aggregated statement about a child's behavior (generalization), or to gather information about a particular behavior at a particular time or in a specific setting (specificity or directness)? The reason for needing the data not only drives the type of assessment that is called for, but also the methods and practices used in the assessment.

What Question Am I Trying to Answer?

Although assessment tool selection should be guided by a multimethod, multisource, and multisetting perspective, making decisions is not a matter of simply adhering to this guiding principle— particularly as related to social, emotional, and behavioral domains. For behavior in particular, context matters in the expression of (what the student is doing) and the perception regarding (how it is being interpreted) what is being exhibited (Dirks, De Los Reyes, Briggs-Gowan, Cella, & Wakschlag, 2012). Thus, it is often appropriate to use multiple assessment methods (e.g., direct observation or rating scales) in collecting data from multiple sources (e.g., teachers, parents, and peers) across a variety of settings (e.g., cafeteria, hallways, and restrooms). One limitation of this approach, however, is that more does not always mean easier or better. Collecting lots of information can be time consuming and cumbersome, and the quality of the data might therefore be affected. Furthermore, in our field, we have not resolved how to reconcile conflicting data from distinct sources (Dirks et al., 2012). Thus, a balance must be achieved between collecting enough information to understand a problem situation and develop an intervention plan and ensuring high quality, accuracy, and relevance. For example, a teacher's daily homework record that is maintained in the classroom grade book may be more efficient and just as relevant as a daily written log that is completed by the student, parent, and teacher that duplicates the recording of homework completion. In this example, some precision might be lost with regard to understanding the context in which homework is or is not being completed; however, feasibility may outweigh precision. We might also consider a multimethod approach, using both sources of information to gain information on work completion; we could compare the results and consider the implications of the data from both sources that agree or how to move forward if the data disagree. In summary, we highly recommend that multimethod, multisetting, and multisource assessment practices be given priority; however, each assessment situation should be evaluated carefully to maintain precision in the context of quantity that could diminish usability.

The chosen assessment tools should provide relevant information about the target behavior(s), the contexts in which the behaviors are observed, and the distal events that, although not in the immediate context, may affect the occurrence of the target behaviors in the problem context. For example, attendance data likely will not help inform intervention decisions related to increasing proactive skills on the playground. Riley-Tillman and colleagues (2005) referred to the match between the assessment tool and the behavior and context as "goodness of fit." Not all assessment tools appropriately measure the same behaviors. As an example, behavior rating scales that assess a student's general state or status relative to a wide range of behaviors likely would not be useful when rating "out of seat" behavior events per hour during math instruction. Similarly, within a class of tools such as Systematic Direct Observation, a good fit between what behavior is measured and how to measure it must be considered. For example, a direct observation duration recording method (e.g., What percent of class time did the student spend out of seat?) would yield different data than an event recording method (e.g., How many times during a class period was the student out of seat?).

Which Data Will Best Answer the Question?

Determining the type of decision to be made guides selection of the assessment tool(s). High-stakes decisions, like curriculum adoption or individualized behavior support planning, require accurate and relevant data that provide users with a high degree of confidence. Confidence is related to the degree of inference needed when interpreting the data. One indicator for determining directness is the extent to which the collected information is removed in time and place from the actual occurrence of the behavior (see Cone, 1978). For example, comprehensive behavior rating scales are considered indirect because the information is collected by another person, who responds to items based on a retrospective perception of the student's behavior. In contrast, Systematic Direct Observation is considered direct, in that the assessments occur as the behaviors are observed. As a general rule of thumb, "high-stakes cases" (e.g., a serious disruption or potential harm to the student or others or a consideration of change in placement to a more restrictive setting) should include a combination of direct assessment tools. In general, the more direct the measure, the more resource intensive the data collection can be—but this is a good example of a reasonable rationale for allocation of intensive assessment resources.

What Resources Are Available to Collect These Data?

As previously stated, although asking the first two questions serves an important function in identifying the problem to be addressed and the potential data that can facilitate a solution, the available resources are also an important consideration. Determining the resources required to collect and interpret data is equally necessary when selecting assessment tools (i.e., how feasible is it to collect the data in a given situation?). Feasibility refers to a consideration, for example, of the time needed to train someone to accurately use the tool, of the intrusiveness of using the tool in the required setting, of scheduling a time for data collection, of the complexity of using the tool, and so forth. For example, asking a teacher to monitor student behavior every day for a full semester may not be possible given the class size, the training required, and fluency with assessment, given other instructional responsibilities. Together, these examples help to define the overall usability of the proposed assessment plan. For example, the factors that influence usability of an assessment could also include acceptability, family–school collaboration, system support, system climate, and understanding of its instrumentation and procedures (see Briesch, Chafoulas, Neugebauer, & Riley-Tillman, 2013). In summary, it is important to consider that resources are finite, and that wasting them on assessments that go beyond what is needed to answer a question can be a mistake that is just as problematic as not providing adequate resources for assessment in the first place.

PURPOSE OF THIS BOOK

Behavior matters: for students, for the adults that they become, for teachers, for parents, for schools, and for communities. Schools need efficient and effective ways to ask questions, approach problems, and determine solutions that support student success in social, emotional, and behavioral domains. Throughout this introductory chapter, we have provided initial considerations for school behavioral assessment guided by the conviction that (1) schools can and should work to support positive student behavior, (2) data are necessary in order to make effective decisions about what is or is not working, and (3) assessment practices must balance defensibility and usability. In Chapter 2, we introduce multi-tiered systems of support (MTSS) as a critical framework for integrating data-based decision making into supports that can effectively meet the needs of all students by expanding specific assessment considerations. Consistent with MTSS frameworks, our focus throughout the entire book is on school-based assessment as aligned with screening and progress monitoring purposes of assessment. As such, the reader should consult other sources for detailed information related to the functional, diagnostic, or evaluative purposes of assessment. Chapter 2 also describes how to drill down to and conceptualize the target behavior of interest that you'll be assessing. Chapter 3 examines the what, why, and how of extant data, which are data created as a byproduct of some other ongoing activity that can be used to assess student behavior. Chapter 4 describes the wide-ranging options utilized in Systematic Direct Observation, which has historically been referred to as the "gold standard" for directly observing student behavior yet might not always be the best choice in terms of usability. In Chapter 5, we introduce Direct Behavior Rating as an assessment option that relies on observers' perceptions of behavior during a larger observation period. Chapter 6 describes traditional behavior rating scales, wherein individuals provide retrospective ratings of student behavior across multiple items. Chapter 7 focuses on data integration, which involves taking the information derived from multimethod, multitrait, and multisource assessments and bringing it all together. Finally, in Chapter 8, we introduce a framework to guide you through conducting behavioral assessment in your own context and case studies that demonstrate practical applications.

For students or school personnel who are new to school-based behavioral assessment, we recommend reading the book all the way through in order to gain a more complete understanding of the various pathways decision making in assessment takes. For those readers who are approaching the book with some background knowledge in behavioral assessment and perhaps have an interest in specific behavioral assessment methods, we would still emphasize reviewing Chapters 2 and 7, given that assessment decisions that are defensible and usable undergird good decision making. By the time you have reached the end of this book, readers who engage in school-based behavioral assessment should have the knowledge needed to guide defensible and usable assessment decisions and an understanding of the tools they can use to make those decisions about student social, emotional, and behavioral needs.

CHAPTER 2

Getting Out of the Gate
Asking Questions to Drive the Assessment Process

Problems need solutions. The "best"—or most efficient and effective—way to identify a solution is to first understand the problem by collecting information that is directly relevant to the specified problem. Although the benefits of collecting direct evidence may seem obvious, school-based behavioral assessment practices often do not follow this simple maxim. We administer a rating scale because, well, historically we have always used a rating scale when we are evaluating a student. We use specific observation procedures because, well, they are what we always use when we conduct an observation. When we consider assessment as a practice unto itself, and not an inextricable part of a larger decision-making process, we can lose sight of the purpose of the data that we are collecting.

To be able to identify the types of problems we seek to solve, and what information is relevant in assisting to solve a given type of problem, we need to have a sense of the system in which we are functioning. We might ask questions such as: "How am I conceptualizing students in this school and the services that they receive?" "Do I think about issues, such as general versus special education or easy versus tough students, as separate problems?" "How are my recommendations usable for all students, staff members, and families?" In this chapter, we discuss multi-tiered systems of support (MTSS) as a critical framework for integrating data-based decision making into supports that meet the needs of all students. Then, we discuss specific assessment considerations within MTSS. We end this chapter with guidelines on how to "drill down" to and conceptualize target behavior(s) for assessment.

MTSS AS A FRAMEWORK FOR BEHAVIORAL ASSESSMENT

MTSS emphasizes the prevention of problems by establishing a continuum of positive practices to support success for all students. MTSS provides a useful way to organize the planning, implementation, and evaluation of different kinds of assessment that inform service delivery. Prevention-focused models like MTSS have long been integrated into medicine and public health (Institute of Medicine, 2012), with educationally based systems focusing on the range of intervention and prevention options, from schoolwide supports to data-based individuation. The continuum of services available within MTSS for behavior has been commonly operationalized into three tiers of intensity (Walker et al., 1996): universal, targeted, and select (intensive) (see Figure 2.1), although two-tiered systems have also been proposed (Fuchs & Fuchs, 2017).

Typical conceptualizations of tiered models of service delivery articulate three tiers of support intensity: universal (Tier 1—all students), targeted (Tier 2—some students), and select (Tier 3—a few students). However, from this point forward in the book, we refer to these three subsets and the assessment and intervention decisions that are directed toward them as "whole groups," "small groups," and "individual students." "Whole groups" refers to a defined set of people who are not differentiated based on need. This set might be a classroom, a grade, or a school. "Small groups" refers to a subset of "whole groups" that have some identified difference from the rest of the group. In the context of MTSS, this group typically has been formed on the basis of shared indications of risk for a problem, whether the risk is higher-than-average scores on a behavior screener or teacher nominations based on general social skills concerns. When we assess and intervene with "individual students," we are focusing on individualized practices that require more resources to implement. We use this language instead of "universal," "targeted," and "select" in order to emphasize the importance of the underlying principle that guides service delivery, *data-based decision making,* rather than a one-size-fits-all approach driven by placement within specific tiers or levels of service delivery.

> **Service delivery can occur across tiers of intensity, such as whole groups, small groups, and individual students.**

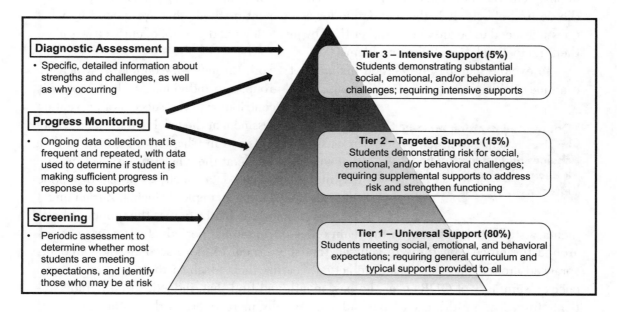

FIGURE 2.1. Illustration of assessment emphasis within an MTSS model.

A "whole-group" level encompasses efforts aimed at all the staff and students in a school or classroom. Prevention models suggest that approximately 80% of students will respond positively to this level of service delivery and will not need additional supports. However, this assumption is not necessarily appropriate for all settings, like communities that experience substantial adversities such as poverty and violence. At the whole-group level, prevention strategies are focused on explicitly creating, and not just assuming the existence of, environments that promote student learning and engagement. These environments are created from practices like identifying common behavioral expectations and explaining, teaching, and supporting the demonstration of these socially appropriate behaviors (Hulac & Briesch, 2017). "Small-group" assessment and intervention are provided for students who display at-risk behavior and may benefit from more behavioral support than just what is being provided to the whole group (e.g., classwide). Typically, it is assumed that approximately 15% of students will need additional supports (again, with the same caveats as mentioned for whole-group supports). These students may be first identified as at risk according to data generated from the whole-group level. As in the small-group level, "individual-student" strategies are allocated for students who are not responding to instruction and intervention at the whole-group and small-group levels. Approximately 5% of students will need this type of highly individualized intervention. Given their high-risk status, corresponding assessment strategies are also likely to be more detailed and highly individualized and may include a comprehensive functional behavioral assessment (FBA).

The Core of MTSS: Data-Based Decision Making

What is *data-based decision making*? Simply put, it's learning how to *think*, not just learning how to *do*. It is the framework that we use to approach problems and understand how we're going to work through them. It is the process that allows us to make decisions based upon a detailed understanding of a problem *and* to understand if those decisions produced the desired effects. It is the foundation for assessment methods that are guided by what questions need to be answered, rather than by just following the script of our well-worn "if-then" recipe books for student problems.

To explore data-based decision making, let's work through an example in which we examine problems rooted in whole-group, small-group, and individual-student concerns.

> **Data-based decision making involves making informed choices *and* understanding if decisions produce desired effects.**

An important contributor to the success of prevention is formative assessment at the level of the whole school or class. As we discuss in Chapter 3, assessment data that can be valuable at the whole-group level include existing schoolwide data, such as office discipline referrals (ODRs). For example, Principal Zurich might call you to share his frustration at the number of elementary students being sent to the main office during lunch periods. In fact, as you look around the office, you think to yourself that there seem to more second-grade students sprawled around the space than are actually eating their lunch in the cafeteria! So, you check a summary of ODRs over the past month and find that, indeed, second-grade students from Mr. Smith's class have had substantially more referrals than other groups of students. Thus, you propose a plan that entails teaching the expectations for cafeteria behavior to Mr. Smith's students along with enhanced monitoring of those students in the cafeteria to support positive behavior and reduce inappropriate behavior. In the end, you have saved the day in Principal Zurich's eyes—without exerting significant assessment effort or developing multiple individual student intervention plans.

However, perhaps your discipline referral data indicate that four students comprise 70% of the total number of cafeteria referrals following implementation of the intervention for Mr. Smith's class. Thus, this group of students might serve as the focus for small-group supports. In this situation, it might be appropriate to continue using ODRs as an assessment tool. However, additional data might also be considered, depending on the intervention strategy employed. For example, imagine that you develop a self-management intervention for these students with regard to cafeteria behavior, which is implemented by the cafeteria aide. The intervention involves a daily rating of the degree to which expected cafeteria behaviors were displayed, using a scale from 1 (not displayed) to 10 (completely displayed). In this case, it could be useful to use the self-management data as another data source because (1) the data already exist and thus resources are not burdened by additional collection (it's *efficient*) and (2) it may be more sensitive than discipline referrals in capturing behavior that is not severe enough to warrant an office referral, yet may be on the path toward it (it's *effective* at telling us what is or is not working). Thus, using the existing rating data to identify areas (e.g., times or particular behaviors) in need of further support can be considered efficient and effective data-based decision making.

For students with intensive needs, assessment tools that are capable of providing specific and detailed information regarding an individual's behavior, such as Systematic Direct Observation or comprehensive behavior rating scales, may also be helpful. For instance, in the cafeteria example, we may find that one of the students in Mr. Smith's class continues to have difficulty following the targeted intervention. A further examination of schoolwide data for this student suggests that challenging behaviors exist across multiple settings. Thus, it could be helpful to further investigate the significance of and reason for the behavior problems; this inquiry might include asking the student's teacher and parent(s), as well as the student, to complete norm-referenced rating scales, in addition to conducting direct observations of the student as part of an FBA. These additional data, coupled with our existing schoolwide data and daily cafeteria behavior ratings, should lead us to a better understanding of the reason for the problem behavior as well as potentially successful intervention options. Thus, assessment at the individual-student level is characterized by a direct focus on the individual student and should also involve ongoing assessment to monitor the effectiveness of an intensive intervention plan.

As illustrated by the earlier example, when Principal Zurich shared a concern about high referral rates during lunch period, we began with the question: "What do I need to know?," which was answered with "I need to identify the source of the problem of high referrals in order to determine what change would be most effective." Then we asked, "How am I going to find out?" Fortunately, accurate ODR data were available, and we graphed the data across multiple variables like grade, setting, and time of day. In examining the graphs, we noted that the second-grade cohort had much higher rates of referrals during lunchtime than any other large group, and we were able to use these data to focus our intervention on the second-grade lunch period rather than on pursuing an option, such as having a schoolwide assembly during lunch to reteach expectations for every grade in every setting. Critically, *this is not the end of our decision-making processor of our evaluation of relevant data.* Instead of considering this case closed and moving on, we will monitor the referral data after implementing our whole-grade lunch period intervention to determine whether second-grade lunchtime referrals do indeed decrease to reasonable rates and if other grades begin to exhibit similar problems during specific periods. If it's working, great! Let's figure out if it's something that should remain in effect or be faded from use. If it's not working, that's ok! Let's figure out why. Do we need to rethink our hypotheses about why these problems are occurring? Is the intervention being implemented as we discussed? Are there issues that we didn't plan for that the lunch staff have to contend with? Could we have prevented some of these issues by being more collaborative with the lunch staff from the start when we designed this intervention?

As a final note related to this example, although Principal Zurich's concern about high referral rates prompted our investigation into schoolwide ODR data leading to an intervention, was there a way that we could have been made aware of the problem without just happening to be in the office to witness the principal's frustration? Could we have identified a problem *before* it got to this point? Indeed, if we had been reviewing ODR data from the beginning of the school year, we likely would have noticed a spike in referrals starting in the second month of the school year, and could have collaborated with the second-grade team and the lunchroom staff on an action plan to remediate this problem before it escalated in intensity. After reteaching lunch period expectations and initiating a group contingency for appropriate behavior across the second grade, we might have provided an early intervention before the lunchroom behavior became a bigger issue for the school. Here, as with every problem we encounter when we use a framework of data-based decision making, we were presented with a problem and asked ourselves two guiding questions: "What do I need to know?" and "How am I going to find out?"

Data-based decision making permeates the practice of school psychology and special education. Whether engaging in behavioral consultation (e.g., Kratochwill & Bergan, 1990) or the positive behavior support process (e.g., Bambara & Kern, 2005), each model contains a similar framework of stages that include problem identification, problem definition, intervention development, intervention delivery, and intervention evaluation. In their book on response to intervention, Burns and Gibbons (2012) describe the origins of the general problem-solving model, and include the IDEAL (Identify, Define, Explore, Act, and Look Back) model as proposed by Bransford and Stein (1984) as a seminal template. Anyone working within MTSS frameworks would quickly point out that this model is cyclical, not terminal; we don't move from problem identification to intervention evaluation and then stop. If, during an intervention evaluation, we determine that an intervention has been effective, then we still have a number of decisions to make: Should we continue the intervention as is? Should we begin systematically fading it out? When will we revisit progress again? If the intervention hasn't been effective, then we need to revisit the steps we took along the way: Is the intervention being delivered with integrity? Is our hypothesis about why the problem is occurring incorrect? Did we design the intervention in such a way that it's unable to result in a change for this student? As we discussed in the example of Principal Zurich, intervention evaluation provides a jumping-off point for more decision making. It does not end the conversation. Because intervention evaluation provides the touchstone of data-based decision making, it should come as no surprise that this step is fully articulated in the commonly used phrase for MTSS in education: response to intervention.

As reviewed here, it is critically important that we work within a *process* for thinking about decision making along with developing and implementing *data systems* to facilitate that decision making. Next, we review the four main purposes of the data that we collect in school settings and begin to link these general purposes to their roles within MTSS and to data-based decision making.

ASSESSMENT CONSIDERATIONS WITHIN MTSS

Data are collected for four main purposes: (1) evaluation, (2) diagnosis, (3) screening, and (4) progress monitoring.

Evaluation

Evaluative assessment, like district- or state-mandated year-end testing, provides a general summary of student skills. The results can serve as an indicator of the overall effectiveness of an intervention, whether the focus is global (e.g., adherence to schoolwide expectations by the entire second grade) or specific (e.g., the outcomes of a 4-month intensive social skills program for a student with attention-deficit/hyperactivity disorder [ADHD]). Evaluative assessment is used to determine outcomes at a specific point in time that act to summarize growth or a lack thereof that has occurred over a longer period, rather than to inform day-to-day decisions about student performance and instruction. Thus, evaluative assessment is best suited for answering questions like "Overall, did this strategy work in reducing our hallway transition time?" or "Generally, how well are our students meeting our schoolwide behavior expectations?," but not questions like "Is this student making progress toward our goal of increased active engagement during math instruction?" In order to answer these questions in a reliable and valid fashion, evaluative assessments may be comprehensive in scope and format. Evaluative assessments are one of the most salient examples of what are called "summative assessments," wherein decisions are made on the basis of data collected at a specific time. By comparison, in "formative assessments," data are collected over a longer period of time.

Diagnosis

When referencing diagnosis in educational settings, we are often talking about identifying an underlying difficulty and providing more detailed analyses of the problem so that we can allocate appropriate services to the student. Said another way, diagnosis occurs so that effective treatment can take place. Historically, treatment for significant academic and behavioral challenges in schools has occurred within the context of special education, such as determining support services for a student identified as having autism spectrum disorder. However, MTSS frameworks also provide a defensible method for determining the severity of a problem and for informing subsequent intervention decisions. This method for identifying student need has also been recognized in federal special education law (Zirkel, 2011, 2017, 2018). If *diagnosis* is defined as "identification of a problem with sufficient specificity to enable intervention," we would also categorize data collected as part of an FBA as belonging to the diagnostic family of assessments. For example, let's say that our FBA data support that self-injurious behavior occurs most often after a disruptive bus ride that is followed by a task demand. Diagnostic assessment is therefore aligned with making "conceptually relevant intervention decisions," wherein instructional strategies are selected according to a student's identified needs rather than on the basis of a trial-and-error approach (see Erchul & Martens, 2010, or Van der Kleij, Vermeulen, Schildkamp, & Eggen, 2015, for a discussion of conceptual relevance in school-based consultation).

Screening

The purpose of screening assessments is to identify students who are either at risk for or already experiencing difficulty in a particular area (e.g., self-regulation or social skills). Typically, screening tools are administered to a preidentified whole group or a targeted set of students on a periodic basis to determine levels of performance that indicate those students who may benefit from intervention. For example, a social–emotional screening form might be completed for all students by their general education teacher, and the results would be used to determine if any students should be considered for additional support. In other words, screening can provide data to derive "small groups" or "individual students" from "whole groups."

Glover and Albers (2007) identified three overarching considerations for evaluating screening assessments: (1) appropriateness for intended use, (2) technical adequacy, and (3) usability. We refer readers to this comprehensive article for more details on each of these considerations but summarize two particular issues in screening here. With regard to appropriateness for intended use, numbers are just numbers until we decide how to use them; if I use the results of my most recent cholesterol test to evaluate whether or not I should buy a new computer, this information clearly is irrelevant for this purpose. It does not make the numbers "wrong," but the use of those numbers in this decision-making process is flawed. Similarly, a screener's appropriateness for its intended use and its technical adequacy both rely on considerations regarding the constructs of interest and how they align with the context within which the screener is administered. In the real world, decision making and data cannot be considered independent of one another.

Perhaps most important, screeners prioritize the efficiency of administration alongside the validity and reliability of their resulting data. Thus, although evaluative and diagnostic assessment tools can be, and often are, lengthy and time-consuming processes for accumulating defensible data, screeners attempt to produce reliable and valid data through a quick and easy-to-complete process. The rationale for this is fairly self-evident: if a teacher is asked by the school psychologist to complete a screener for every child in a class of 30 students, the screener should probably not take 25 minutes per student to complete. The efficiency of both the tool and the process within which the resulting data will be used needs to be considered if we expect to implement a sustainable screening system in a school.

Progress Monitoring

Progress monitoring refers to the collection of information on a frequent and repeated basis, otherwise known as "formative assessment." These data are collected over time to determine whether a change in behaviors has occurred and whether or not goals are expected to be met. The collection of repeated information enables intervention decisions to be made early and formatively during the process of evaluating student supports, rather than having to wait until the end of a semester, when enhancements or changes may be less effective, efficient, or feasible. For instance, we would probably like to know whether a classwide intervention is working before the end of the school year arrives so that we can make informed decisions that will materially impact the students in this class. Given limited resources and time, as well as the implications of allowing behavior problems to continue unabated, schools cannot afford to waste days, months, or years on the delivery of ineffective student supports.

The frequency of data collection for progress monitoring can vary (e.g., three times per quarter to three times per day). However, just as the utility of screening instruments are dependent on their efficiency, progress monitoring measures must be repeatable in order to actually function as formative assessments. This means that we have to ask questions about a measure's resulting data, such as "If a meaningful change occurred, would this instrument detect it?" This sort of question refers to the data's sensitivity to change. Just like screening instruments, we also need to attend to the efficiency with which we can implement a progress monitoring assessment method. Instead of needing to be efficient because we are measuring multiple students, we now need to prioritize efficiency because we are using the tool multiple times.

Finally, just as screening tools require a robust decision-making framework in order to implement and defensibly use them, we need to understand how we will contextualize and interpret the multiple data points that result from progress monitoring before we begin collecting the information. As we discuss in Chapter 7, single-case design is one robust system for interpreting the formative data that result from progress monitoring. In this experimental method, we use formative data to predict how a student or group of students would continue to behave in the absence of any change. We then implement a change, such as an intervention, while continuing to collect data to evaluate if the data that we observe are different from the data we predicted we'd see.

This Book

Tiered systems of support rely on all four purposes of assessment. If we need to answer the question "What is the student's overall pattern of behavioral functioning compared to other students of the same age?," as we might ask if we are considering a student for special education services, we must identify the tools that can be defensibly used in a *diagnostic* fashion. Similarly, if we want to communicate the summative effects of our schoolwide positive behavior support plan to the school board, we may *evaluate* this program by summarizing data at two points in time: for example, the average annual number of ODRs.

Both of these purposes of assessment are valuable; simply put, these are questions that make sense and deserve to be answered. However, MTSS emphasizes a shift from looking only at a specific time and relying exclusively on diagnostic methods to identifying problems and determining solutions. A plethora of resources are available for professionals who want to learn about these methods, which require a significant amount of time and exper-

MTSS requires a focus on assessments that can be used for screening and progress monitoring.

tise to administer. For readers seeking more detailed treatments of these topics to facilitate individualized intervention development, we suggest consulting books on the FBA process such as O'Neill, Albin, Storey, Horner, and Sprague (2014) and Bambara and Kern (2005).

Although all assessment purposes can serve a critical role in MTSS frameworks, this book focuses on tools that can be used for the purposes of *screening* and *progress monitoring*. These two purposes of assessment have always mattered in school-based behavior support, but have received short shrift in the literature in comparison to the historical focus on assessment for evaluation and diagnosis. Screening and progress monitoring matter intensely within a prevention- and intervention-focused system of support. Simply put, if we want to prevent problems before they get worse, we need to *screen* the students in our school to identify who needs help, and if we want to know if an intervention is working with enough time to actually respond to the data we see, we need to *monitor the progress* of students whose behaviors we are trying to change.

PRIORITIZING AND CONCEPTUALIZING BEHAVIOR FOR ASSESSMENT

Now that you have an understanding of how to use data-based decision making to select assessment tools based on where and why you are engaging in assessment, we discuss what you need to know in order to effectively ask questions to find answers. As previously noted, regardless of which tier of intensity is involved, the first step is to identify the target behavior, or the construct you are looking to assess. In order to do so, we must ask ourselves: what is the problem at hand? To answer this question, we need to determine where discrepancies exist between current levels of behavior and behavioral expectations (Burns & Gibbons, 2012). We can identify these discrepancies, or problems, by comparing whole-group, small-group, or individual-student data to a criterion that objectively establishes the expectation.

Once all problems have been identified, we need to "drill down" to prioritize a target behavior for assessment. The highest-priority problems are those that have a harmful or negative impact on critical learning and social outcomes (Bambara & Kern, 2005). Specifically, the student's consideration of student and staff safety, the student's participation in learning and extracurricular activities, and their development of positive adult and peer relationships should take precedence when considering the impact of a problem or potential problem. For example, truancy or excessive school absences may not directly put a student or staff member in danger, but they do directly affect a student's ability to access the curriculum and engage in positive interactions with peers and school staff—two necessary building blocks of positive learning and social outcomes. As such, this is an important social/emotional concern. Bambara and Kern (2005) provide three levels of priority for intervention that we have adapted, given that they are useful as a guideline for identifying a primary target for assessment:

- Level I. The first level includes destructive behaviors, or those that are directly harmful or threatening to oneself or others (e.g., self-injury, hitting, kicking, or bringing a weapon to school).
- Level II. The second level includes disruptive behaviors, or those that are not imme-

diately dangerous but interfere with learning, participation in activities, and/or social relationships (e.g., destroying materials, screaming or crying, or refusing to share with others).

- Level III. The third level includes distracting behaviors, or those that deviate from expected behaviors but do not significantly interfere with learning or social development (e.g., dressing inappropriately, poor hygiene, or fidgeting with materials).

After you have identified the target behavior(s), it is critical to define the behavior, as the defined behavior is the construct you are going to assess. In the following chapters, we discuss considerations for defining target behaviors within specific assessment methods. For example, Chapters 4 and 5 provide additional information about and examples of behavioral definitions. But, generally speaking, how do we define key characteristics of behavior that can be measured using assessment? For all assessment methods, it is critical to have an operational definition of each target behavior, meaning that the behavior is defined using specific and measurable terms. When a behavior is operationally defined, anyone reading the definition should be able to differentiate between the defined behavior and all other behaviors without ever having seen the behavior in person. Including examples and non-examples of the target behavior in the definition provides further clarification. Briesch, Volpe, and Floyd (2018) provide a summary of the steps for operationally defining behavior based on the work of Barton and Ascione (1984):

- Step 1. Write down an initial definition based on what first comes to mind when you picture the target behavior.
- Step 2. Make a list of all possible examples of the behavior, both as directly observed and as reported by teachers and other relevant school staff members.
- Step 3. Make a list of non-examples of the behavior, specifically in borderline scenarios in which an occurrence of the behavior might be questionable.
- Step 4. Organize any examples and non-examples that cannot be neatly incorporated into the definition into a list format.
- Step 5. Test the operational definition by having untrained observers record instances of the behavior using only the definition.

These procedural steps can be applied within multiple assessment methods. For an example of how these procedures might be used in practice, refer to Figure 2.2.

Many methods of assessment require the definition of a problem to contain observable characteristics, or those components of behavior that we can see or hear directly. For example, we can observe when a student has used their hand to pick up a writing utensil or when a student is screaming profanities. Assessment options, such as direct observation, are primarily used to measure externalizing behavior. Externalizing behaviors are actions that are directed outward, such as hyperactivity, aggression, calling out in class, and antisocial behavior. When we conceptualize problem behavior in schools, most of us probably think of those students who are frequently out of their seat wandering around the classroom, calling out while a teacher is talking or saying mean things to other students. This type of behavior is most clearly disruptive

It is important to both identify and define the target prior to engaging in the assessment.

Step	Example
1. Write down an initial definition based on what first comes to mind when you picture the target behavior.	Leo engages in behaviors during math that are potentially disruptive to his teacher and peers.
2. Make a list of all possible examples of the behavior, both as directly observed and reported by teachers and other relevant school staff members.	• Yelling or loudly saying things related or unrelated to the lesson without being called on • Talking or attempting to talk to peers when not permitted • Throwing paper or writing utensils • Banging on his desk • Getting out of his seat • Singing during independent seatwork
3. Make a list of non-examples of the behavior, specifically in borderline scenarios in which an occurrence of the behavior might be questionable.	• Loudly providing related response after being called on • Talking to peers during assigned group work • Providing a choral response to a teacher's question or directive • Leaving his seat to throw something away and promptly returning to his seat • Leaving his seat to get materials required for an activity following a teacher's directive • Kneeling on or hovering above his chair
4. Organize any examples and non-examples that cannot be neatly incorporated into the definition into a list format.	**Examples:** Yelling or loudly saying things related or unrelated to the lesson without being called on, talking or attempting to talk to peers when not permitted, throwing paper or writing utensils, banging on his desk, getting out of his seat, singing during independent seatwork **Non-Examples:** Loudly providing a related response after being called on, talking to peers during assigned group work, providing a choral response to a teacher's question or directive, leaving his seat to throw something away and promptly returning to his seat, leaving his seat to get materials required for an activity following a teacher's directive, kneeling on or hovering above his chair
5. Test the operational definition by having untrained observers record instances of the behavior using only the definition.	The school psychologist asks a general education paraprofessional to keep a tally of instances of Leo's disruptive behavior during math using the operational definition.

FIGURE 2.2. An example of the procedural steps completed to create an operational definition for disruptive behavior. Adapted from Briesch and colleagues (2018).

to both that student's learning and the ability of other students to learn, and thus tends to be prioritized in assessment and intervention by teachers and administrators.

However, given the increase in prevalence of child and adolescent internalizing disorders (Splett et al., 2018), it is critical to expand our definition of behavior to include social and emotional components. In the chapters ahead, we use this expanded definition to consider the utility of social, emotional, and behavioral (SEB) assessment tools in measuring both externalizing and internalizing problems. Internalizing problems occur within the self and include anxiety, somatization, depression, and withdrawal (von der Embse, Scott, & Kilgus, 2015). These internalizing constructs can be measured by external indicators. For example, a student who frequently complains of a stomachache and asks to go to the nurse's office before having to make a presentation in class may be experiencing somatic symptoms associated with performance anxiety. In this example, if we were to use the five procedural steps to define the internalizing concern, we might identify "requests to go to the nurse" as our SEB target. For internalizing problems that do not have a clear corresponding behavior, assessment methods that employ direct observation may not be appropriate. In these cases, the use of a rating scale that clearly defines the internalizing problem may provide a clearer picture of the frequency or intensity of the concern. In Chapters 4, 5, and 6, we discuss SEB assessment methods that can be used to measure both externalizing and internalizing concerns.

CONCLUDING COMMENTS

In this chapter, we introduced MTSS as an important framework for integrating data-based decision making into supports that meet the needs of all students. Specifically, we provided a general overview of MTSS frameworks that serve students at the whole-group, small-group, and individual-student levels. We followed up this overview with a definition of data-based decision making and worked through an example of how schools can use data to make decisions about student supports across MTSS levels. We then discussed specific assessment considerations within MTSS. In other words, we reviewed the four main purposes of assessment (evaluation, diagnosis, screening, and progress monitoring) and how these purposes fit within an MTSS framework. Finally, we provided guidance on how to effectively identify and conceptualize targets for assessing both externalizing and internalizing problems. Perhaps most important, we discussed the need to expand our definition of behavior to include social and emotional concerns when thinking about using assessment to identify interventions that most appropriately support student SEB needs.

CHAPTER 3

Using Extant Data in Behavioral Assessment

In Chapter 2, we discussed using MTSS as a framework for behavioral assessment to identify supports for whole groups, small groups, and individual students. Although it is typical to think of assessment as some measure or test process, there is a class of assessment consisting of sources of data that are already available, called **extant data**. The use of such data in assessment using an MTSS framework may not be obvious, and thus may be overlooked, as a valuable data source. However, since extant data are often readily available, particularly for schools utilizing MTSS, they can be informative about previous patterns of behavior.

WHAT ARE EXTANT DATA, AND WHY USE THEM?

Extant data can be important for a variety of reasons. First, this information can complement more formal assessments in providing a comprehensive picture of a student. That is, these data can serve an informative role in multimethod, multisource, and multisetting assessment practices by offering a contextual source of information that might be missed in the use of standardized, norm-referenced measures. Second, these data often are collected in a formative fashion: that is, the collection is ongoing or repeated over time, so they serve as an excellent tool in progress monitoring. For example, a teacher who records student performance on weekly spelling quizzes can review the data to reveal error patterns (e.g., "*i* before *e* except after *c*" rule not mastered). This source of outcome data could then be used to document the effectiveness of an intervention, with the goal of mastering this rule. Third, and perhaps most helpful, extant data serve as a readily available source of information. A significant challenge of conducting behavioral assessment for various purposes in applied settings is achieving a balance between preci-

> **Extant data are often already collected by schools, which can reduce the strains on time and resources.**

sion and feasibility. As such, it is critical that before adding new measures and increasing our workload, we first consider data that do not require significant additional effort to use.

One final unique advantage of extant data is that the information is already being collected for some purpose; that is, a reason for collecting the data has already been determined. Given that assessment can be considered a burden because time and resources are finite, it can be wise for schools and districts to garner data from available sources. For example, schools have collected and utilized attendance data for a variety of purposes for decades. Thus, the application of attendance data for measuring an intervention focused on school truancy would not be viewed as additional work, and the data would likely be considered valid for that purpose. The same logic can be applied to a classroom where a teacher has already decided to collect data for some purpose. Using that classroom data not only requires fewer resources, but also is beneficial given the perception that it is already useful in that setting.

Although the characteristics of extant data may be appealing, a disadvantage of working with preexisting data is that there is often insufficient information to appropriately analyze a problem. For example, simply examining the grade recorded (i.e., percent correct) on weekly math quizzes over the past month does not provide information on how students attempted to solve problems or if interfering problem behaviors were present (e.g., peer distractions or difficult tasks). These additional types of information often are not collected and reported while the student is actually engaged in the task. In addition, unlike assessments that have been developed and researched in relation to their reliability and validity for a specific purpose, extant data rarely have known psychometric properties. Despite these limitations, given the potential advantages of extant data, a thoughtful and appropriate application can have substantial benefits in an educational environment.

WHAT TYPES OF CLASSWIDE EXTANT DATA MIGHT BE AVAILABLE?

A variety of extant data (also known as permanent products) are available for academic behaviors, for example, videotapes, audiotapes, computer logs, or paper-and-pencil formats. For example, teacher grade books and student homework and report cards represent forms of academic data that are routinely recorded by teachers, and are often, but not always, collected and stored in a formative manner to allow for progress monitoring. Academic permanent products may be grouped into two categories: (1) performance summaries, such as scores recorded in teacher grade books or the results of district or state norm-referenced testing and (2) work samples, such as worksheets, writing assignments, or art projects. See Table 3.1 for additional examples.

Performance Summaries

Performance summaries are available sources of data that are typically already aggregated and presented in a "formal" format; for example, grades on quizzes and tests recorded in a teacher's grade book, quarterly progress reports, and results of district- and/or state-level assessments. However, to be useful for making instructional decisions, these data must be organized in meaningful ways. In one situation, for example, it may involve graphing weekly

TABLE 3.1. Examples of Possible Extant Data for Academic Behaviors

Academic permanent products	Examples
Work samples	• Worksheets • Homework • Daily journals • Writing assignments • Art projects • Portfolios
Performance summaries	• Grades on quizzes and tests • Other information recorded in teacher grade books (e.g., number of homework assignments completed) • Progress reports • Results of district-/state-level assessments • Results of curriculum-based measurement

or monthly grades on math homework assignments to understand the frequency with which a student has attained a goal of 85% correct or better. In another situation, it may involve organizing yearly state-mandated testing scores or end-of-year grades in specified subjects over the past 3 years into a single chart to provide a global, long-term picture of academic performance. Enhancing the meaning of these types of data begins with an overall record review. See Appendices 3.1–3.3 for examples of forms that may be useful in organizing extant data. Completed examples of these forms are provided in Figures 3.1, 3.2 (in Case Example 3.1), and 3.3 (in Case Example 3.1).

Although permanent products may provide an excellent source of everyday student data, the challenge is identifying what data to use and how often to use it. Nearly all teachers use grade books to input and organize student data; yet little is done with this information after it is recorded. Many teachers only look at the recorded grades when computing averages at the end of a grading period. However, a grade book can serve as an extensive database for the ongoing monitoring of performance at the individual-student or whole-class level. For example, graphing grades on a simple chart can provide a useful picture of how individual students, or the class as a whole, are performing academically. In addition, teachers can chart student progress before and after the introduction of a new instructional technique to visually determine its effectiveness. In Case Example 3.1, we further illustrate this point.

Although grade books are most often used to record academic performance information, they can also be used to track information about students' social behavior. For example, participation ratings (e.g., high, medium, or low engagement) or measures of appropriate or inappropriate behavior (e.g., number of conflicts avoided or time out of seat) can enhance the utility and meaning of extant information. One critical consideration when using grade book data is the nature of the original task demand. In an ideal situation, the original task will be highly consistent in each application. For example, a spelling test given every Friday that always consists of 20 similarly difficult words can be considered consistent from week to week, and, therefore, the results are more useful for progress monitoring. If, on the other hand, there is significant variability in the original task demand, some caution should be taken if each data point is evaluated similarly. This consideration should be a part of the records review when determining the utility of data for some intended purpose.

Record Review

Date: <u>1/20/2019</u>

Student's Name: <u>Ellie Martin</u>

Grade: <u>5</u>

Student's overall level of performance/progress (circle one):   Typical

⟨ Below progress/performance expected ⟩   Above progress/performance expected

---

Background/Health Information: *Ellie's family recently moved, causing her to change schools midyear (from South to North Elementary School). Ellie's file shows that she received a referral to the Planning and Placement Team at her former school due to problems with attention. Although the team tried to implement a prereferral intervention, Ellie's family moved before the team was able to see any results.*

Academic Information:

Reading: *For the past 2 years, Ellie has received C's on progress reports.*

Writing: *Ellie generally receives grades in the B–C range.*

Math: *Ellie's progress reports reveal a mixture of A's and B's.*

Results of Standardized Testing (fill in name of measure used and relevant scores):

<u>X</u>   District-/State-Level Assessment: *CTBS (Comprehensive Test of Basic Skills): Reading (45th percentile), Writing (55th percentile), Mathematics (80th percentile), Science (72nd percentile), Social Studies (65th percentile)*

Aptitude Testing: _____

_____

_____

Achievement Testing: _____

_____

_____

FIGURE 3.1. Example of a completed Record Review form.

Work Samples

Another source of academic data comes from work samples, such as daily homework, worksheets completed during independent work time, writing assignments (e.g., a daily journal), and creative arts projects (e.g., drawing or building with blocks; Mandinach, 2012). These sources of data are often used by teachers to determine the overall scores or grades discussed in the previous section on performance summaries. However, work samples also can and should be used to provide specific information about the reason for a particular problem or achievement—such as the information needed when engaging in diagnostic assessment. For example, a review of the types of errors made on previous math quizzes reveals that Maria has not mastered the basic facts for multiplication by 4. A review of math quizzes for the entire class suggests that more than half the students had the same type of error. As a result of these reviews, the teacher decides to reteach and practice the skill with the entire class. Data obtained from work samples can be summarized in a graphic format to determine whether progress is adequate or if an instructional change is indicated (see Chapter 7 for a discussion of data analysis strategies).

CASE EXAMPLE 3.1

Mr. Jones is a third-grade teacher at Sunnydale Elementary School. Over the past 2 weeks, the focus of his math lessons has been on multiplication. Every other day, Mr. Jones gives his students a 2-minute timed quiz involving single-digit multiplication problems. Although there has been a range of student performance on these quizzes, Maria has had particular trouble, often scoring at or below 40% correct. Maria's mother, Mrs. White, meets with Mr. Jones to discuss what she can do to help her daughter learn the multiplication tables. After much discussion, Mrs. White agrees that she will spend 15 minutes each night reviewing multiplication flash cards with Maria. They plan to meet in 2 weeks to determine whether Maria has made any progress.

As Mr. Jones gives math quizzes and tests to his class, he records each of Maria's scores on a permanent product recording sheet (Figure 3.2). In preparation for meeting with Mrs. White, Mr. Jones plots each of Maria's quiz scores on a simple chart presented in Figure 3.3.

In reviewing the data together, it was clear that the supplemental time spent reviewing the flash cards at home had been worthwhile. Although Maria started off answering fewer than half of the problems correctly, by the end of the second week she had scored an 83% on her test. Very pleased with the results, Mrs. White decided to continue reviewing the flash cards with Maria every night after dinner but also asked Mr. Jones if there was anything else she could do to help Maria. Simply by looking at the test scores, however, Mr. Jones was unable to recall what specific types of errors Maria had made. In order to find this out, it was necessary for Mr. Jones to turn to the actual work samples.

Permanent Product Recording Sheet

Date(s): _September 7_

Student's Name: _Maria_

Subject: _Math_

Behavior: _Math problems solved correctly_

Permanent Product: _Weekly math quizzes & tests_

Date	Type of Permanent Product	How Many Times Behavior Occurred	Total Opportunities for Behavior to Occur	Percentage of Observed Behavior (Observed/Total × 100)
10/1	Math test #1	8	20	40%
10/7	Math test #2	10	20	50%
10/10	Math quiz	5	10	50%
10/14	Math test #3	15	20	75%
10/21	Math test #4	15	18	83%
10/25	Math quiz	8	10	80%

FIGURE 3.2. Example of a completed Permanent Product Recording Sheet.

(continued)

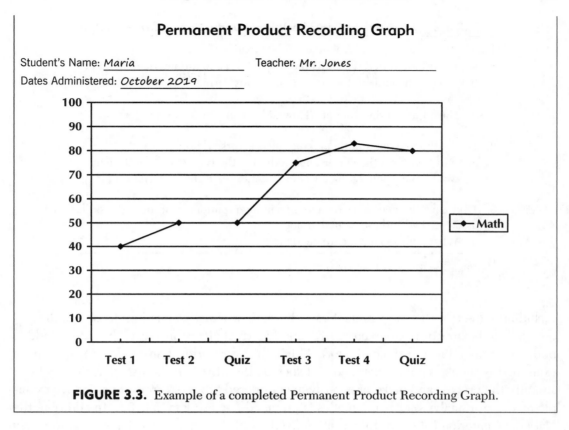

Permanent Product Recording Graph

Student's Name: *Maria*   Teacher: *Mr. Jones*

Dates Administered: *October 2019*

FIGURE 3.3. Example of a completed Permanent Product Recording Graph.

Another benefit of taking this approach toward examining students' work samples or products is the ability to determine a student's work efficiency and accuracy. Although the grade at the top of an assignment provides useful information, determining the way the student approached an assignment and the types of errors made can be particularly useful. For example, a teacher may have two students who both correctly answered 50% of the problems on a math worksheet. Whereas one student worked slowly and deliberately and only answered half of the questions, the other student quickly attempted to solve every problem but made consistent errors in decimal placement. Both students earned the same overall grade, but certainly not for the same reason—thus, different approaches are needed for remediating the problem for each student. A teacher might give the first student more practice with developing mathematical fluency and the second student more explicit instruction on the rule for decimal placement.

Work samples can also be an important source of information for conducting an error analysis, which, in turn, would inform reteaching. The type of error analysis employed is generally dependent on the type of skill being examined, and a variety of questions can be addressed (see Table 3.2). The Multilevel Academic Skills Inventory–Revised (MASI-R; Howell, Hosp, Hosp, & Morehead, 2007) exemplifies one tool that can assist in the analysis of errors in academic subject areas. For example, in the area of mathematics, the MASI-R can be used to identify several possible errors,

Extant data for academic behavior can be obtained from performance summaries, work samples, and curriculum-based assessment.

TABLE 3.2. Questions to Consider When Conducting an Error Analysis

1. Are there patterns in errors the student made? If not:
   a. Have I identified the skills the student did and did not demonstrate?
   b. Have I encouraged the student to try answering all problems and to show their work?
   c. Have I asked the student, "How did you arrive at this answer?"

2. Is the student consistently making these errors? If not:
   a. Can I confirm the pattern by predicting the type of error a student would make and giving an assessment to see if the pattern occurs?

3. Do I have the necessary data to inform interventions to address the skills associated with these errors? If not:
   a. What additional data are needed?

Note. Based on Howell and Nolet (2000).

including sign errors (i.e., the student uses the sign incorrectly), missing steps (e.g., the student fails to borrow or regroup correctly), and incorrect algorithms (e.g., the student added both the numerator and denominator). Although error patterns in work samples can be examined without use of a reference tool such as the MASI-R, the use of such a tool can simplify the process and make previously unconsidered types of errors apparent. An example of an error analysis for mathematics is provided in Case Example 3.2. In addition, the National Center on Intensive Intervention (NCII) website (*www.intensiveintervention.org*) offers resources and web-based training on conducting error analysis.

Curriculum-Based Assessment

Given its planned and purposeful use in academic assessment and monitoring, *curriculum-based assessment* (CBA) is not typically used as a permanent product source of information. However, CBA information can serve a useful purpose in performance summaries and as work samples. For example, CBA data can be summarized and aggregated to provide evaluative and normative information about overall performance within or across individuals, classes, or entire schools. Although norm-referenced standardized tests may be useful for evaluating long-term progress, these measures are generally not designed for frequent repeated assessment. In contrast, CBA data can provide a specific picture of what kind of performance should be expected from students in a particular environment, what types of error patterns exist, and whether students need specialized or remedial instructional supports (i.e., for at-risk screening purposes). Most CBA approaches involve measures that can be quickly and repeatedly administered to an individual or group for progress monitoring in order to select an appropriate intervention in a multi-tiered system of support.

Hintze, Christ, and Methe (2006) note that CBA actually represents a number of diverse assessment practices, but is commonly defined as including measurement activities that incorporate a direct recording of performance in the local curriculum for informing instructional decisions. The manner in which the curriculum is sampled to create the assessment items differentiates one CBA approach from another. For example, in the general outcome

---

CASE EXAMPLE 3.2

Let's return to the case of Maria and her multiplication tables. After his parent–teacher conference with Maria's mother, Mr. Jones returned to his desk to more closely examine Maria's last multiplication test in order to identify additional areas upon which interventions might be focused. Although Maria was performing at a significantly higher level since she began reviewing the multiplication facts at home, her rate of improvement had slowed over the past couple of quizzes. Mr. Jones wondered whether there was a specific skill (or skills) that Maria still lacked. In order to answer this question, he chose to conduct an error analysis. Results of Maria's last test are presented below:

Math Test #4

Student's Name: *Maria*   Date: *October 21*

3	2	6	9	4	6
× 4	× 5	× 7	× 8	× 4	× 1
12	10	42	72	16	6
3	7	8	5	9	3
× 9	× 2	× 1	× 6	× 2	× 3
72	14	8	30	18	9
8	3	1	6	2	7
× 5	× 2	× 4	× 3	× 6	× 9
40	6	4	18	3	36

When Mr. Jones reviewed the test, his first inclination was to examine whether all of Maria's mistakes involved the same number (which would indicate that Maria and her mother should devote extra time to reviewing those particular facts). However, he found that the three problems that she answered incorrectly (3×9, 2×6, and 7×9) all involved different digits, so he examined the problems more closely. On the first and last problems, it appeared that Maria multiplied correctly, but simply reversed the digits in her answer (i.e., $3 \times 9 = 27$ written as 72). The other error Maria made was in multiplying correctly but then adding the digits together in her answer (i.e., $2 \times 6 = 12$, $1 + 2 = 3$). When Mr. Jones then looked back at Maria's previous quizzes, he found several of the same errors. Although she did not make these errors consistently, Mr. Jones decided that it would be worthwhile to devote extra instructional time to reviewing digit placement in multiplication.

---

measurement approach, items from across the entire year might be sampled in one model. In contrast, specific subskill mastery measurement approaches involve sampling items from a particular aspect of the curriculum. See Hintze and colleagues (2006) and the references in Table 3.3 for further information about the characteristics of various CBA methods and their similarities and differences.

Curriculum-based measurement (CBM) is an example of a general outcome measurement approach to CBA that fits into a multi-tiered model of assessment. For example, when an entire school adopts CBM, the performance of all students might be assessed three times a year to obtain normative information for the entire school (i.e., the whole-group level). The

TABLE 3.3. Useful Resources for Additional Information on Curriculum-Based Assessment/Curriculum-Based Measurement

Resource	Description
aimswebPlus: *www.aimsweb.com*	aimsweb®Plus is a web-based CBM and formative assessment tool that includes a battery of tests to assess reading (early literacy, reading comprehension and fluency, vocabulary) and math (early numeracy, computation, concepts, and applications) for students in grades K–8. The cost to use the complete aimswebPlus platform is currently between $7–9 per student per year.
DIBELS: *dibels.uoregon.edu*	This website sponsored by the University of Oregon allows users to download DIBELS and easyCBM assessment materials addressing multiple reading and math skills. Data can be electronically entered into the web-based database in order to produce both graphs and automated reports. The cost to use the DIBELS database is about $1 per student per year, although testing materials are available to download for free.
Intervention Central's Curriculum-Based Measurement Warehouse: *www.interventioncentral.org*	The Curriculum-Based Measurement Warehouse provides a number of materials for learning about and conducting CBM. CBM assessment materials and administration manuals are available for reading, math, spelling, and writing. Users can also create probes for each of these four content areas. The website's ChartDog tool converts electronically entered CBM data into progress monitoring graphs. In addition, materials are available to help train large groups of teachers and other educators in CBM. All materials on the Intervention Central website are currently free.
Academic Skills Problems— Fourth Edition Workbook (Shapiro, 2011)	The final three chapters in this workbook are dedicated to progress monitoring, particularly CBM. In the first chapter, the authors provide guidelines and practice in creating and visually analyzing graphs. The second chapter is dedicated to describing how educators can develop local norms (i.e., in individual classrooms or schools) for measures such as CBM. Finally, the development and use of goal charts and tools for data-based decision making are discussed.
The ABCs of CBM: A Practical Guide to Curriculum-Based Measurement, Second Edition (Hosp, Hosp, & Howell, 2016)	This book is part of The Guilford Practical Intervention in Schools Series. In addition to providing background information on what CBM is and when it should be used, this book presents accessible information and hands-on instruction for conducting CBM in grades K–8. In addition, using the information gleaned from CBM to make sound decisions regarding instruction and intervention, along with the role of CBM within a response-to-intervention model are explained.

performance of those students who are found to be at risk for academic difficulty (i.e., the small-group level) is assessed monthly to ensure that effective instruction is being provided. Students whose performance does not improve sufficiently would receive specialized and individualized instruction and be assessed on a weekly basis (i.e., the individual-student level). In general, the more intensive the instructional need, the more frequently data are collected to monitor student progress and inform instructional decision making.

The following example illustrates the CBA approach to multi-tiered systems: Mr. Greenberg has recently begun implementing an academic intervention intended to increase the speed (fluency) with which a group of students can recite the multiplication tables. He wants to know if the intervention is effective and worth the extra implementation effort. Using the percentage of tables recited correctly (accuracy) would not provide enough information about student fluency (number correct per minute). Nor would weekly quiz administration be sufficient to inform day-to-day intervention decisions. Therefore, Mr. Greenberg changed to 2-minute CBM probes involving multiplication facts, which were administered twice a week over a 3-week period. This more timely and specific information improved his assessment of student learning and teaching effectiveness.

WHAT TYPES OF SCHOOLWIDE EXTANT DATA MIGHT BE AVAILABLE?

A multitude of extant data sources are available for assessing and intervening with behaviors at the schoolwide level. In this section, we review five sources of data: attendance data, office discipline referrals (ODRs), student records, school climate, and behavior management plans.

Attendance Data

One of the most consistently collected forms of extant data, attendance information (i.e., absences, tardies, and early dismissals), can identify students who have a variety of social behavior challenges like poor health, lack of transportation, avoidance of academic failure, competing social distractors (e.g., friends), and work outside of school. The resulting information can assist teachers, parents, counselors, and school psychologists in developing more effective and relevant behavior support plans. In addition, because this information is collected daily, it is well suited for progress monitoring purposes to evaluate the effectiveness of interventions in which the primary or secondary outcome is related to attendance. These data offer an excellent example of a source that is readily available, has a high degree of integrity, and has multiple related benefits within a school setting. Further, it is unlikely that anyone would need to argue that increasing attendance is an important outcome!

Office Discipline Referrals

Another widely used method of estimating rates of problematic behavior is the collection of office discipline referrals (ODRs). A number of researchers have demonstrated that ODRs can be a useful form of extant data for decision making if the definitions are clear, the referral processes are standardized, the school staff are supported in the accurate use of these processes, and the procedures for inputting and summarizing these data are efficient (Cavanaugh, 2016; Flannery, Fenning, Kato, & McIntosh, 2014; McIntosh, Campbell, Russell Carter, & Zumbo, 2009; Pas, Bradshaw, & Mitchell, 2011; Predy, McIntosh, & Frank, 2014).

> **Schoolwide extant data sources can be used in assessment and decision making for whole-group, small-group, and individual student behavior.**

Although in most public schools it is assumed that teachers will manage minor disciplinary incidents in the classroom (e.g., being out of seat or talking out of turn), teachers are often expected to complete ODRs when they believe that a student's behavior should be addressed by someone outside of the classroom. The need for an ODR may occur in situations wherein the behavior is highly intense (e.g., violent physical behavior) or recurring (e.g., this is the third "strike" against a student). ODRs are often delivered to a building administrator (e.g., principal or assistant principal), who then handles the problem behavior and determines the appropriate administrative action (McIntosh et al., 2009). However, in systems like positive behavioral interventions and supports (PBIS), some classes of minor teacher-managed behaviors result in an ODR that is logged in a schoolwide information system.

ODRs can provide a useful source of information for schoolwide social behavior. For example, consider the principal of a middle school who is concerned about the number of physical fights occurring among seventh-grade students, especially in nonclassroom settings. To determine specifically where to increase active supervision, the principal reviews ODRs for the last 2 months and learns that most fighting incidents are occurring outside the cafeteria and in the bus loading area. Knowing this information, the principal can organize school resources to increase adult proximity and active supervision in those nonclassroom locations. In addition, the principal can continue to monitor ODRs to determine whether the changes in supervision have resulted in fewer fights in those settings.

Although ODR data may not be sufficient for assessment at the individual-student level, they can be used to screen for students in need of further assessment and provide a context for a student's level of behavior within the school. For example, ODR information may provide a general description of a student's violation of behavioral expectations and where these problems behaviors occurred, but more data are needed to develop individualized behavior intervention plans (e.g., data about antecedent and consequence events, the possible function of behavior, the setting and time of day). Additional examples of social behavior measures are illustrated in Table 3.3.

For ODRs to be a useful tool, some guidelines related to standardization need to be followed. First, to facilitate the collection of ODR data, schools commonly use a "discipline referral" slip or form to record information about the rule violation. The content and data requested on this form should be consistent with behavioral definitions, discipline referral procedures, and so forth. In addition, the form should be simple and easy to complete and not require a great deal of time or attention from the teacher. Further, schools can collect more consistent (and therefore more defensible) ODR data on a schoolwide basis by using the School-Wide Information System (SWIS), which is a web-based system for collecting standardized ODRs (Molloy, Moore, Trail, Van Epps, & Hopfer, 2014).

Second, if data are going to be used for decision making at the school level, procedures for collecting and summarizing information must be simple, logical, and time-saving. Data are not likely to be used for formative or ongoing decision making if, for example, information is entered into a database at the end of each month and the data are not displayed in visually simple and informative graphic formats. As such, data need to be consistently entered into a system that is easily accessible for both reviewing specific ODR data and reviewing larger patterns of ODRs over time and across settings. Although standardizing ODRs and establishing a data recording system can be a challenge, the results can be quite useful. In addition, a recent body of research indicates disproportionality in ODRs among Black students and other students of color (Bottiani, Bradshaw, & Mendelson, 2017; Gion, McIntosh, & Smolkowski, 2018; Girvan, Gion, McIntosh, & Smolkowski, 2017; Martinez, McMahon, & Treger, 2016), particularly in schools with fewer financial and staff resources. It is critical that schools continuously monitor the individual- and school-level factors that may be contributing to ODRs to ensure that the data are reliable and valid indicators of problematic behavior.

Review of Student Records

A continuously growing body of research supporting the link between academic difficulties and problem behavior (e.g., Ashdown & Bernard, 2012; Lane, Oakes, Carter, & Messenger, 2014; Sayal, Washbrook, & Propper, 2015; Wang & Fredricks, 2014) suggests that academic sources of information can be important in informing the development of behavior support plans. A quarterly review for students who have a dramatic decline in their academic grades can reveal, for example, that they have experienced a significant change in their school, family, or community situation or are not benefiting from the instruction that is being provided. Through early intervention with instructional accommodations and/or behavioral supports, the occurrence of problem behaviors and future risk status might be reduced.

School Climate Surveys

Although the concept of school climate emerged in the literature in the early 1900s, its importance has been increasingly recognized by educators and researchers over the past 30 years (Cohen, McCabe, Michelli, & Pickeral, 2009; Thapa, Cohen, Guffey, & Higgins-D'Alessandro, 2013; Wang & Degol, 2016; Zullig, Koopman, Patton, & Ubbes, 2010). In particular, the topic of school climate has been receiving national attention as a result of evidence supporting the link between school climate and academic achievement, school attendance, and multiple social, emotional, and behavioral concerns (Bear, Yang, & Pasipanodya, 2015; Reaves, McMahon, Duffy, & Ruiz, 2018). For example, the Safe and Supportive Schools program has provided funding to states to conduct assessments of school climate and safety (Huang et al., 2015).

As noted by Wang and Degol (2016), school climate "is a broad, overarching construct consisting of multiple dimensions and is, as a result, measured in multiple ways" (p. 333). However, the primary method for measuring school climate is the collection of survey data, with self-report surveys used most frequently in both research and practice (Wang & Degol,

2016). Researchers have also begun to develop and adapt school climate surveys to evaluate teacher, school staff, and parent perspectives (Bear et al., 2015; Huang et al., 2015). The majority of school climate surveys measure four broad dimensions of school climate: safety (e.g., perception of safety, safety rules); teaching and learning (e.g., social and civic knowledge development or perceived use of supportive teaching practices); relationships (e.g., supportive/caring adult and peer relationships); and environmental and structural characteristics (e.g., physical environment or school connectedness; Bradshaw, Waasdorp, Debnam, & Johnson, 2014; Cohen et al., 2009; Reaves et al., 2018; White, La Salle, Ashby, & Meyers, 2014).

Given recent findings suggesting that students with emotional and behavioral disorders (EBDs) are more likely to indicate a negative perception of school climate on self-report surveys (La Salle, Peshak George, McCoach, Polk, & Evanovich, 2018), these extant data can be a source of meaningful information about student behavioral risk and challenges. However, the findings from a recent review of longitudinal school climate literature indicate that many school climate measures lack rigorous development and validity (Reaves et al., 2018). To ensure that decisions based on school climate survey data are valid and reliable, it is important to use a psychometrically sound instrument. The National Center on Safe Supportive Learning Environments (NCSSLE) provides a compendium of evidence-based and psychometrically sound school climate surveys, assessments, and scales that are available for free at *https://safesupportivelearning.ed.gov/topic-research/school-climate-measurement/school-climate-survey-compendium*. Of note, the NCSSLE highlights the School Climate Surveys developed by the U.S. Department of Education (EDSCLS), which has an associated free-of-cost and adaptable web-based platform, available at *https://safesupportivelearning.ed.gov/edscls*.

Outcomes from Behavior Management Plans

Existing behavior management plans implemented at individual, classwide, and/or schoolwide levels represent another important source of information for decision making. For example, many effective educational environments include a clearly articulated plan for promoting positive behavior, commonly in the form of a token economy. In turn, the distribution and trade-in of tokens (e.g., points, certificates, or tickets) for displays of appropriate social behaviors (e.g., sharing, taking turns, problem solving, or being on time) represent an excellent source of information for evaluating the effectiveness of schoolwide or classroom behavior management systems. This information can be used to approximate the extent to which the school staff are acknowledging appropriate student behavior at desirable rates and whether students are displaying appropriate school and classroom behaviors.

Similar assessments and evaluations can occur at the classroom and individual student levels. Teachers commonly establish classroom management systems that involve teaching typical classroom routines, strengthening cooperative group behaviors, and managing classroom rule violations. When systems are established to collect information on the number of teacher acknowledgments and reprimands, teachers can evaluate the effectiveness of their overall instructional and behavior management practices and the general status of student behavior in their classrooms.

When students require individualized behavior interventions (e.g., targeted social skills instruction, behavioral contracts, or a function-based behavior support plan), the data are usually collected on the student's behavior in relation to the effectiveness of the interventions. ODRs, attendance patterns, tokens earned, and other information can be used at the individual-student level. In addition, assessment decisions can be facilitated by examining the information available in current and/or previous intervention plans. For example, Mr. Liao refers one of his eighth-grade students, Joe, to the student support team for "inattention." When the team asks Mr. Liao if he has tried any interventions with Joe, he describes a self-monitoring program using a Direct Behavior Rating (DBR), in which Joe is asked to evaluate how well he had been paying attention. The team immediately identifies DBR information as potentially useful in assessing Joe's behavior. When the school psychologist reviews these data, they can determine what behaviors might be important to observe during a classroom visit to evaluate whether changes are needed in the current behavior intervention plan.

Data collected outside of the school setting may also be helpful. For example, Ms. Klein has worked with Ivan's father to establish a consistent homework routine to increase Ivan's homework completion rates and academic achievement. Since beginning this intervention, Ivan's father has kept a nightly log of the time Ivan spends on his homework. Together, Ms. Klein, Ivan, and Ivan's father can use this information to evaluate whether instruction needs to be modified and/or his homework routine is effective. Examples of other types of data for informing decisions related to social behavior can be found in Table 3.4.

Whether data are collected at the schoolwide, classroom, or individual student levels, the information needs to be collected, summarized, and analyzed on a regular schedule. For example, if a token economy (i.e., tokens or items provided as reinforcers for specific behaviors that can then be redeemed for a larger reward) is established and the number of tokens are not counted and reviewed on a weekly basis, determining intervention effectiveness and making timely adjustments may not be possible. We have experienced situations in which teachers are not consistently recording this information, but when the potential usefulness in doing so is pointed out to them, they begin to record the data more consistently. One repeated theme that applies to all extant data is the need to help educational professionals understand the potential utility of the data, and to work with them to standardize procedures and more consistently record and review the data.

TABLE 3.4. Examples of Possible Extant Data for Social Behaviors

- Data from current and/or previous attempted intervention plans
- Office discipline referrals
- Reward slips/prize tickets
- Suspension/expulsion records
- Request for assistance forms
- Health records
- Records of meetings held about the student
- Class absences
- Direct behavior ratings

HOW DO YOU DECIDE
WHICH INFORMATION MIGHT BE USEFUL?

Given the variety of existing data types, the next question is to determine which information might be the most useful in decision making. The general answer will depend on why the data are needed or on what available data would best match the existing problem. To facilitate answering this question, a number of guidelines should be considered.

First, extant data must be easily accessible in a timely manner by those individuals who use the information to make decisions. From an efficiency perspective, extant data, by definition, have the advantage of already existing; however, it is important to determine if the data are readily accessible. For example, the information might not be helpful if a student's grade scores are archived in a password-protected file or confidentiality policies restrict access to individual student data.

Second, extant data should be clearly organized and easily summarized. Even if the data are accessible, the degree to which the data have to be manipulated and made readable affects their utility. For example, information that must be collected from each student's personal file, compiled, and sorted from a box in which behavior slips have been accumulating for the year or information that is submitted by individual teachers and then needs to be summarized are examples of systems that are costly with respect to the time, effort, and personnel involved.

Third, the existing data must be trustworthy to be useful in decision making. If teachers and office staff do not agree about what behaviors should be referred to the office, about when and how to disseminate tokens, or about what information fields to complete on behavior incident reports, then these information sources lose their value and utility in decision making. The inconsistent collection of extant data is not only a challenge in terms of assessment, but also undermines the original purpose of the data collection. For instance, if tokens are given out inconsistently, the desired intervention effect is unlikely.

Finally, at least one staff person, but preferably an entire team, must have the time, expertise, and resources to use summarized data to guide decision making. Even the most accurate and accessible data are pointless if they are not used to guide instructional and behavioral decisions that improve the outcomes for students and the quality of interventions.

HOW DO YOU SUMMARIZE THE COLLECTED DATA?

A prerequisite to being able to summarize extant data is to determine what is considered a correct versus an incorrect response. For example, if Mrs. Gonzalez considers not raising a hand before responding worthy of an ODR, but Mr. Jones completes ODRs only for physical altercations, counting the number of referrals in 1 week will not provide an accurate picture of a student's behavior in the school. The need to develop specific, operationalized definitions of correct and incorrect behavior becomes particularly important when more than one individual works with a student. However, even if a student spends most of the day with a single staff member, the time spent clearly identifying what constitutes the

For use in assessment and decision making, extant data must be accessible, organized, reliable, and usable.

problem behavior is necessary to make certain that everyone is on the same page. Different perceptions and levels of tolerance about problem behavior exist, and both affect how we interpret or rate student behavior. However, to the greatest extent possible, the school staff should strive for consensus on what constitutes prosocial (desirable) versus problematic (undesirable) behavior.

Once agreement has been established, a number of possibilities for summarizing the data are available. Case Example 3.3 illustrates how one might utilize methods of summarization with regard to extant data, including the following:

- *Frequency count.* One of the easiest ways to summarize data is to keep a running tally of how many times the behavior occurs. For example, a principal may be interested in how many times a particular student has been late to school over the past month. Two conditions must be met when using a frequency count. First, a similar number of opportunities must be possible for the behavior (e.g., spelling problems or opportunities to be called upon) to occur within a specified time. Second, the length of each observation session must be equal. For example, five tardies in 5 days would be interpreted differently from five tardies in 5 months. If these conditions are not met, the rate or percentage (correct/incorrect) is calculated.

- *Rate.* Rate is calculated as a way to standardize a frequency count by dividing the number of observed responses by the length of the observation. With regard to academics, we are accustomed to seeing rates (e.g., number of words read correctly per minute or number of assignments completed in a week). An example of a rate calculated for a social behavior would be the number of tokens a student has earned for positive behavior each week. Rates, however, can be artificially inflated or deflated if the number of opportunities to respond are exaggerated or restricted, respectively. Richards (2018) indicates that fewer than 10 response opportunities can affect rate accuracies. Although a shorter time period can be selected to provide an estimate of behavior (e.g., 5 minutes), teachers must ensure that the period accurately represents the overall rate of behavior. See Case Example 3.3 for an example of summarizing and graphing data using rate (blank forms can be found in Appendices 3.2 and 3.3).

- *Cumulative responses.* Recording the cumulative number of responses is similar to conducting a frequency count. However, rather than recording the number or rate of behavior for individual observation sessions, a running total or cumulative record of the number of behaviors is maintained. For instance, a high school principal might reward students who receive an accumulated total of 10 positive referrals with a special parking spot in the campus lot.

- *Trials to criterion.* Recording the number of trials to criterion is particularly relevant when assessing skills that are still being learned (i.e., in the acquisition phase). The number of responses that an individual makes before reaching a performance criterion on the target behavior is emphasized. For example, a student learning to throw a basketball into a hoop will probably make several attempts before succeeding. In determining the number of trials to criterion, we are interested in how many shots it takes before the basket is made. Or a student learning to independently follow a recipe may successfully complete only half of the recipe instructions independently. In this case, the trials to criterion would be expressed as a percentage (e.g., 50%) of the steps completed.

CASE EXAMPLE 3.3

It is only October and Dr. Clark, the school psychologist, has already received multiple referrals regarding a 10th-grade student, Luke, because of struggles across academic areas. On the last progress report, Luke received D's in all of his core content classes (e.g., English, history, science, math, and foreign language), which was not consistent with his academic performance in previous years. Although Luke had not been an A student in the past, he had consistently received a mixture of B's and C's.

Dr. Clark approaches each of Luke's teachers and asks them to compile some information for him. First, he asks for a frequency count of the number of times that Luke has been absent from their classes each week since the beginning of the school year. Second, he asks each teacher to calculate a percentage (rate) of the number of homework assignments that Luke has completed thus far (Dr. Clark asks for a rate in case teachers did not assign homework every night). Third, he asks for the results (in percentages) of any quizzes or tests that Luke has taken in each class. Last, he asks each teacher to share a copy of his or her syllabus, including information regarding how grades are calculated.

Once Dr. Clark receives the requested information, he sits down to summarize and evaluate it. He is surprised to find that Luke has earned satisfactory grades on his quizzes and tests (typically B's and C's). What then catches his eye, however, is the fact that Luke has been absent an average of 2 days a week in each of his classes. In addition, he has only completed approximately 33% of the total number of homework assignments. When Dr. Clark looks at Luke's course syllabi, he discovers an important piece of the puzzle: Across subjects, both homework and class participation (e.g., discussion, presentations, and science labs) contribute significantly to the overall course grade. Dr. Clark quickly realizes that efforts must focus on identifying factors that are affecting Luke's attendance and how those problems can be overcome.

WHAT ARE THE STRENGTHS ASSOCIATED WITH USING EXTANT DATA?

Already Available and Accessible

Perhaps the greatest strength of extant data relates to their ready availability. As noted by Sheridan, Swanger-Gagne, Welch, Kwon, and Garbacz (2009), information gleaned from extant data can be collected throughout the day without placing any additional burden on the classroom teacher, such as remembering to conduct ratings at specific intervals or to collect assessment information while engaged in other classroom responsibilities. Additionally, the fact that it is possible to review these permanent products at a later point reduces the demands on teachers' time.

Reduced Risk of Reactivity

Collecting permanent product data can mitigate the risk of reactivity, or the likelihood for an individual to display atypical behavior in the presence of an outside observer. A basic example of reactivity is a scenario in which an external observer enters the classroom to observe a student with disruptive behavior, and the student does not act out because they know that they are being watched. With permanent products, typically the classroom teacher is simply utilizing existing data and is not altering the classroom environment in a way that students would notice. Therefore, reactivity is diminished. Although reactivity seems like a relatively minor issue, it is critical in relation to behavioral assessment. Reactivity has the potential to change both student and teacher behavior. In this situation, even the most reliable measure will not be valid because the environment being monitored is not representative of what typically happens. This can end up being a significant issue if the data collected in the atypical environment are considered accurate, resulting in inappropriate decisions.

Contextually Relevant

Another strength of extant data is the insight they provide into the everyday functioning of student behaviors. Since the data often are taken from existing sources, they paint a picture of student behavior that is relevant to the particular classroom or school. In addition, since these outcome measures are typically selected by the classroom teacher, they should be more socially valid. Data from sources like standardized tests or Systematic Direct Observation are often not relevant to the immediate classroom or instructional context. Considering that we often utilize data in working with teachers to modify how they are intervening with a student, their belief that the data are socially valid and relevant is critical.

WHAT ARE THE WEAKNESSES ASSOCIATED WITH USING EXTANT DATA?

Potentially Time-Consuming to Summarize

Although the time required for data collection can be dramatically reduced when using extant data, the process of summarizing the data has the potential to become time-consuming. In addition, if an error analysis is conducted, the process could be significantly lengthened. One important step toward ensuring efficiency is to determine which data are necessary to answer the questions posed. When summarizing the data, efficient systems for data display must be used. For example, if the data are graphed, an easy graphing tool such as ChartDog (see *www.interventioncentral.org/teacher-resources/graph-maker-free-online*) can be utilized. A quick Google search for "free online graphing tools" provides several alternative options as well, thanks to recent advances in open technology. Guidelines for visually displaying data in charts and graphs are presented in Chapter 7.

May Provide a Limited Picture

As is the case with any assessment tool, extant data may not be useful in all situations. With preexisting data, an accurate representation of what the student knows or can do may not be possible. In these situations, an assessment would not reveal an entire picture of a student's skills. Therefore, this type of data should not be used in isolation, particularly when making high-stakes decisions, such as those related to placement or diagnosis. Extant data should be one part of a multimethod assessment practice.

Challenge in Maintaining Consistent Use

For extant data to be useful, consistent and accurate data collection must be established. For example, if a school contains four classrooms in the same grade, it is highly unlikely that all four teachers will utilize identical grading systems. Teacher A might base 50% of a student's grade on homework, whereas Teacher B might base 25% of a grade on homework. A similar problem exists for social behaviors, such as when two teachers possess different tolerance levels for problem behavior. Although this weakness is not of as much concern when assessing student performance within the classroom, it is an important consideration when making interclassroom comparisons or assessing at the whole-school level.

Unknown Psychometric Adequacy

With most forms of extant school data (the exception most often being norm-referenced standardized tests and ODRs), psychometric properties have not been investigated. For example, it is unlikely that teachers put their math tests through statistical analyses to ensure that they are reliable and valid. Given that it is technically impossible to establish the psychometric adequacy of extant data, the utility of this class of assessment is typically restricted to less intensive cases *or* the assessment should be paired with tools that have well-defined psychometric characteristics.

CONCLUDING COMMENTS

In this chapter, several options are presented for using data that already exist in schools but may be overlooked in assessment. We reviewed the potential sources of extant data for academic and social behavior, along with how the data might be used for various assessment purposes. The use of extant data is appropriate for a particular situation if the need for using this information and this particular type of data are clear. The primary advantage of using extant data is its feasibility; that is, it has already been collected. The use of existing data can reduce the burden on data collection resources and enhance the goodness of fit within the natural environment. However, caution must be exercised when using extant data, particularly regarding the need for an efficient method of summarizing the data and the potential limitations for their use in high-stakes decisions.

Record Review

Date: _____

Student's Name: _____

Grade: _____

Student's overall level of performance/progress (circle one):   Typical

    Below progress/performance expected   Above progress/performance expected

Background/Health Information:

Academic Information:
Reading:
Writing:
Math:

Results of Standardized Testing (fill in name of measure used and relevant scores):
___ District-/State-Level Assessment:

Aptitude Testing: _____
_____
_____

Achievement Testing: _____
_____
_____

Permanent Product Recording Sheet

Date(s): _____

Student's Name: _____

Subject: _____

Behavior: _____

Permanent Product: _____

Date	Type of Permanent Product	How Many Times Behavior Occurred	Total Opportunities for Behavior to Occur	Percentage of Observed Behavior (Observed/Total × 100)

Permanent Product Recording Graph

Student's Name: _____   Teacher: _____

Dates Administered: _____

Comments: _____

_____

_____

_____

_____

_____

_____

_____

_____

_____

_____

CHAPTER 4

Systematic Direct Observation

In the previous chapter, we focused on extant data as a feasible way to collect information pertaining to students, classrooms, and entire schools. Extant data capitalizes on information that is already being collected, and does double duty in a multi-tiered framework for data-based decision making. As long as the extant data are defensible in addition to being easily collected and are interpreted and presented in a manner consistent with their noted strengths and weaknesses, they can provide an outstanding source of information. However, as the remaining assessment methods that we cover in this book reflect, there can also be questions that are not easily answered by data that already exist. These questions might include: "How long is Xiao Mei typically disruptive during a class period, and does this change as the day progresses?" "What is a good classwide estimate for the amount of time students are academically engaged in Mrs. Grippon's third-grade class?" or "How many times does Leo curse each day, and what is the average number of curse words he says by period?" When we have questions about specific behaviors during specific time periods, we often turn to an assessment method called Systematic Direct Observation (SDO). In this chapter, various techniques for conducting SDO are reviewed, along with the procedural guidelines and examples supporting each technique. We also offer some guidelines for selecting behaviors and techniques and for summarizing data. Finally, the general strengths and weaknesses of using SDO are discussed.

> **Using SDO techniques can assist in answering questions about specific behaviors during specified periods.**

WHAT IS SDO AND WHY USE IT?

SDO is exactly what it sounds like: systematic rules for data collection that are used to count, measure, time, or otherwise quantify a behavior while it is being directly observed by the person collecting the data. This may seem like a no-brainer, but it is important to specify that we consider SDO to be a strictly quantitative method of data collection, wherein rules about how to conduct the observation and collect the data are imposed prior to beginning the observation (Suen & Ary, 1989). *Systematic procedures are different from qualitative or "naturalistic" data collection methods, wherein the goings-on during the observation drive how the resulting data will be understood, categorized, and ultimately interpreted* (Hintze, Volpe, & Shapiro, 2002). In an example of naturalistic data collection, an observer enters a classroom during morning math instruction and writes down descriptions of behaviors as they occur, later summarizing them to provide a complete account of the behaviors and their context. The detail with which the behavior is recorded may vary from a global description of an event (e.g., "Rohini said 'Hi' to John") to a narrow, more specific descriptive recording that involves context as well as antecedents and consequences (e.g., "During recess today, Rohini said 'Hi' to John after he approached her group while they played soccer").

> **SDO offers a quantitative method for repeated data collection, as procedures are prespecified and used consistently during the time the data are being collected.**

Although naturalistic observation techniques have the potential to provide important information, depending on the reason for conducting the observation, they also have drawbacks that can limit their application in behavioral assessment and monitoring. The lack of a predetermined, specified behavior and an associated standardized definition makes it very difficult to combine data across observations. In addition, qualitative observation techniques are highly vulnerable to inferential judgments and to greater variance from observer to observer (Suen & Ary, 1989). Given the difficulty inherent in quantifying these data, the information gathered from naturalistic observation might be helpful in initially identifying and analyzing the stages of problem solving but may not be useful in monitoring behavior over time or across settings.

Thus, at first we may utilize naturalistic observation techniques when we need to familiarize ourselves with a target student or classroom and specifics of the target behaviors before finalizing an operational definition and beginning formal data collection. For example, Lucia was asked to consult with Mrs. Chen, a sixth-grade teacher at another school in the district, to support Paul, a student who has started exhibiting some disruptive behavior. Lucia spoke with the district special education coordinator, who filled her in on the general referral concern but wasn't too familiar with this specific teacher and her classroom management style. Lucia also spoke to Mrs. Chen to get some more information about Paul and to schedule her first visit to the classroom. During the initial conversation, Mrs. Chen was not very specific regarding what Paul's disruptions looked like (i.e., the topography of the behavior), even when asked some probing questions. So, under pressure to start her observations but still unsure about the specifics of the situation, Lucia arrived for her observation session with her tablet computer and decided to sit in the back of the classroom and take narrative notes on (1) the overall classroom environment, including classroom management techniques and the factors associated with instruction and the curriculum and (2) the times when Paul is disruptive and what those disruptive behaviors look like. Thus, Lucia decided to engage in some naturalistic observation to familiarize herself with the case and inform her development of a more systematic observation method for when she returned to the classroom later that week.

In contrast to naturalistic observation, SDO refers to the observation of explicit behavior that is predefined and collected in prespecified settings (thus, it is "systematic"). Salvia, Ysseldyke, and Witmer (2017) describe five characteristics that distinguish the systematic nature of SDO from naturalistic approaches:

1. The specific characteristics of behavior are attended to.
2. These behaviors have been defined in operational terms.
3. The data are collected under standardized procedures.
4. The time and place for observations are specified.
5. Interobserver agreement can be assessed.

Taken together, these five characteristics reduce the amount of inference making needed to connect the numbers on the page to the actual student's behavior, and thereby increase our confidence in the resulting data when they are interpreted appropriately. We can comprehensively and explicitly explain why these specific numbers are used to describe a student's behavior, and articulately respond to questions regarding what these data do and do not represent. In other words, being specific regarding what is being observed and standardizing the procedures and presentation of the data can enhance our confidence that the data are a reflection of the student's behavior. For example, Sammy may have been referred by his teacher for not paying attention in class. After further discussion, the teacher and school psychologist decide that the behavior is most likely to occur during independent seat work. Thus, observation sessions are scheduled to collect baseline information during those times, with academic engagement identified as the target behavior to be observed. Further specification of academic engagement is needed (Shapiro, 2011), so the teacher decides to mark the target behavior as present if Sammy is either passively (e.g., listening to a lecture or reading silently) or actively (e.g., writing or raising a hand) engaged. A standardized system for collecting data about Sammy's academic engagement is specified, and the school psychologist agrees to summarize the information prior to their next meeting.

As discussed by Hintze et al. (2002), the rationale for the use of SDO over other procedures lies in the need to gather relevant information about students using assessment practices that result in reliable and valid data. In addition, SDO that incorporates explicit definitions of target behaviors can reduce ambiguity or subjectivity. Ambiguity or subjectivity in defining problem behavior can contribute to implicit bias (unconscious stereotypes), which has been identified as a contributor to disproportionality in our decisions about behavior based on student characteristics, such as race and ethnicity (McIntosh, Girvan, Horner, & Smolkowski, 2014). Strong evidence points to the disproportional application of exclusionary practices in K–12 public schools, particularly toward students who are Black, male, or identified with a disability (U.S. Government Accountability Office, 2018). It is critical that we recognize the significance of this issue, the failure that it represents in ensuring equitable access to education and positive life outcomes for all students, and our role in enacting change. Given our emphasis on sound assessment practices that can serve multiple purposes, including the capacity for progress monitoring, support for the use of SDO procedures is emphasized in this chapter.

WHAT ARE SPECIFIC TECHNIQUES THAT UTILIZE SDO?

After reviewing the five characteristics of SDO just mentioned, you might be wondering how one method of measurement can be defined using such broad strokes. Indeed, we prefer to discuss SDO as a general methodology for measurement, or a set of rules that can be applied to distinct problems, out of which a variety of different ways for measuring behavior can be derived. In other words, we consider SDO to be an umbrella term for many different types of measures, just like the term "rating scale" describes an overall methodology for measuring the characteristics of a person but doesn't tell us exactly what a specific rating scale might look like. To say "I'm doing SDO" is akin to saying "I'm doing a rating scale"; we generally understand what the person is referring to but need clarification on what specific measurement techniques are actually being utilized.

The specific SDO technique that one might choose depends entirely upon the questions that are posed. We walk through a specific decision-making process for choosing an SDO method later in the chapter, but first, we present some foundational SDO techniques, each of which serves a specific purpose and has unique strengths and weaknesses. As we described in depth in Chapter 2, the selection of a particular technique begins with operationally defining the behavior or group of behaviors of interest and specifying the question or questions that need to be answered about the behavior.

> **There are many options to choose from in selecting a specific SDO technique, which can be described by features that are continuous or noncontinuous.**

Within the literature, different methods of categorizing SDO techniques have been described. Some methods emphasize the way in which observation is conducted by the observer (e.g., Suen & Ary, 1989), whereas other methods emphasize the dimension of behavior that is being targeted (e.g., Cooper, Heron, & Heward, 2007). Here we present a simplified version of the categorizations as described by Suen and Ary (1989) in their seminal text on direct observation, with two general buckets of techniques: those that use **continuous** (constant and unceasing) observation, and those that use **noncontinuous** (interrupted and interval-based) observation. This categorization and a description of each method is provided in Table 4.1.

Continuous observation techniques depend upon paying constant attention to the subject during the specified observation period. In other words, if I am conducting a frequency count intended to measure Nico's hand-raising behavior during math class, I should be focused on Nico during the entirety of math class.

Continuous observation techniques include:

- *Frequency count:* the number of times a specific behavior occurs (e.g., four initiations of a conversation).
  - If you also record *the length of time you were observing,* you can convert this number to a *rate,* which is the number of events per unit of time (e.g., nine self-injurious hits per minute) by dividing (1) the number of events by (2) the total length of the observation. If I saw 30 self-injurious hits during a 60-minute observation, I could report that value as 0.5 hits per minute (30 hits/60 minutes), or 5 hits every 10 minutes (30 hits/six 10-minute periods in an hour), which might be easier for others to interpret since "half a behavior" can be difficult to describe.

TABLE 4.1. Systematic Direct Observation Methods

Method	Dimension	How?	Example
Continuous observation			
+ Frequency count	Event	Count the number of times a behavior happened.	Julio raised his hand four times.
+ Rate	Event	Count the behaviors, and then divide the number of times they happened by the amount of time you observed them.	Julio raised his hand twice an hour.
+ Percentage of opportunities	Event/locus	Divide the number of times the behavior happened by the number of times it could have happened.	Julio raised his hand in response to 50% of teacher prompts.
+ Duration recording	Time	Measure the length of time the behavior occurred during the observation period.	Julio was engaged for 30 minutes, or Julio was engaged for 75% of the class period.
+ Latency	Locus	Measure the length of time between a prompt and a response. You'll usually want to divide the length of time by the number of times it happened.	On average, 5 seconds elapsed between a teacher prompt and Julio raising his hand.
Noncontinuous observation			
+ Time sampling and interval recording	Time	Chunk an observation period into intervals (i.e., a 10-minute period into sixty 10-second intervals). During each interval, record the interval as an "occurrence" only if . . .	We estimated that Julio was engaged for 60% of the 15-minute observation period . . .
− Momentary time sampling	Time	• the behavior was happening at the beginning of the interval.	using momentary time sampling with 10-second intervals.
− Partial-interval recording	Time	• the behavior occurred at any point during the interval.	using partial-interval recording with 10-second intervals.
− Whole-interval recording	Time	• the behavior occurred throughout the entire interval.	using whole-interval recording with 10-second intervals.

46

- *Duration:* the time spent engaging in a specific behavior (e.g., actively engaged in reading for 12 minutes). We can think about duration in a few different ways:
  - *Total duration* provides the total amount of time the behaviors were occurring throughout the observation period. In other words, you are measuring the total time (in seconds or minutes) that a student engages in a target behavior during an activity. An observer could use a stopwatch to record the total duration by pressing "start" when the behavior begins, "stop" when it stops, and "start" again when the behavior next occurs, and so on. At the end of the activity, the stopwatch will indicate the total length of time the student was observed to be engaging in the target behavior.
  - If you also record *the length of time you were observing,* the total duration can be converted into *percentage of time* (e.g., out of seat for 35% of the reading period) by dividing the total duration of the behavior by the total duration of the observation. This calculation makes these percentages comparable across observations of different lengths, which can be extremely useful when comparing data collected across multiple sessions!
  - Finally, if you also record *the number of times the behavior happened* (either just by counting separately, or [and we recommend this method] by recording the duration of each individual instance of behavior), the total duration can be converted to *average time per event* (e.g., each temper tantrum lasted an average of 7.5 minutes) by dividing the number of times the behavior happened by the total duration of the behavior.
- *Interresponse time:* the length of time between the end of one instance of behavior and the beginning of the next instance of behavior (e.g., 84 seconds elapsed between the first and second slap).
  - Like duration, both interresponse time and latency (described next) can be described as a *total* or as an *average time per event.* Just follow the same procedures described to record duration.
- *Latency:* the length of time for (1) an instance of a target behavior to begin, after (2) a prompt or antecedent cue is provided (e.g., it took 2 minutes to begin the task after the teacher's direction was given).

In contrast to these continuous observation techniques, noncontinuous techniques are used when continuous observations are too difficult to conduct, such as when (1) you need to continuously observe multiple behaviors, multiple students, or the behaviors of a group of students (i.e., teaching while observing or keeping track of multiple behaviors); (2) behaviors are occurring at rates that are too fast to count accurately (e.g., profanity during a temper tantrum); or (3) individual behaviors vary drastically in duration (e.g., 20 seconds out of seat vs. 15 minutes out of seat). In noncontinuous techniques, the data are recorded during prespecified intervals of time within a specified observation session; they are then summarized as a percentage of intervals of behavioral occurrences and nonoccurrences. Unlike continuous-observation systems in which each behavioral event is observed and measured as precisely as possible, noncontinuous methods result in approximations because behavioral occurrences are assessed only at specific intervals of time. In noncontinuous observation, behavior is sampled in one of three basic ways:

1. *Momentary time sampling.* A behavioral occurrence is indicated if the behavior occurs at a single point in time relative to an observation interval. This is almost always at the beginning or the end of the interval (we use the "beginning of the interval" throughout this book for convenience).

2. *Whole-interval recording.* A behavioral occurrence is indicated if the behavior occurs throughout the entire duration of an observation interval.

3. *Partial-interval recording.* A behavioral occurrence is indicated if the behavior occurs at any point during an observation interval.

In the next section, we review each method in detail; a summary of each technique is also presented in Table 4.1.

Continuous Observation Techniques

Frequency Counts (and Their Cousin, Rate)

Frequency count is the technical term for counting how many times something happens. Data from frequency counts can answer the question "How many times did this behavior occur?" and frequency counts are a good choice when the target behavior is relatively discrete (i.e., has an observable start and end point), when each behavioral event is comparable in duration or in other dimensions of interpretative importance (e.g., intensity), and when logistics permit continuous observations. Frequency counts require a simple tallying or counting of each behavior occurrence during a specified observation period and place. For example, you might count the number of times Rez raises his hand during whole-class math instruction. One of the most straightforward methods for conducting a frequency count is to just make tally marks on a piece of paper, but other creative ways to conduct a frequency count exist and are really only limited by your imagination. Some ideas include moving a rubber band from one wrist to the other, using a frequency counter or "clicker" similar to that used by museum docents, or making a small rip on the edge of a card or piece of paper.

At their most basic, frequency count data are summarized by totaling the number of times the behavior occurred during the observation period. If the observation period is always the same length (e.g., 48-minute science period), the counts alone can be presented and interpreted (e.g., 4 hand raises on Monday, 3 on Tuesday, 9 on Wednesday, 0 on Thursday). If the observation period varies in length, however, the frequency is typically converted into **rate**, as seen in Figure 4.1. Rate is calculated by dividing the number of observed events by the length of the associated observation period (e.g., 2.0 talk-outs per minute on Wednesday, 0.5 talk-outs per minute on Thursday, and 3.0 talk-outs per minute on Friday). To facilitate interpretation, frequency data can be presented in bar or line graphs (see Figure 4.4 for an example with a different type of data). In Chapter 3, an example of converting frequency to rate for academic data can be found in Case Example 3.1.

A frequency count summary can be made across the entire observation period or divided into smaller intervals that represent the observation period, such as every 15 minutes during morning instructional activities. One advantage to dividing the period into intervals is that patterns of behavior across time can be examined. To enhance the contextual meaning of event data, additional information could be collected, for example, (1) infor-

In the past 2 weeks, Sammy, a third-grade student, has been throwing tantrums during the day. Sammy's teacher, Mrs. McIntyre, is concerned by this behavior and seeks the guidance of the school psychologist. Although she promises that she will be in to observe Sammy as soon as possible, the school psychologist asks Mrs. McIntyre to keep a *frequency count* of how many times Sammy tantrums over the next few days. Mrs. McIntyre agrees to keep a tally throughout the entire school day (8:00–2:30), and then the school psychologist will graph the data using a bar chart. Mrs. McIntyre's data are provided below:

Day	Mon.	Tues.	Wed.	Thurs.	Fri.
# of tantrums	4	2	1	2	1

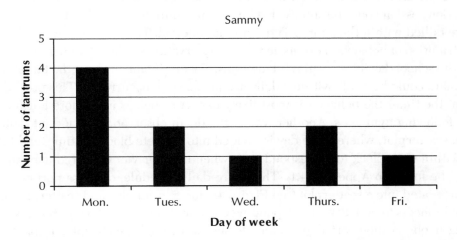

In the above example, keeping a frequency count worked well because Mrs. McIntyre monitored Sammy's behavior over the same period of time each day (8:00–2:30). How would this situation change if Mrs. McIntyre were unable to record Sammy's tantrums for the same amount of time each day? If the observation periods from day to day are not of equal length, Mrs. McIntyre must calculate a ratio of the number of behavioral occurrences in a designated time period (most often number per minute). These calculations are illustrated below:

Day Time	Mon. 8:00–10:00	Tues. 8:30–10:00	Wed. 9:15–9:45	Thurs. 8:00–9:00	Fri. 8:30–9:50
# of tantrums	4	2	1	2	1

Monday's rate = 4 tantrums/2 hours = 2 tantrums per hour

Tuesday's rate = 2 tantrums/1.5 hours = 0.75 tantrums per hour

Wednesday's rate = 1 tantrum/0.5 hours = 2 tantrums per hour

Thursday's rate = 2 tantrums/1 hour = 2 tantrums per hour

FIGURE 4.1. Summarizing frequency data through a bar chart.

mation about the setting (e.g., curriculum, number and demographic of peers or physical arrangements); (2) antecedent events that precede behavioral events (e.g., teacher directives/ instruction or peer behaviors); (3) consequences that follow behavioral events (e.g., teacher or peer attention, removal of instructional materials, or being removed from the room); and (4) nonroutine stimulus events or conditions (sometimes referred to as "setting events" when used with a specific behavioral meaning) that affect the value or influence of consequences (e.g., illness, social conflict, or missed medications).

In addition, information about the distribution of behavioral events can be obtained by further dividing an observation session into smaller intervals. For example, a 40-minute observation session could be subdivided into eight 5-minute intervals, and as events occur, they are tallied within the appropriate 5-minute interval. The result is a general pattern of the distribution of behavioral events across the observation session. Another tactic is to sub- divide the school day into meaningful intervals. That is, if tantrums are the target behavior, a tally mark could be made within a daily agenda for each occurrence. This procedure may pinpoint the times the behavior is most likely to occur, such as just before lunch or imme- diately following gym class. Another way to divide an observation period into intervals is to use a **scatterplot**, wherein the day is divided into discrete blocks of time, and tallies are made within each block to correspond with when the behavior occurred (a blank scatter- plot can be found in Appendix 4.1). The entire daily schedule, or just a portion of it, may be incorporated into a scatterplot (see Figure 4.2 for an example), and scatterplots can vary from daily sheets to entire weeks, depending on your preferences. An additional strength of dividing an observation period into intervals, such as through a scatterplot, is that the occur- rence of infrequent yet serious behaviors, such as a physical altercation between students, can be captured within days and across weeks with corresponding time-of-day information.

In summary, the frequency count technique is appealing because of its relative ease of use, intuitive interpretation (i.e., most stakeholders will be very comfortable with how to make, count, and understand tally marks), and flexibility. However, the information that is gathered can be limited, and it is most meaningfully interpreted when events are fairly comparable across occasions (e.g., of similar intensity/duration across time); therefore, in many situations, frequency count information may best be used as a complement to another procedure. An additional caution regarding the selection of a frequency count procedure is that it can be exceedingly difficult to use *in vivo* (or live and in-person) with behaviors that occur with very high frequency. For example, if "speaking swear words" is the behavior of concern, but this behavior occurs at extremely high rates throughout the day, attempts to record each individual swear word may preclude an accurate count of swearing behaviors, as well as interfere with your ability to teach or support your students, and may exacerbate the swearing behavior that you're trying to measure and intervene with! Thus, the *in vivo* frequency count procedure may best be used for behaviors that occur at low-to-moderate rates and are relatively discrete and equal in duration or other dimensions of interest.

If behaviors are happening at a very high frequency, like individual swear words dur- ing a 10-minute tantrum, you might consider a few different options. First, you could set up a video or audio recording device in the classroom, which would likely permit a more accurate count of a high-frequency behavior, but also often poses its own set of roadblocks precluding its usage (e.g., district/school policy, parent permission, or students reacting to the presence of a video camera in their classroom). Second, you could change the way you

Mrs. McIntyre could also use a scatterplot to record when Sammy tantrums during the school day. Each time Mrs. McIntyre observes a tantrum, she simply makes a tally mark in the box representing the day and time at which the tantrum occurred.

Student's Name: _Sammy_   Date/Time: _November 3–7_

Behavior: _tantrums_   Setting: _classroom_

Time	Mon.	Tues.	Wed.	Thurs.	Fri.
			Day		
8:00–8:30					
8:30–9:00	III	II		I	IIII
9:00–9:30	recess	recess	recess	recess	recess
9:30–10:00	II	I	II	I	II
10:00–10:30					
10:30–11:00					
11:00–11:30	III	I	II		III
11:30–12:00	lunch	lunch	lunch	lunch	lunch
12:00–12:30					
12:30–1:00	I			II	II
1:00–1:30					
1:30–2:00					
2:00–2:30					
2:30–3:00	I			I	II

After Mrs. McIntyre examines the scatterplot, patterns begin to emerge. Not only does Sammy have more tantrums on Mondays and Fridays, but he also is more likely to have one immediately before and/or after recess and lunch breaks. Knowing this information should be helpful to Mrs. McIntyre in designing an appropriate intervention.

FIGURE 4.2. Recording frequency data using a behavioral occurrence scatterplot.

define the behavior of interest. Are you really interested in counting every single swear word that McKaila says, or are you more interested in how long these swearing periods go on for? Finally, you could consider the use of noncontinuous recording methods to estimate instances of the behavior, as described in the section on noncontinuous methods.

Duration and Interresponse Time

The second type of continuous observation technique is the logical next step in measuring some dimension of the target behavior: we can measure how many times something happens (frequency count), and we can measure for how long it occurs (**duration**). In measuring duration, the length of time over which the behavior occurred is recorded in some manner. Thus, the most basic question that we can answer with data derived from a duration recording is "For how long did this behavior occur?"

The simplest method of recording duration, just starting and stopping a stopwatch or cell-phone timer when the behavior is occurring, requires the least amount of effort but also results in the least amount of information. We learn how long the behavior was going on during the observation period (e.g., Javier was engaged in silent reading for 50 minutes during English), and are able to convert that time into a percentage of the total time if we know the length of the observation period (e.g., Javier was engaged in silent reading for 50 minutes during the 55-minute English period, or 91% of the period), but nothing else.

However, the types of questions we can answer with a duration recording can be expanded by including more detail in the duration recording procedure. By recording frequency data within the duration recording, we significantly expand the types of questions we can ask. A recording can be as simple as using rows on a sheet of paper to indicate the length of each individual instance of behavior; for example, tantrum 1 occurred for 45 seconds, tantrum 2 occurred for 90 seconds, and so on. Thus, the duration recording procedure also becomes a frequency count procedure; we can say how many tantrums took place and how long each one was, thus allowing us to answer a question like "What was the average length of each individual tantrum during morning meeting?" To go one step further, if we noted the start and end times of each individual tantrum, we could ask "When do tantrums typically occur during morning meeting?"

This final procedure for duration recording brings us to a discussion of **interresponse time**, or the amount of time that elapses between instances of behavior. By noting the start and end times when recording duration, we can also calculate the amount of time from the end of one tantrum to the beginning of the next, answering the question "What's the average length of time between tantrums? What are the longest and shortest gaps between tantrums?" Although interresponse time is seemingly just "one more thing" in the world of SDO, it is the critical variable of interest when we are trying to lengthen or shorten the amount of time between instances of a behavior. For example, if we are trying to lengthen the amount of time between requests for a bathroom break or shorten the amount of time between hand raises, interresponse time is going to serve as our primary measure.

Latency

In **latency recording**, we measure the length of time between an event of interest (i.e. an antecedent, or triggering event) and the start of the target behavior. Often, latency recording is used to measure the length of time that elapsed between (1) a prompt and (2) the behavior that was prompted, thereby answering questions like "How long does it usually take for Carolina to begin her worksheet after her teacher provides her with a verbal prompt?" If a completion time for the behavior is needed, duration and latency recording can both be used. Some sort of timing device, like a stopwatch or cell-phone timer, is most commonly used to record duration and latency data. As with all continuous observation techniques, behavioral events must have a clearly defined start and stopping point. For example, if you're recording teacher transition prompts, and a teacher casually tells a student to get ready to go to lunch without a clear directive (e.g., specifying to immediately put books away and get in line), determining when to begin latency recording may be difficult. When these kinds of ambiguities arise, the most important rule to remember is *consistency*. As long as you are consistent in your definition of the target behavior, you can coherently describe what these data mean when interpreting and presenting them.

Data for duration, interresponse time, and latency can be summarized by reporting an average or total time, depending on whether you're interested in the length of time relative to another activity (e.g., a comparison of response time across instructional activity transitions during a day) or the average response time (e.g., during the transition to lunch). As in frequency count recording, collecting concurrent information about setting, antecedent, and consequence events can contextualize the observation data that are obtained. In the previous example, a pattern might be found in the observational data that relates to the nature of the instruction provided by the teacher. A passive, nonspecific prompt (e.g., "Who's hungry for lunch?") may be more likely related to a longer latency than a specific prompt (e.g., "Get ready for lunch by clearing your desks and sitting quietly"). In this example, if the difference in the antecedent is not noted, the data won't reflect the importance of the quality of the prompt.

When we use SDO, we are developing a measurement system that we expect to yield meaningful data and facilitate clear and transparent decision making. As we have discussed, one important component of this system is that we clearly define a conceptually meaningful observation period, such as the first 30 minutes of math class or an entire morning meeting. Chapter 2 discussed the importance of matching our generalizations about data to the level of inference we feel comfortable making, of being explicit about why those generalizations make sense, and of being forthright about the weaknesses of the data and about our interpretations of them. Continuous observation techniques, like those we just discussed, have the conceptual advantage of requiring us to be constantly attending to a target student while we record data pertaining to their behavior. However, maintaining constant attention on a particular student for the purpose of recording behavioral data can be extremely challenging at times, for reasons we discuss next.

Noncontinuous Observation Techniques

When multiple behaviors or multiple students need to be observed at the same time or in the same session, or when the observer needs to be engaged in other activities during the observation period, it can be challenging to near-impossible for an *in vivo* observer to accurately use a continuous observation technique. Inevitably, if I am running a social skills group and trying to simultaneously collect data on the duration of each student's social appropriateness and level of engagement, at some point I am going to be looking at my materials when a student politely smiles at a peer, or focusing on some students more than on others, or taking notes on specific conversation topics I just thought of for our next meeting, and neglect to record a critical piece of data. Or if I am in the back of the classroom strictly focused on my observations for the next 30 minutes, but I am trying to keep three timers going simultaneously for each of the three behaviors I am observing for a target student, inevitably I am going to mess up my careful stopwatch juggling.

Faced with the mundane, logistical, and very human challenge of keeping our tasks manageable while also collecting defensible data, we turn to the noncontinuous observation techniques. They consist of three major methods: **whole-interval recording**, **partial-interval recording**, and **momentary time sampling** (a blank momentary time-sampling form is provided in Appendix 4.2). When using a noncontinuous recording technique, the observation period is divided into prespecified intervals of time. In applied settings, and depending on the observer, each interval is typically set at between 10 seconds and 1 to 5 minutes. In general, the smaller the interval, the finer grained the observation and the higher quality the data will be; however, the smaller the interval, the more difficult it can be to conduct observations. For instance, if I decide to use a 10-second interval to record on-task behavior during the social skills group I'm leading, I might quickly realize that my constant need to look down at my notes to record a behavior is impeding my ability to lead the group. Keeping track of small intervals and teaching at the same time or recording more than one behavior and/or student can be challenging.

The occurrence of target behaviors is recorded (coded) during each interval on the basis of a prespecified rule for when and what to record. Only one code (e.g., yes or no, + or −, 1 or 0) is recorded in a single interval, regardless of how many behavioral events occur within an interval. At the end of the observation, the number of intervals in which the target behavior was marked as "observed" is divided by the total number of possible observation intervals, and a percentage is calculated. The summary is always a percent of intervals in which the behavior is observed (or not) and represents an **estimate** of the actual percentage of time during the observation period that the behavior is occurring. For example, Felix was observed to be on task during 68% of the observed intervals, Penny was talking with neighbors for 35% of the observed intervals, and Padma had her head down and her eyes closed during 45% of the observed intervals. It is important to restate that these results are estimates; they are not exact measurements of time or of a behavioral occurrence. Therefore, it is inaccurate to report data from noncontinuous methods as "45% of the time."

Perhaps the most critical issue with respect to noncontinuous observation techniques is that they require even more inference making than parallel continuous methods like duration recording. Although we understand that duration recording, like all assessment measures, is indeed an estimate that corresponds to the actual behavior we're measuring, it does give us the most robust and direct rules to follow in order to get as close to the target behavior as possible. With noncontinuous sampling, we sacrifice some of this "closeness" in order to gain the convenience of being able to observe multiple behaviors or students at one time or to do other tasks during an observation period.

The behaviors to be observed in noncontinuous observation techniques can be coded as simply on task or off task, or multiple codes can be included to provide more specific detail about the behaviors occurring. For example, the definition of off-task behavior can be extended to include out of seat (O), looking around (L), calling out (C), and/or talking to peers (T) (descriptions of some of the behaviors most commonly used in observational systems can be found in Table 4.2). Similarly, continuous and noncontinuous systems can be combined if a range of behaviors is being recorded; a blank observation recording template is provided in Appendix 4.3. For example, on-task and off-task behavior could be coded using time sampling, while simultaneously recording instances (events) of hand raising during each interval. An observer might then report that a student was observed to be on task for 57% of the observed intervals and to have raised her hand seven times throughout the observation, or 0.25 times per minute.

Noncontinuous Decision Rules

The three major noncontinuous observation methods, whole-interval recording, partial-interval recording, and momentary time sampling, simply represent three different decision rules that can be applied to the individual intervals that comprise a divided-up observation period. Let's take the example of a 30-minute observation period with 15-second intervals.

TABLE 4.2. Commonly Observed Behaviors and Associated Definitions

Observation system	Behaviors	Definitions
State–Event Classroom Observation System (SECOS; Saudargas, 1997)	*State behaviors only*	
	Schoolwork	Student has head and eyes oriented toward assigned schoolwork.
	Out of seat	Student is out of his or her seat.
	Looking around	Student is looking around and not engaged in any other activity.
	Motor behavior	Student is engaged in repetitive, stereotyped body movements.
	Play with object	Student is repetitively playing with an object.
	Social interaction with child	Student is interacting with one or more other students.
	Social interaction with teacher	Student is interacting with the classroom teacher.
Behavioral Observation of Students in Schools (BOSS; Shapiro, 2011)	Active engagement	Student is actively and visibly attending to assigned work. Examples include writing, reading aloud, raising hand, discussing responses with peers in a cooperative group.
	Passive engagement	Student is listening to a lecture, looking at an academic worksheet, reading silently, or listening to a peer respond to a question.
	Off-task motor	Student's motor activity is not directly associated with an assignment, such as out-of-seat activity, aimless flipping of pages in a book, drawing, or writing unrelated to the activity.
	Off-task verbal	Student is making audible verbalizations that are not allowed and/or not related to the activity, such as calling out when not asked for a response, forced burping, whistling.
	Passive off-task	Student is not attending to required work (sitting quietly, looking around the room, staring out the window).
Preschool Observation Code (POC; Bramlett, 1993)	*State behaviors only*	
	Play engagement	Student is oriented toward play materials, games, and/or activities.
	Preacademic engagement	Student is oriented toward activities designed to teach specific skills (e.g., numbers, concepts).
	Nonpurposeful play	Student is not engaged in, or is in between, activities.
	Disruptive behaviors	Student is yelling, throwing objects.

(continued)

TABLE 4.2. *(continued)*

Observation system	Behaviors	Definitions
Preschool Observation Code *(continued)*	Self-stimulating behaviors	Student is mouthing objects, twirling hair.
	Social interaction—peer	Student is verbally interacting or playing with a peer.
	Teacher monitoring—interacting	Teacher is monitoring activities.
Behavior Assessment System for Children—Third Edition: Student Observation System (BASC-3; Reynolds & Kamphaus, 2015)	*Adaptive behaviors only*	
	Response to teacher/lesson	Student is listening to teacher/classmate or following directions, interacting with teacher in class/group, working with teacher one on one, standing at teacher's desk.
	Peer interaction	Student is playing/working with other student(s), talking with other student(s), touching another student appropriately.
	Work on school subjects	Student is doing seatwork, working at blackboard or computer.
	Transition movement	Student is putting on/taking off coat, moving around room (appropriately), preparing materials for beginning/end of lesson, or out of room.
Kehle, Clark, & Jenson (1986)	Disruptive behavior	Student is engaging in behavior involving touching, vocalizing, aggression, playing, disorienting, making noise, and/or out of seat.

For a whole-interval recording, we would watch the behavior during each 15-second interval, and if the behavior occurred during the "whole" interval, we score that interval as an occurrence (e.g., +, 1, "yes"). In a partial-interval recording, we would score intervals based on whether the behavior occurred during any "part" of the interval, and in momentary time sampling, we would score intervals based on whether the behavior occurred at one specific "moment" during the interval. Figure 4.3 provides an overview of how these different methods compare to one another.

General recommendations for choosing between these three types of noncontinuous observation techniques have been provided, but in order to understand why these recommendations exist and what general conclusions can be made about each technique, we'll first briefly touch upon a core idea in behavior observation discussed by Suen and Ary (1989): the concept of the behavior stream and the importance of **mixed intervals**. Picture your sidewalk which, if it is like ours, is one long walkway that is divided along its length into rectangles of concrete separated by cracks. Jokes about mothers' backs aside, imagine that we played a game in which we colored in every other concrete rectangle to be green, and that as you walked at a steady pace along the sidewalk, you had to sing whenever you were in a green rectangle. If you stood along the edge of the sidewalk, you could easily observe where you were singing and where you were not. This is a pretty good representa-

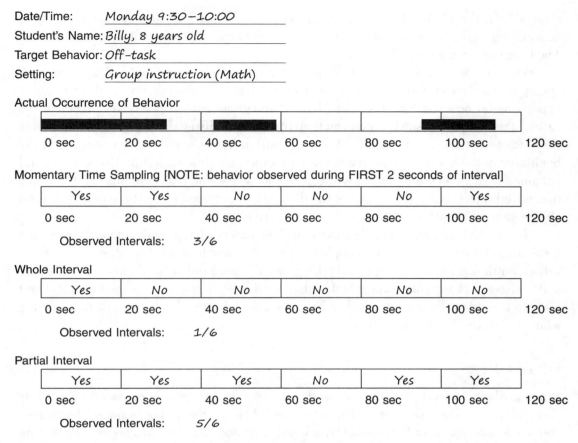

Date/Time: Monday 9:30–10:00

Student's Name: Billy, 8 years old

Target Behavior: Off-task

Setting: Group instruction (Math)

Actual Occurrence of Behavior

| 0 sec | 20 sec | 40 sec | 60 sec | 80 sec | 100 sec | 120 sec |

Momentary Time Sampling [NOTE: behavior observed during FIRST 2 seconds of interval]

Yes	Yes	No	No	No	Yes
0 sec	20 sec	40 sec	60 sec	80 sec	100 sec	120 sec

Observed Intervals: 3/6

Whole Interval

Yes	No	No	No	No	No
0 sec	20 sec	40 sec	60 sec	80 sec	100 sec	120 sec

Observed Intervals: 1/6

Partial Interval

Yes	Yes	Yes	No	Yes	Yes
0 sec	20 sec	40 sec	60 sec	80 sec	100 sec	120 sec

Observed Intervals: 5/6

This example highlights potential discrepancies that may arise when information is collected using each of the available time-sampling methods. The first graph indicates that off-task behavior *actually* occurred during approximately half of the observation period. This information is most accurately estimated using momentary time sampling (3/6 intervals), whereas the occurrence of off-task behavior is underestimated if only whole intervals are recorded (1/6 intervals) and overestimated if partial intervals are recorded (5/6 intervals).

FIGURE 4.3. A comparison of momentary time sampling, whole-interval recording, and partial-interval recording using a 20-second interval.

tion of the core features of a "stream" of behavior; we know where (or when) we started and ended each instance of singing, and we could count the number of individual times we sang to easily calculate the amount of time we were singing with a fairly high degree of accuracy.

Now, let's chunk this length of time into individual intervals by laying a ladder down on top of the sidewalk; each rung of the ladder separates one "interval" of the sidewalk from the next. Depending on how we laid the ladder down, we might have some intervals that are all green, some that are all gray, and some that have a bit of gray and a bit of green. If we wanted to test our noncontinuous decision rules, we could get three scores for each of these intervals as "singing" or "not singing" based on each of the three types of decision rules, and see if our estimate was close to the actual value. The all-green and all-gray intervals are easy to score, because whole-interval, partial-interval, and momentary time sampling all provide the same values. In the case of an all-green square, we were singing the whole time, so we score a + for the whole interval; we sang at least once, so we score a + for partial interval; and we sang at the beginning of the interval, so we score a + for momentary time sampling. The reverse is true for an all-gray square.

Where the scoring gets tricky is in the part-green and part-gray rectangles. These rectangles are the "mixed intervals," and the results of our individual decision rules will differ depending on how the colors are distributed throughout each concrete rectangle. In the case of a rectangle that starts green and then turns gray halfway through (i.e., 50% singing), we sang at least once, so we score a + for the partial interval; and we were singing at the beginning of the interval, so we score a + for momentary time sampling. However, we did not sing for the whole interval, so we score a − for whole-interval sampling. Thus, we see that mixed intervals are the source of the distinctions between these three noncontinuous observation techniques, which we'll discuss in turn next.

Here's one final point to make about chunking observation periods into intervals: what if we pushed the ladder over by a couple feet? In other words, what if we started our observation a little later? Now the intervals that were all green might have some gray in them, and we have to change our estimates. In other words, depending on how the intervals lined up with the sidewalk, our estimates of behavior could drastically change just by changing when we "started" our observation.

Whole Interval

When a whole-interval procedure is used, the behavior is recorded or coded only if it is observed continuously throughout the entire (or "whole") interval. For example, if a 30-second whole-interval recording method was being used and Xiao Mei was observed fidgeting during the entire interval (i.e., all 30 seconds), the interval would be scored with a "+." An interval would be recorded with a "−" in any other instance, such as: (1) she did not start fidgeting until 10 seconds after the beginning of the interval but then fidgeted for the rest of the interval, (2) she was observed fidgeting at the beginning of the interval but stopped 2 seconds before the end of the interval, or (3) she was observed fidgeting at the beginning and end of the interval but was appropriately on task for 5 seconds in the middle of the interval. We can attempt to enhance the accuracy of the scoring by selecting the smallest interval size possible that is logistically manageable for the observer. However, of the three noncontinuous techniques presented here, the whole-interval procedure is the most likely to *underestimate* the actual prevalence of the target behavior.

Partial Interval

Partial-interval recording differs from a whole-interval procedure in that the behavior is marked as occurring if it is observed *at any time* during the interval. Using the previous example, if Xiao Mei displayed fidgeting behavior during 3, 10, 20, or 30 seconds of a 30-second interval, a "+" would be scored, indicating that the behavior had occurred. The same score would be provided if within a given interval Xiao Mei fidgeted for 5 seconds, went "on task" for 10 seconds, and then fidgeted again for 4 seconds. Partial-interval recording may be a better choice than whole interval when the behavior is a low-frequency behavior or if observers are not able to observe continuously. In contrast to whole-interval recording, a partial-interval recording is more likely to *overestimate* the true occurrence of the behavior, because behavior is recorded if it occurs during any portion of the interval. Therefore, shorter interval lengths (e.g., 10 seconds) are more desirable and recommended to minimize any overestimation that may result from the presence of mixed intervals.

Momentary Time Sampling

The third technique, momentary time sampling, is similar to whole- and partial-interval recording in that the intervals are prespecified. However, the recording of behavior occurs only at one specific point during the interval, typically at the beginning or the end. At that specific point, the observer watches the student and marks whether the behavior was or was not occurring at that moment. For example, using a 20-second interval with momentary time sampling, Xiao Mei's fidgeting behavior would be observed during the first second of each new interval and then is recorded as occurring or not occurring. This method has two main advantages. First, in contrast to the potential for overestimating or underestimating the occurrence of behavior by other time-sampling methods, momentary time sampling may provide a more accurate estimate of true occurrence (see Saudargas & Lentz, 1986), especially if the interval size is relatively small (e.g., 20 seconds) and the duration of the observation is long (Suen & Ary, 1989). A second advantage to momentary time sampling is the simplified nature of simultaneously recording numerous behaviors and/or students, along with having a sufficient opportunity to record the information between each interval mark. A brief scan of the room at the specified mark can allow the observer to make any and all relevant ratings before the beginning of the next interval. Indeed, some methods capitalize on this advantage to allow for a 20-second period to record frequency count data. In Figure 4.3, a visual comparison of the three time-sampling techniques is provided.

WHAT IS THE EVIDENCE FOR SDO?

Given that SDO is an umbrella term for different methodologies ranging from frequency counts to momentary time sampling, it's difficult to make a blanket statement about the evidence for SDO. Furthermore, even within a specific method like momentary time sampling, the numerous assessment decisions that need to be made may impact the evidence for that method. For instance, is the evidence suggesting that the data demonstrate a high reliability for academic engagement when measured in a specific way relevant to a situation examining disruptive behavior? Next, we highlight specific considerations that practitioners should be aware of when utilizing SDO. To wit, what should I be thinking about when I design or select an SDO measurement tool, and how can I use that information to make robust decisions?

Defensibility

We can unpack the defensibility of SDO in two major ways: theoretically and empirically. First, the theoretical underpinnings of SDO methods have been articulated for decades, perhaps in the greatest detail by Suen and Ary in their 1989 book *Analyzing Quantitative Behavioral Observation Data*. Others, like Rogosa and Ghandour (1991) and Pustejovsky and Swan (2015), have advanced more fully elaborated statistical models for data derived from methods within SDO. Most of these conversations exceed the scope of what we summarize in this book, but they do provide critical information for understanding how to think about data derived from SDO.

As in our sidewalk example described earlier, "mixed intervals" are the source of differences between noncontinuous observation methods; if an interval includes both the presence and the absence of a behavior, then noncontinuous methods (whole interval, partial interval, or momentary time sampling) differ as to whether an interval is considered to be an "occasion" or "nonoccasion" (e.g., + or –, or 1 or 0). Let's think about that ladder we placed over our sidewalk; the farther away the rungs are from one another, the more likely it is that we'll have a "mixed interval" between those rungs that have both green and gray within it. But what if we made the distance between the rungs shorter? In other words, what if we shortened the length of time that each interval captured: for instance, from 45 seconds' worth of sidewalk to 15 seconds' worth of sidewalk? Well, depending on how the blocks of green and gray are distributed along the sidewalk, we might now be able to make an estimate that's much closer to the actual length of time that the behavior happened!

This property of noncontinuous observation methods is critical to understanding how to design a robust and defensible SDO tool. As described in detail by Suen and Ary (1989), three major components affect the estimate derived from a noncontinuous measurement method: interval length, the shortest amount of time that one "event" of behavior occurs for (also known as a "bout"), and the shortest amount of time that passes between the end of one bout and the beginning of the next (also known as interresponse time). Stated very simply, if your interval length is shorter than the shortest bout and the shortest interresponse time, an estimate of duration derived from momentary time sampling should be accurate! It's somewhat more complex for partial-interval and whole-interval sampling, but *as a rule, shorter intervals are going to produce better estimates.*

Reliability becomes a fairly tricky concept when we are working with any data that are collected over time. Before we dive into that side of the conversation, let's start with the example of a good old-fashioned rating scale. To make an instrument more reliable using a metric like coefficient alpha, I can add more items to my measure. As long as the items are generally related to one another (or "intercorrelated"), my alpha value will increase, and I can be more confident that my overall score represents the variance that I want to see. Critically, the *average value* that I calculated from these items will have more reliability associated with it. The scores from individual items are not getting more reliable, but the average score is.

Now let's consider reliability with respect to SDO. I sat in the back of the room, did my 30-minute observation wherein I counted the number of times Alcides raised his hand, and now want to use that single data point for my interpretation. In other words, I want my estimate of "22 hand raises" to be reliable! How do I get there? There are two central ways to address the reliability of data derived from SDO. First, you can have someone else conduct interobserver agreement checks with you to make sure that they agree with how you're observing the behavior. Second, you can aggregate your observations across some other dimension: more than one rater, more than one observation that you then average to become one "average" observation, or more than one method. One study suggested that estimates of academic engagement can be reliable with just one or two raters when momentary time sampling is used, or with two to three raters when whole-interval recording is used (Johnson, Chafouleas, & Briesch, 2017), whereas other studies suggest that two 30-minute observations may result in one aggregate estimate with desirable reliability (Ferguson, Briesch, Volpe, & Daniels, 2012).

Usability

Direct observation can be relatively cost free or inexpensive with regard to material resources. For individuals using a paper-based recording method, the cost could be limited to photocopies and writing utensils. As the use of technology increases, however, so do the costs related to hardware, software, technical assistance, and maintenance. Decisions to invest in more expensive data recording, storing methods, and equipment should be guided by other cost variables, such as time, intrusiveness, ease of use, and the steps or manipulations required to go from raw to summary data.

However, using SDO in applied settings can have limited feasibility. Individual observation sessions may not seem overly burdensome, as they may only last 15 or 20 minutes; however, rarely would a single observation be considered appropriately representative of student behavior. Most situations require repeated observations over an extended period. The time required to collect the data can quickly add up, particularly if the time needed for summarizing and interpreting the information is included. In addition, SDO usually requires the presence of an external observer in situations when it is difficult for a classroom teacher to instruct the whole class and collect data on a particular student at the same time. Depending on the staffing resources in a given school, finding sufficient personnel to conduct needed observation sessions also can be difficult. As a result, in environments with limited staffing resources, SDO methods might be reserved for high-stakes situations.

Repeatability

Unlike behavior rating scales, which provide a global assessment of behavior over a longer period, SDO allows for repeated measurement—which is needed in progress monitoring. For example, the use of a momentary time sampling technique may reveal that disruptive behavior occurred in 30–50% of observed intervals before some intervention and in 0–15% of observed intervals postintervention. Such information is critical when analyzing behavior change over time. Because the range of measurement is not limited, any changes in behavior that occur from one observation to the next are easier to detect.

Flexibility

Another highly attractive feature of SDO is the ability to tailor SDO methods to fit individual situations. Although some examples of established observation systems are designed to target specific behaviors (e.g., Behavioral Observation of Students in Schools [BOSS]; Shapiro, 2011), less specialized direct observation methods can be used to monitor virtually any behavior from off-task to aggressive behavior. Basically, you can use SDO to record any behavior that is observable, has a discrete beginning and end, and is operationally defined. Furthermore, depending on the complexity of the observation system, SDO procedures can be used to monitor the behavior(s) of an individual or a group of individuals simultaneously.

WHAT CONSTRUCTS ARE MOST APPROPRIATE FOR THIS MEASUREMENT METHOD?

As previously noted, the goal of SDO is to quantify behavior. The target behavior to be quantified can vary depending on the specific situation. However, the first consideration is to define the specific behaviors in observable and measurable terms—that is, to answer the question "What behaviors am I interested in, and what outcome data do I need?" Consideration should be given to narrowing and defining the behaviors. Narrowing refers to selecting the smallest number of behaviors that are of particular interest or that answer a specific question. Although trying to monitor a long list of behaviors is tempting, the longer the list, the more difficult it is to look for, evaluate, and record the behaviors. A general guideline is to limit the list to two or three target behaviors and monitor those behaviors with integrity. After the number of behaviors to be observed has been narrowed, each behavior must be defined in specific, observable, and descriptive terms. These definitions must be "comprehensive," in that all variations of the behavior are included, and "mutually exclusive" in that nontarget behaviors cannot be mistakenly included.

To ensure that definitions are comprehensive and mutually exclusive, behavioral definitions must be operational in nature: that is, an observer must be able to clearly distinguish between the target behavior and nontarget behaviors during an observation. Similarly, a strong operational definition is one that allows two independent observers to agree whether they saw or did not see the target behavior because the topography or appearance of the behavior is specific and observable. Although general definitions might be interpreted as being appropriate because they "catch" more behaviors, they can make it difficult to determine what should and should not be scored. For example, if the behavior is called "aggression" without further specification, confusion can result about whether to include verbal and physical forms as well as aggressive acts toward persons and objects. As another example, even though "on task" has been defined as "student is oriented toward the teacher and/or is actively engaged in instructional activities," observers may question whether to mark a student "on task" if they are looking at a teacher who is speaking but not acknowledging questions, or if it is difficult to see what the student is writing, or if the student displays a hand raise in response to a teacher question but is looking out the window. In all of these examples, behavioral definitions need to be narrowed, and multiple examples and nonexamples are needed to ensure agreement about how to score.

Examples of behaviors and possible associated definitions are provided in Table 4.2 to illustrate how behaviors might be selected and defined. The examples were taken from a range of SDO publications used for practice and research purposes. When selecting and defining the behavior(s) of interest, some further considerations are in order. First, the observation setting should guide behavior selection. The behaviors and definitions included in Table 4.2 are common in classroom-based settings. Similar and different behaviors and definitions may be selected for other settings, like the playground, the school bus, school hallways, and the home. In addition, developmental considerations in behavior selection may be in order. For example, although they are similar in intent to other behaviors listed in the table, the behaviors indicated under the Preschool Observation Code (Bramlett, 1993) were modified to be more age appropriate for a preschool population.

For a particular clinical population, such as students with ADHD, common clinical descriptors and definitions should be considered. For example, the Attention Deficit Hyperactivity Disorder School Observation Code (ADHD-SOC; Gadow, Sprafkin, & Nolan, 1996) involves behavioral categories for both the classroom and lunchroom and/or playground settings. The class-based observations include interference, motor movement, noncompliance, verbal aggression, symbolic aggression, object aggression, and off-task behavior. Lunchroom and playground behaviors include noncompliance, nonphysical aggression, verbal aggression, and physical aggression.

Observing interactions between the target student and others (such as the teacher and/or parent) may be necessary to obtain a complete picture of the context surrounding the behavior. In these instances, having clear definitions for the behaviors of the student and the other target individuals would be important. A few example behaviors for teacher observation are included in Table 4.2. Whitcomb (2017) provides a review of useful observation systems for home- or clinic-based settings, including observations of behavior, such as child noncompliance during parent interactions, and aversive family behavior.

Finally, it is critical to remember that the decisions we make when we operationally define a behavior are not value free. In other words, I may be using very clearly defined methods to measure behavior, but that does not mean that I am now a robot that lacks the implicit biases that we all carry with us. Silva (1993, p. 63) put it well when he stated, "We may believe, for example, that saying 'Record the number of times that Jimmy gets up from his chair' does not result in any conceptual problem. But it does. . . . The record will not be a simple reflection of reality, but the result of decisions, agreements, or conventions that have subtle aspects, such as the influence of sociocultural norms." My choice of that specific behavior to target, the specific operational definition I wrote for it, and the way I apply that definition when I measure the behavior all matter. If I write "respectful" operational definitions for mostly Black students and "academically engaged" operational definitions for mostly White students, I need to consider what the choice of behaviors means for how all children are seen, treated, and valued within my school. As discussed in the introduction to this chapter, incorporating explicit definitions offers one strategy for reducing ambiguity or subjectivity that can influence implicit bias (McIntosh et al., 2014). In summary, we must always carefully consider the influences of the sociocultural context within which we and our children live if we are going to make decisions that help all students succeed.

HOW WOULD I COLLECT DATA USING THIS METHOD?

Selecting a system for collecting SDO data begins with determining (1) the behavior(s) of interest (e.g., hand raises) and (2) an appropriate type of data-recording method aligned to the question of interest for the chosen behavior (e.g., for frequency counts, "How many times did Wallace raise his hand during math and reading?"). These two decisions should guide the next step, which is identifying the modality of recording: paper and pencil, computer, a smartphone app, or some other method. Let your modality choice be guided by your questions of interest, not the other way around. I might buy a really cool espresso maker because it's on sale and I'm feeling like making a sympathy purchase for myself, but I just drink normal drip coffee in the morning. What the heck am I going to do with this espresso maker? The same goes for behavioral assessment: find the product that matches your specific needs, don't invent needs because you found a cool product.

A lot of us still use paper-and-pencil forms to record data in schools. They are cheap, easily customizable, do not require us to have our phones out in class, and many of us are just more comfortable with them. This method is obviously going to give way to digital technology, as it becomes even more tightly integrated into our lives, but for simplicity's sake, we describe the creation of a paper-and-pencil observation tool below. Following this description, we provide some examples of digital methods for conducting observations.

In recording frequency data, basic background information (e.g., student name, date, activity, and observer name) is written at the top of the paper, and tally marks are made for each observed occurrence of behavior. A more elaborate way to collect frequency data throughout an entire day could be through the use of a scatterplot (see Appendix 4.1). The time or activity could be indicated in the left-hand column as a way to represent the entire school day. In Appendix 4.2, a sample form for recording on-task and off-task behavior is provided, whereas the form in Appendix 4.3 includes space to select and define other behaviors. Procedures for using each of the time-sampling techniques are included on the sample forms.

An alternative to creating your own observation forms is to use an existing, published system. Again, the appropriateness of a particular system depends in large part on the behaviors of interest. A summary of several existing systems for recording school-based behavior is given in Table 4.3; a more comprehensive review is provided in Briesch et al. (2018) on behavior observation. The BOSS (Shapiro, 2011) is perhaps the most well known by school psychologists; a survey asking about SDO protocol use for FBAs suggested that over 50% of the school psychologists who responded used the BOSS (Johnson, Goldberg, Hinant, & Couch, 2019). As described extensively in *Academic Skills Problems Workbook* (Shapiro, 2011), this protocol uses momentary time sampling and partial-interval recording to assess student engagement in on-task (passive or active) and off-task behaviors (motor, verbal, or passive), respectively. Although the official BOSS app is no longer available, multiple apps are available to facilitate systematic direct observation including BehaviorSnap ($10; *behaviorsnapapp.com*) and Insight: Observation Timer (free; available on Apple app store). Note that it's likely best practice to use pseudonyms for students when entering data into an app in order to avoid any potential for breaches of confidentiality.

The ADHD-SOC (Gadow et al., 1996), mentioned previously, is a well-established measure that has particular applications for children who display significant externalizing behaviors. It is described as straightforward and easy to learn. The Peer Social Behavior of the Systematic Screening for Behavior Disorders (SSBD-2 PSB; Walker, Severson, & Feil, 2014) is another established system with an impressive record across several large-scale studies. The PSB is a playground-based observation system that serves as one piece of the SSBD three-stage screening process for children at risk for serious behavioral disorders. Although described as a highly acceptable and cost-efficient system, the PSB is primarily considered to be a screening tool and is typically used in conjunction with the entire SSBD process. The Preschool Observation Code (POC; Bramlett, 1993), presented in Table 4.3, is an example of a code that is appropriate for observing preschool children.

TABLE 4.3. Some Examples of Existing Systems for Conducting Systematic Direct Observation in School Settings

Observation system	Brief description	Recording system
Attention Deficit Hyperactivity Disorder School Observation Code (Gadow, Sprafkin, & Nolan, 1996)	Described as useful for screening and evaluating ADHD intervention effects across multiple school settings (e.g., classroom, lunchroom, or playground). Target behaviors emphasized include disruptive and aggressive areas. Peer comparison recommended.	Partial-interval recording.
Behavior Assessment System for Children—Third Edition: Student Observation System (BASC-3 SOS; Reynolds & Kamphaus, 2015)	Appropriate for observing adaptive and maladaptive classroom behavior of children in preschool through high school. Available in a paper-and-pencil format or for use on a computer or tablet/iPad.	Momentary time sampling. Also includes sections for narrative comments of teacher–student interaction and observer's overall rating of behaviors observed.
Behavioral Observation of Students in Schools (BOSS; Shapiro, 2011)	Emphasis on academic behavior in the classroom, particularly engagement (passive and active). Also allows for peer comparison and estimation of amount of time teacher engaged in direct instruction.	Momentary time sampling for engagement, partial-interval time sampling for off-task behaviors.
Peer Social Behavior of the Systematic Screening for Behavior Disorders, Second Edition (SSBD-2 PSB; Walker, Severson, & Feil, 2014)	The PSB component offers a playground-based observation system for use in the final stage of the SSBD, a screening process to identify children at risk for serious behavioral disorders. Target behaviors include social engagement, parallel play, and alone time; not codable.	Partial-interval recording.
Preschool Observation Code (POC; Bramlett, 1993)	Allows simultaneous observation of multiple classroom-relevant behaviors for preschool ages. Also provides opportunity to code interactions with teacher.	Momentary time sampling for state behaviors, frequency counts for event behaviors.

A final example worth mentioning is the Behavior Assessment System for Children—Third Edition: Student Observation System (BASC-3 SOS; Reynolds & Kamphaus, 2015), which was first developed in the initial iteration of the BASC (Reynolds & Kamphaus, 1992). The SOS is an observational tool designed to measure positive and negative classroom behaviors of children ages 2 through 21 and is available in both web-based/digital and paper formats. It can be used to observe and analyze the behavior of individual students and teachers and for diagnosis, intervention planning, and evaluating intervention effectiveness (Briesch et al., 2018; Reynolds & Kamphaus, 2015). Although this observation code is likely to be of great value to school psychologists, particularly alongside the rest of the BASC-3 system, the SOS can be expensive, given that the manual and a package of 25 paper forms costs close to $200. However, the test publishers suggest that minimal training (i.e., one 30-minute session) is required to effectively and appropriately use the SOS, which may make it a more desirable observation code (Briesch et al., 2018; Reynolds & Kamphaus, 2015).

HOW WOULD I SUMMARIZE AND REPORT DATA USING SDO?

A significant advantage of using SDO over other direct observation techniques is the ability to analyze and present information in useful ways. Specifically, multiple data points can be quantified, compared, combined, and summarized for both summative and formative purposes. For example, a weeklong recording of the frequency of Manny's tantrum behavior can be summarized into a statement of total occurrences (10 per week), average daily occurrence (2 per day), most likely time of occurrence (morning after math instruction), and so on. In addition, and perhaps more significant, Manny's tantrum behavior before an intervention was implemented can be compared to the data collected after the intervention starts. The opportunity to compare data across two conditions allows for a preliminary evaluation of the impact of an intervention on a target behavior. In each of these examples, a standardized observation method is required.

Options for summarizing data depend on the type of data recording system. As in the example of Manny just noted, frequency data can be tallied and organized as desired and then may be presented in a visual format using a bar or line graph (see Figure 4.4 for an example of a bar chart). Generally, the data from time-based recording systems are presented as a percentage of observed intervals in which the behavior of interest was or was not observed. Because noncontinuous methods involve determining the presence or absence of behavior within an interval, they result in approximations of the actual occurrence of behavioral events (indirect). Thus, results are reported as "Behavior was observed to occur in X percentage of intervals," rather than "Behavior was observed to occur X percentage of the time." As with continuous methods, data can then be summarized and graphed as appropriate (e.g., using bar or line graphs). Typically, the y-axis would be labeled with what is being described (e.g., "percentage of observed intervals"), and the x-axis would be labeled with the time (e.g., session or day). An example is provided in Figure 4.4. When deciding how much data should be collected to represent actual student behavior, a general rule of thumb is to have at least three stable data points. If the data are highly variable and the data points available for interpretation are limited, the evaluation of results is difficult, particularly when making decisions about intervention effectiveness.

Ms. Kaufman, the school psychologist, has been asked to observe Sara's behavior during independent work time. Sara's teacher is concerned that she spends a significant amount of class time staring out the window and doodling instead of working on her assignments. Ms. Kaufman agrees to observe Sara over the next week. During these observation periods, she will utilize a momentary time sampling procedure (15-second intervals) to record the percentage of intervals in which she observes Sara engaging in on-task behavior (defined as "Sara is oriented toward the teacher and/or is actively engaged in instructional activities"). Ms. Kaufman also plans to collect the same data for a same-sex peer in order to examine Sara's behavior in comparison to her classmates. Ms. Kaufman's data are provided below:

	Sara			Peer (comparison)		
Session	Number of on-task intervals	Total number of intervals	Percentage of on-task intervals	Number of on-task intervals	Total number of intervals	Percentage of on-task intervals
Day 1	18	40	45	28	40	70
Day 2	21	60	35	51	60	85
Day 3	44	80	55	72	80	90
Day 4	24	60	40	51	60	85
Day 5	39	60	65	57	60	95

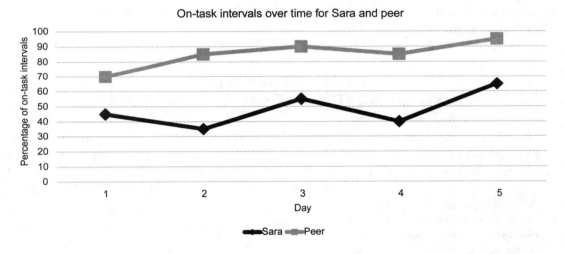

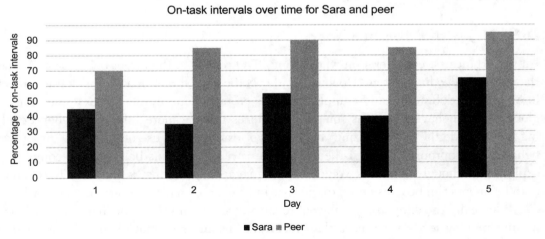

FIGURE 4.4. Summarizing momentary time sampling through line series and bar graphs.

WHAT STRENGTHS
ARE ASSOCIATED WITH SDO TECHNIQUES?

> **The strengths associated with SDO include a high usefulness in progress monitoring, flexibility in technique choice, and minimal material cost.**

The central feature of SDO is the **direct observation** of behavioral occurrences by an observer/recorder. In contrast, when raters are asked to retrospectively assess behavior (e.g., with behavior rating scales), accuracy can be affected by such factors as time, memory, and intervening experiences. Thus, the closer in time to actual occurrence that the behavior is recorded, the greater the potential for more objective data, especially if definitions and procedures are clearly described. Objective data require less inference making and fewer steps to interpretation. The numerous options available when developing an SDO instrument give this methodology flexibility, and its ability to be repeatedly administered over time provides significant usefulness in progress monitoring. Another advantage of using SDO for collecting and summarizing behavioral data is that standardized procedures allow for direct comparisons across observation sessions and other dimensions as well (e.g., raters, students, or settings). SDO methods generally have a minimal cost for materials.

WHAT WEAKNESSES
ARE ASSOCIATED WITH SDO TECHNIQUES?

Although the advantages of using SDO are clear, the procedures are not without their flaws. As reviewed by Whitcomb (2018), even strong advocates of direct observation would concede the existence of various threats to the data. Without careful attention to the potential

> **SDO offers many strengths, but users must be aware of and appropriately respond to its limitations.**

sources of influence, the reliability and validity of the obtained data can become questionable. Thus, we provide an overview of various sources of influence and discuss ways to reduce the effects of each one.

Difficulty with Definition Specificity

An important first consideration when using SDO relates to the target behavior itself and the associated coding system. How well and specifically a target behavior is defined affect how well the definition can be applied to a given behavioral event. For example, a more global target behavior, such as "on task," requires making more inferences when deciding how to code the "hand-raising" behavior. For example, the use of the term "disruptive behavior" is appropriate only if the acceptable variations of this behavior are completely explained. Although most of us would not tend to equate "belching" with "throwing chairs," both behaviors can be considered disruptive and each one may be important to record.

Practically speaking, using an event recording to note instances of "hand raising" may require making fewer inferences than recording instances of "out of seat" behavior displayed by the child who frequently moves around the vicinity of their seat (picture a backside "hovering" 4 inches above and next to the actual seat!). On the other hand, defining a behavior with too much specificity (e.g., 10 different subcategories of "on-task" behavior) may make recording too cumbersome, and, as a result, the data obtained may be too narrow to be important in understanding the full picture of student behavior. In addition, such extreme specificity can narrow the behavior to the point of irrelevance, or errors could occur because of the added complexity associated with collecting data on a large number of behaviors. In the end, the goal is to establish a careful balance between being too specific and too global when operationally defining behaviors to be observed and recorded.

Reactivity

SDO generally requires the presence of an external observer within a natural setting (e.g., classroom or playground). Unfortunately, a target child (or teacher) who knows that they are being observed may react by changing their behavior and thereby decreasing the likelihood that the observation is representative of the way that the individual typically behaves. This phenomenon, known as *reactivity,* affects not only the behaviors of the target student and the teacher but also the whole class, as other children notice a rater sitting in the room. Some signs of student reactivity include, for example, staring, waving, or directing questions at the observer.

In a related manner, changes in the "typical" class (e.g., a large number of new students or visitors, a high number of absences, or a substitute teacher) can affect a student or teacher's typical behavioral occurrences. Options for limiting potential reactivity include entering the setting at a natural transition point, avoiding the use of equipment that may attract attention, and familiarizing yourself with the classroom prior to the official observation to allow students to adjust to the observer's presence (Whitcomb, 2017). Regardless, the rater must remember that teachers may be correct when they say "the class was totally different with you in the room."

Observer Error and Observer Drift

Whenever humans are involved in scoring or measurement, the potential for error exists. A first general concern relates to the person who scores or codes the data. Observers differ in such areas as their personal characteristics, previous knowledge and expectations about the child or situation, or experience with the technique (e.g., McIntosh et al., 2014). One important source of observer error is called "observer drift," which occurs when observers deviate from the original definitions of behavior and change their recording habits. Observer drift can be associated with fatigue, forgetfulness, decreased motivation, or loss of interest. The potential for observer drift can be limited through careful attention to high-quality initial training as well as through periodic retraining in the observation system. Although the subject of training is often overlooked, even experienced educational professionals need periodic skill tune-ups. In addition, reliability checks, such as through a calculation of interobserver agreement, may be important in alerting the observer to potential influences in the data.

One simple formula for calculating interobserver agreement when using data that were collected interval-by-interval (i.e., time sampling or interval recording) with a categorical judgment (yes/no, poor/good/great) involves dividing the number of agreements by the number of agreements plus the number of disagreements, multiplied by 100. However, this method has one very significant flaw. With a binary outcome (e.g., yes/no, 1/0), there are four potential score pairs that the two raters can produce: 0/0 (e.g., Rater A scored a 0, and Rater B scored a 0), 0/1, 1/0, or 1/1. Both 0/0 and 1/1 would be marked as an agreement, and 1/0 and 0/1 would be marked as a disagreement. However, this also means that if both raters were just scoring each interval randomly, there's a 50% chance that both raters would agree on any given interval (i.e., have a 0/0 or 1/1 even though they were just randomly guessing).

Despite these flaws, this "agreement index" is still very popular in the literature. However, there's a better way: calculating a **kappa** value. Kappa measures the agreement between two raters on a categorical outcome (yes/no, poor/good/great) after correcting for chance. For this reason, kappa is a lot more stringent than the agreement index, but it also results in more defensible conclusions about agreement. An agreement index value of 80% or higher or a kappa value of .60 or above is generally viewed as favorable (Kratochwill et al., 2010). As shown in Figure 4.5, kappa is fairly straightforward to calculate by hand,

Interval	1	2	3	4	5	6	7	8	9	10
Observer 1	+	–	+	+	+	–	–	+	+	+
Observer 2	+	+	+	+	+	–	–	+	+	–
Agreement?	Y	N	Y	Y	Y	Y	Y	Y	Y	N

Formula: % Agreement = [Number of Agreements/(Number of Agreements plus Disagreements)] × 100

% Agreement = [8/(8 + 2)] × 100

% Agreement = 80%

	Observer 1 Behavior Present	Observer 1 Behavior Absent	
Observer 2 Behavior Present	6	1	7
Observer 2 Behavior Absent	1	2	3
	7	3	10

Kappa = $(P_O - P_C)/(1 - P_C)$

P_O (percent agreement) = agreements/(agreements + disagreements)

P_C (chance agreement) = $[(X_1 \times Y_1)/N^2] + [(X_r \times Y_r)/N^2]$

P_O = 8/(8 + 2) = 8/10 = .80

P_C = $[(7 \times 7)/10^2] + [(3 \times 3)/10^2]$ = (49/100) + (9/100) = .58

Kappa = (.80 − .58)/(1 − .58) = .22/.42 = .52

FIGURE 4.5. Calculating percent agreement and kappa. The kappa example is adapted from Watkins and Pacheco (2000).

but web-based calculators are also freely available with a quick internet search for "kappa agreement calculator."

There are numerous ways to measure interobserver agreement for data that were collected using frequency or duration recording, and all require some general sacrifices in precision. It is very hard to calculate agreement with respect to frequency data for the simple reason that, if I counted four instances of behavior and you counted five, I don't know if you saw four of the same instances that I did and then one extra one that I missed, or if you saw five completely different instances than the four that I saw. I could divide the smaller count by the larger count and multiply the result by 100 to get something like a percent agreement index (e.g., 4/5 × 100 = 80%). However, I have no idea if any of the four instances that I saw are represented in the five instances that you recorded. For this reason, using intervals to subset event data can be one way to feel more, but never completely, confident in an estimate of interobserver agreement. If we chunk an observation period of 10 minutes into 1-minute intervals, and then record the events we saw in 10 separate blocks (e.g., minute 1 = three instances, minute 2 = five instances), then we can calculate agreement for each individual interval and then average across them ("mean count per interval") or just ask how many intervals for which we had perfect agreement ("exact count per interval"; Cooper et al., 2007). The same ideas apply when we're thinking about comparing duration recordings to one another.

In summary, whether during initial training or retraining, observers must thoroughly understand the definition of the target behavior, and the systems for recording behavior and data collection must be monitored to ensure adequate agreement.

Difficulty Monitoring Low-Frequency Behaviors

Problem behaviors that occur infrequently and/or inconsistently may be difficult to monitor using SDO. For example, if Michael has been referred for demonstrating "aggressive outbursts," but if this behavior only occurs once or twice per month, it may be difficult for an outside observer to schedule an appropriate observation session. If Michael typically has these outbursts right before lunch, scheduling would be less of a problem. On the other hand, when no apparent pattern to his outbursts exists, the probability of the behavior occurring during the observation session will be low to zero. Rather than depending on an external observer to collect the data, the collection might be conducted, for example, by existing classroom personnel (e.g., a classroom teacher or aide).

Generalizability

Given that each observation session typically occurs for a relatively short period of time (e.g., 15–30 minutes), the behaviors observed may not be representative of what occurs throughout the typical school day. For example, if Mr. Jones conducts momentary time sampling during math instruction and finds that Nick was off task during 55% of the intervals measured, it's difficult for Mr. Jones to assume that Nick would exhibit similar rates of off-task behavior during reading instruction or even during independent math seat work. SDO provides information about behavior at a specific time and under specific setting or environmental conditions. Repeated measures within and across different settings can increase our ability to generalize what we saw to the student's general level of functioning, but we always have to be clear on *what* we're generalizing the specific data to and *why* we believe that we can generalize those data.

CONCLUDING COMMENTS

In this chapter, we have described several techniques for conducting systematic direct observation (SDO). In particular, we provided guidelines for determining which recording techniques are appropriate for specific types of behaviors. The questions that need to be answered to guide SDO are why the data are being collected, how to define a behavior, what data to collect, and which recording technique should be used. However, the process always begins with understanding what questions need to be answered. In summary, regardless of the specific SDO technique that is selected, the following guidelines apply when using SDO:

> SDO choice should always be guided by questions such as which data do we want to collect and which behaviors do we want to address.

1. Specify the question or problem that needs to be addressed.
2. Define the behavior in observable terms, that is, its topography (appearance), beginning and end, typical duration, and so forth.
3. Identify and describe the times when and the places where the behaviors are most and least likely to occur.
4. Determine whether a continuous or noncontinuous method is most appropriate given the behaviors and the setting and select one.
5. If possible, record the proximal setting, antecedent, and consequence events that relate to behavioral occurrences.
6. Implement the observation system consistently in the same time and location.
7. Check for the accuracy of the data recording on a regular basis and retrain as needed.
8. Summarize the data in terms that answer the initial question or that solve the problem.

Behavioral Occurrence Scatterplot

DIRECTIONS: This graph can be used to record event behaviors (when interested in simply recording the occurrence or nonoccurrence of a behavior). List the days of the week across the first row (e.g., Mon., Tues., Wed.) and times or activities down the first column (e.g., 9:00–9:15, Spelling lesson). When a target behavior occurs, place an X in the box that corresponds with the appropriate day and time. After completing the chart, look for any patterns that emerge (i.e., are most of the X's clustered in the morning? before recess or lunch?).

Student's Name: _____   Date/Time: _____

Behavior: _____   Setting: _____

Day

Time										

Comments:

_____

Time-Sampling Recording Form
for On-Task/Off-Task Behavior

Student: _____   Date/Time: _____

Teacher: _____   Observer: _____

Observation Activity: _____

DIRECTIONS: Momentary time-sampling procedures are used to code on-task (+) or off-task (–) behavior. Using a stopwatch, observe the target student (white boxes) and a same-sex peer (shaded boxes) and record the observed behavior *at the beginning* of each 20-second interval. (Record the target student observation data first.) Compute the percentage of intervals of on-task or off-task behavior by calculating the number of +'s divided by 30 and multiplying by 100 [(+'s/30) × 100].

Interval	Target	Peer	Interval	Target	Peer	Interval	Target	Peer
1			11			21		
2			12			22		
3			13			23		
4			14			24		
5			15			25		
6			16			26		
7			17			27		
8			18			28		
9			19			29		
10			20			30		

Percentage on-task behavior:

Combined-Technique Observation Recording Form

Target Student's Name: _____ Date: _____

Teacher: _____ Time: _____

Observation Activity: _____

Observer's Name: _____

DIRECTIONS: This form can be used to code two behaviors during the same observation period for both the target student and a same-sex peer. The first two columns should be used to record any behaviors that do not have a clear beginning and/or end using a time-sampling technique (e.g., momentary time sampling). The second two columns should be used to record discrete behaviors using a continuous observation technique (e.g., frequency count). Record the target student's behavior first.

Noncontinuous behavior: _____

Operational definition of behavior: _____

_____

Continuous behavior: _____

Operational definition of behavior: _____

_____

	Non-continuous		Continuous				Non-continuous		Continuous	
	T	P	T	P			T	P	T	P
1						21				
2						22				
3						23				
4						24				
5						25				
6						26				
7						27				
8						28				
9						29				
10						30				
11						31				
12						32				
13						33				
14						34				
15						35				
16						36				
17						37				
18						38				
19						39				
20						40				

CHAPTER 5

Direct Behavior Rating

In Chapter 4, we discussed how SDO can be used in the assessment of various behaviors of individual students, classes, and teachers. SDO allows educators to collect observational data on student behavior in a systematic way. Direct Behavior Rating (DBR) achieves the same goal in behavioral assessment but adds elements of other methods discussed later in this book. We first review some background on DBR, followed by a brief summary of evidence supporting its use. We conclude with guidelines for determining the appropriateness of DBR as your assessment tool, along with suggestions for instrumentation (designing it) and implementation procedures (using it) in schools.

WHAT IS DBR, AND WHY USE IT?

DBR refers to a category of hybrid assessment tools that combine the characteristics of SDO and behavior rating scales. Like SDO, these tools are designed to be used in a formative (repeated) fashion to represent clearly defined behaviors that occur over a specified period of time (e.g., 4 weeks), under specific and similar conditions (e.g., 45-minute morning independent seatwork). In addition, the recording of the target behavior occurs in close proximity to the time the behavior was observed (Chafouleas, 2011). However, as with behavior rating scales, using DBR requires rating target behaviors with a predefined scale, such as rating the degree to which José was actively engaged. So teachers might be asked to use a scale from 1 (not at all) to 10 (almost always) to rate the degree to which José was actively engaged in work activities during independent seatwork this morning. Thus, in contrast to a traditional rating scale that may ask the rater to summarize behavior over a 1-month period, DBR prespecifies the rating period, and the resulting rating reflects the observed behavior during that period only. In brief, the recording process mimics a rating scale, yet DBR uses direct assessment to rate a target behavior following a prespecified shorter period.

Although the term DBR has become more widely recognized over the last 10 years, other terms have historically been used to describe it. For example, the Home–School Note, Behavior Report Card, Daily Progress Report, and Good Behavior Note, whose origins date back to the 1960s, are all examples of DBR-like tools that may not have included standardized instrumentation, procedures, and assessment as their primary goals (i.e., when used as part of an intervention package). In contrast, terms that have focused on DBR-like tools in assessment have included performance-based behavioral recording (Steege, Davin, & Hathaway, 2001) or Daily Behavior Report Card (Chafouleas, Riley-Tillman, & McDougal, 2002). In the first edition of this book, we established the DBR as a common descriptor that captures the essential characteristics of this category of assessments: that is, a brief rating of target behavior(s) following a prespecified observation period.

> **DBR involves a brief rating of target behavior(s) following a prespecified observation period.**

Chafouleas and colleagues (2002) first described DBR as a flexible procedure that can vary according to the behavior to be rated (e.g., an increase or decrease in academic or social target behavior); the type of rating system (e.g., checklist or scale); the rating frequency (e.g., once daily, throughout the day, or once weekly); the rater (e.g., child or teacher); the target of rating (e.g., individual or entire class); the frequency with which the information is shared with another person (e.g., daily or weekly); the consequence utilized (e.g., positive or negative); and the setting for delivery of the consequence (e.g., home or school). Although much of this description is still accurate, DBR has evolved substantially over the last decade. More recent descriptions of DBR have focused on the defining characteristics of the tool: directness, behavior, and ratings (Briesch, Chafouleas, & Riley-Tillman, 2016; Christ, Riley-Tillman, & Chafouleas, 2009).

When we say that DBR is *direct*, we mean that the actual measurement (or rating) is completed in close proximity to the end of the period of behavior observation (Briesch et al., 2016; Cone, 1978). To ensure that a rating is as direct as possible, it should occur immediately (or as close in time as feasible) following a relatively short period of observation (Briesch et al., 2016; Chafouleas, 2011). *Behavior* refers to an action (e.g., physical movement or nonverbal or verbal communication) that can be defined, observed, and measured with relative ease. Appropriate target behaviors for DBR should be observable, measurable, and responsive to school-based intervention (Briesch et al., 2016). Finally, *ratings* signify a quantifiable measure of an individual's perception of the behavior; the rating provides an estimate of a target behavior's occurrence based on the impression of the rater (Christ et al., 2009). Each of

> **Direct—the rating follows a short observation; Behavior—an action observed and measured; Rating—an estimate of occurrence.**

these features (directness, behavior, ratings) is combined to result in standardized instrumentation (i.e., design) and implementation procedures (i.e., use), so that DBR can be used repeatedly in the same fashion and everyone can clearly understand what data were assembled and what method was used to collect the information.

Two primary forms of DBR have been presented in the literature: single-item scales (DBR-SIS) and multi-item scales (DBR-MIS). Figure 5.1 provides examples of what each type of DBR might look like. A DBR-SIS is a rating of a single behavior using standard

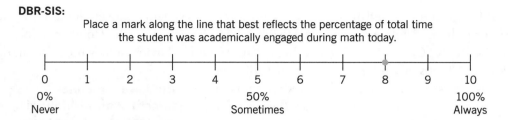

DBR-SIS:

Place a mark along the line that best reflects the percentage of total time
the student was academically engaged during math today.

| | | | | | | | | | | |
|0|1|2|3|4|5|6|7|8|9|10|

0%   50%   100%
Never   Sometimes   Always

DBR-MIS:

Behavior—Academically Engaged	Rating		
Student actively participated in class	1	2	3
Student raised hand when appropriate	1	2	3
Student stayed on task throughout class	1	2	3
Total:			

FIGURE 5.1. DBR-SIS and DBR-MIS examples.

procedures: that is, the recording occurs after a predetermined observation period (Briesch, Chafouleas, & Riley-Tillman, 2010). Multiple behaviors can be rated using DBR-SIS during this period, but each behavior must be rated independently, and thus, the ratings may not be mutually exclusive (Briesch et al., 2010). For example, a student can be both engaged with a class activity and displaying disruptive behavior at the same time, so it is critical to have clear definitions of any target behaviors to prevent rater confusion. A DBR-MIS shares the majority of DBR-SIS features related to procedures, but the instrument is different in that multiple component behaviors are rated for each target behavior construct (Volpe & Briesch, 2012). For example, in order to measure a student's academically engaged behavior, an observer might rate multiple (typically four or five) items related to engagement (e.g., hand raising, looking at instructional materials, or participating in classroom activities). Unless otherwise noted, this chapter focuses on DBR-SIS, given that the volume of current evidence and a freely available online training module (described later) are focused on single-item scales.

The defining characteristics of DBR allow a consistent yet flexible form of assessment tool to be used in many different contexts. That is, the customizable nature of DBR makes it applicable for use across school settings and grade levels to assess behaviors of interest. Flexibility in customization can be important because research suggests that educators are more likely to employ practices that are not resource intensive (in terms of time, money, effort, and staffing), can be used for multiple purposes (e.g., assessment, intervention, and communication), and are contextually relevant (e.g., designed for schoolwide and classwide use and for individual students; Chafouleas, 2011; Severson, Walker, Hope-Doolittle, Kratochwill, & Gresham, 2007). However, as previously noted, to maximize the usefulness of DBR for assessment purposes, it should be structured so as to emphasize the features of SDO (over naturalistic observation). That is, to be considered systematic, DBR tools should include:

1. A definition of the behavior of interest that is operational (clear).
2. Procedures that are standardized to facilitate multiple points of data collection.
3. Observation and recording that occur at a preestablished period (in time and place) and frequency.
4. A summarization of resulting data in a consistent manner.

These criteria set the standards for SDO (Salvia et al., 2017), and are likewise important for DBR. DBR data that are not collected under systematic conditions may not be useful in monitoring behavior because of challenges in comparing information across ratings. Establishing standard instrumentation and procedures may allow for multiple persons in the classroom to rate a student on the same behaviors using consistent procedures. For example, a classroom teacher and an instructional assistant may both collect DBR data on a student's aggressive behavior, and the patterns of those data for both raters could be examined. In summary, standard instrumentation and implementation procedures are critical to being able to use DBR for reliable and valid assessment purposes.

> **Standard instrumentation and procedures are critical features of DBR.**

WHO CAN USE DBR?

When choosing to use DBR in assessment, consideration should be given to who will be responsible for conducting the ratings. Most often, that person will be the classroom teacher or someone who is with the student consistently throughout the day— but most definitely during the specified rating period. The burden on resources is significantly reduced when the rater is someone already present in the student's environment; however, that person must be willing and able to complete the observation and recording as specified. In addition, when evaluating DBR data, research has suggested that having the same rater be responsible for all the ratings collected during the same observation period (see Chafouleas, Christ, Riley-Tillman, Briesch, & Chanese, 2007a; Chafouleas, Riley-Tillman, Sassu, LaFrance, & Patwa, 2007b) is necessary to avoid errors in analysis associated with different raters.

Another option is to have the target student complete the rating, particularly if the data are gathered as part of a self-management intervention. Self-management interventions involve teaching skills that promote the independent monitoring, evaluation, and regulation of individual student behavior (Briesch, Briesch, & Mahoney, 2014; Hoff & Sawka-Miller, 2010; Kanfer & Gaelick-Buys, 1991). Educators often use self-management interventions to target on-task behavior, rule following, and disruptive behavior (Briesch & Briesch, 2016). A critical component of self-management interventions is self-monitoring, in which students are taught to observe and record their own behavior (Briesch et al., 2014; Cole & Bambara, 1992); these data can be used in addition to or in place of a teacher rating.

In addition to providing behavioral data, self-monitoring has been shown to be a powerful intervention for teaching appropriate behavior. As an intervention, self-monitoring has been used effectively for students with learning disabilities (e.g., Crabtree, Alber-Morgan, & Konrad, 2010; Ganz, 2008; Joseph & Eveleigh, 2011; Konrad, Fowler, Walker, Test, & Wood, 2007) and EBD (e.g., Blood, Johnson, Ridenour, Simmons, & Crouch, 2011;

Gulchak, 2008), as well as for students without exceptionalities (e.g., Briesch & Chafouleas, 2009; Rock, 2005). The appropriateness of using a DBR in self-monitoring depends on the student's understanding of the task and follow-through with using the rating procedures. First, students need to learn to identify when they have engaged in a target behavior (e.g., inattention or disruptive behavior) and understand the method that they will use to record their behavior. For example, a teacher might say the following:

> "I would like to work with you to monitor [or check] your behavior in class. We are going to rate how well you pay attention and work on assignments using a scale from 0 to 5, with 1 meaning that you didn't pay attention very well and 5 meaning that you paid great attention. A 2, 3, or 4 rating means that you paid attention for a little, some, or most, but not all, of the time. I would like you to use this card to rate your behavior after math class, and I also will rate your behavior on a separate card. After the class period, we will meet to talk about our ratings. Do you understand what we are going to do? Let's practice with some examples. . . ."

In the initial stages, the student's rating should be compared to an adult rating (e.g., the teacher), and the student should receive feedback on the rating as well as positive reinforcement for its agreement with the adult rating. Once the student's ratings are consistently similar to the teacher's ratings and the teacher is confident about the student's skills to continue rating independently, the comparison might be faded to a point where random and intermittent accuracy checks are conducted. Further suggestions for user-friendly resources on self-monitoring can be found in Table 5.1.

TABLE 5.1. Resources for Using DBR in Self-Management

Resource	Description
www.dbr.education.uconn.edu	The DBR website hosts information briefs and resources for using DBR in self-management interventions.
Hawken, L. S., Crone, D. A., Bundock, K., & Horner, R. H. (2020). *Responding to problem behavior in schools: The check-in, check-out intervention* (3rd ed.). New York: Guilford Press.	In this book, a program targeting students at risk for behavior problems is described. The program involves the daily rating and checking of student behavior. One option is to use self-management when fading supports.
Jenson, W. R., Rhode, G., & Reavis, H. K. (2009). *The tough kid tool box* (2nd ed.). Eugene, OR: Pacific Northwest.	One section of this popular intervention book for practitioners is dedicated to self-monitoring, including suggestions for troubleshooting problems.
www.ebi.missouri.edu	This website provides a printable description of self-management interventions and procedures for implementing them.
www.interventioncentral.org	This website offers an extensive resource on using behavior ratings in the *Classroom Behavior Report Card Manual*.

Training

DBR can be used by just about anyone, but it should be noted that research studies have found that adequate training generally results in more accurate DBR ratings (Schlientz, Riley-Tillman, Briesch, Walcott, & Chafouleas, 2009). Generally, only minimal rater training is needed to produce improved rating accuracy (LeBel, Kilgus, Briesch, & Chafouleas, 2010). For easily observable behavior (e.g., academically engaged or disruptive) or behavior that occurs at more extreme ends of the rating scale (i.e., never or always), minimal training appears sufficient in most situations. For behavior ratings that occur in the middle of the scale (e.g., at a medium level or 30–70% of the observation period) or for behaviors that are more challenging to directly observe, improvements with training have been noted yet are not as pronounced (e.g., with respectful or compliant behavior; Chafouleas, Kilgus, Riley-Tillman, Jaffery, & Harrison, 2012).

Given the positive outcomes associated with minimal training, researchers developed a freely accessible online DBR training module. The module provides an overview of DBR-SIS use in behavioral assessment, modeling of behavior ratings using DBR-SIS, and opportunities to practice and receive feedback while using DBR-SIS (Chafouleas, Riley-Tillman, Jaffery, Miller, & Harrison, 2015). Based on user feedback, the training module was revised in 2018 to include new training clips, a more user-friendly interface, and updated content to reflect current research findings. The DBR training module can be found at *www.dbr. education.uconn.edu.*

WHAT IS THE EVIDENCE FOR USING DBR?

Since the inception of DBR, researchers have published over 50 studies to develop the conceptual and empirical basis for using DBR as a behavioral assessment method. Next we briefly review the main highlights of DBR's development. In addition to our brief review, the book *Direct Behavior Rating: Linking Assessment, Communication, and Intervention* (Briesch et al., 2016) provides a comprehensive review of DBR applications for multiple purposes across different settings. Given that our coverage of the history of DBR, its evidence base, and its use in practice as an assessment tool is limited to this chapter, we recommend referring to Briesch et al. (2016) for more in-depth information about the story behind DBR and its use for different purposes.

Defensibility

Substantial theoretical and empirical evidence exists for the defensibility of DBR. First, the technical adequacy of DBR has been established through studies of reliability, validity, and classification accuracy (Briesch et al., 2016). Classical test theory and generalizability theory have both been used to estimate the reliability of DBR scores. In other words, researchers have used theory-based statistical analyses, to examine how DBR scores might vary depending on individual student characteristics, the environment (e.g., time or location) in which the rating is taking place, and/or the rater. Findings from these studies indicate that DBR scores tend to be highly correlated across six to ten observations, meaning that raters are generally able to use DBR consistently over time (Briesch et al., 2016; Johnson et al., 2016). These studies (Chafouleas et al., 2010; Christ et al., 2009; Christ, Riley-Tillman, Chafouleas, & Boice, 2010) also suggest that some guidelines should be followed to increase our confidence that DBR data are being used reliably:

1. Raters should conduct a minimum of five observations for low-stakes decisions.
2. The number of observations should be increased to improve the dependability of DBR.
3. The same rater should conduct all observations, as different raters can influence the reliability of scores.

Evidence of validity has been obtained through examining how DBR scores compare to existing measures that have been validated for different purposes. Several studies have explored the relationship between DBR-SIS and SDO codes (Multiple Option Observation System for Experimental Studies [MOOSES]), as well as numerous short- and long-version rating scales (e.g., Social Skills Improvement System [SSiS], Behavioral and Emotional Screening System [BESS], Social Skills Rating System [SSRS], and Student Risk Screening Scale [SRSS]; Chafouleas, Jaffery, Riley-Tillman, Christ, & Sen, 2013a; Kilgus, Riley-Tillman, Chafouleas, Christ, & Welsh, 2014; Miller et al., 2015; Miller, Riley-Tillman, Chafouleas, & Schardt, 2017a). Overall, these findings have indicated that DBR scores are highly consistent with scores on other evidence-based measures, supporting evidence for the validity of DBR scores.

Classification accuracy involves the use of statistics, namely probability, to determine the extent to which a measure accurately identifies risk (Briesch et al., 2016). In the case of DBR, classification accuracy indicates that the measure accurately identifies students at risk for behavior problems and that it does not identify students who are not at risk (Briesch et al., 2016). This is a particularly important consideration when using DBR in screening assessments, which we discuss later in this chapter. Further, classification accuracy points to a measure's ability to detect incremental changes in an individual's score over time; this capability is critical when using a measure to monitor student progress (Maggin & Bruhn, 2018). Findings indicate that DBR exhibits desirable classification accuracy across grade levels when a combined summary score is used (Briesch et al., 2016; Johnson et al., 2016). The procedures for obtaining a combined score (i.e., a summary across multiple single-target ratings), along with research-based cut scores, are discussed in the section on summarizing and reporting DBR data.

Usability

DBR was designed to meet a need for a simple, user-friendly, and efficient method of behavioral assessment (Harrison, Riley-Tillman, & Chafouleas, 2014). As discussed earlier, the usability of DBR is enhanced because extensive rater training is not required (Chafouleas et al., 2015; Harrison et al., 2014; LeBel et al., 2010). Overall, teachers have reported that DBR is both easy to understand and feasible to implement independently (Miller, Chafouleas, Riley-Tillman, & Fabiano, 2014a). Research also indicates that teachers have found DBR to be both acceptable and usable in progress monitoring (Smith, Eklund, & Kilgus, 2018).

Further, DBR can be adopted and implemented with minimal resources, in terms of the time, costs, and materials, which makes it a highly usable measure (Briesch et al., 2016). For those using a pencil-and-paper method to collect DBR data, the financial costs incurred are those for the paper, photocopying forms, and writing utensils. The greatest resource expenditure using this method is the personnel time needed to identify and define the behavioral targets, to choose the appropriate DBR scale, and to create the DBR forms. Perhaps the biggest resource challenge relates to data summarization and analysis, which can be "home-grown" in that it depends on school personnel who are skilled in spreadsheet-based software, or which can be integrated into existing systems as appropriate.

Repeatability

Although DBR instrumentation is designed as a rating scale, it shares SDO's features of repeatability. At its core, DBR facilitates repeated measurement both within and across contexts (Chafouleas et al., 2010; Christ et al., 2009). In fact, this repeatability (i.e., standard instrumentation and procedures repeated over many occasions) is critical for the dependability of DBR (Christ et al., 2009), as previously discussed. This feature of repeatability makes DBR ideal as a tool for use in progress monitoring assessment, which we discuss later.

Flexibility

As previously noted, perhaps one of the most attractive features of DBR is the broad array of uses and applications that it has. For example, DBR can be used with preschool through high school populations to generate information about positive and negative behaviors. In addition, it can monitor a wide range of behaviors—from assignment completion to physical aggression. DBR can also be used to rate one individual or a larger group. Finally, the length of the observation period can be determined, depending on the context for assessment (Chafouleas, 2011; Riley-Tillman, Christ, Chafouleas, Boice, & Briesch, 2010). For example, if Joseph exhibits problem behaviors at infrequent or sporadic intervals throughout the school day, it may be most appropriate for his teacher to rate his behavior twice during every school day, taking into account his behavior throughout the morning period and then again for the afternoon period. In contrast, if Crystal is consistently disengaged during math instruction but not during other activities during the school day, it would be reasonable for her teacher to rate her engagement after math instruction has ended, as opposed to conducting one rating at the end of the school day. This flexibility is an important strength of DBR, in that it can be adapted to fit the needs of a variety of assessment situations.

WHAT CONSTRUCTS
ARE MOST APPROPRIATE TO MEASURE WITH DBR?

Although DBR offers flexibility in target behavior selection, it is important to choose target behaviors that appropriately fit your assessment needs. Briesch et al. (2016) outlined five general guidelines for selecting behavior targets with DBR:

1. Determine the level (or tier) of focus for the assessment, such as within a multi-tiered system (e.g., universal, targeted, or selected).
2. Determine whether the behavior of interest is best defined in broad (e.g., disruptive behavior) or specific (e.g., calling out) terms.
3. Ensure that the behavior can be directly observed, so that it is both observable and involves movement.
4. Ensure that the behavior has social validity (i.e., most people would consider it important).
5. Consider whether you want to measure positive replacement behaviors (e.g., hand raising instead of calling out).

Although these guidelines for selecting behavior targets are helpful in customizing DBR instrumentation, particular behavior targets have served as the primary focus in the development and evaluation of DBR-SIS. In particular, three constructs have been identified as core school-based behavioral competencies, or critical indicators of student functioning in school settings. The core behavior targets include academically engaged, respectful, and disruptive behaviors (Briesch et al., 2016; Chafouleas, 2011). Table 5.2 presents operational definitions for these core constructs and several relevant examples and non-examples of each behavior. Next we discuss how these core school-based behavioral competencies relate to student outcomes.

TABLE 5.2. DBR-SIS: Core Behavior Definitions and Examples

Core behavior	Definition	Examples	Non-examples
Academically engaged	Actively or passively participating in the classroom activity.	Writing, raising hand, answering a question, talking about a lesson, listening to the teacher, reading silently when appropriate, looking at instructional materials	Doodling, looking around the room, staring into space, flipping aimlessly through materials, activity unrelated to instructional task
Respectful	Compliant and polite behavior in response to adult direction and/or in interactions with peers and adults.	Following teacher's direction, prosocial interaction with peer(s), positive response to adult request, verbal or physical disruption without a negative tone or connotation	Refusal to follow teacher's directions; talking back; eye rolling; inappropriate gesture, language, and/or social interactions; disruption with a negative tone or connotation
Disruptive	Student action that interrupts regular school or classroom activity.	Getting out of seat, fidgeting or playing with objects, acting aggressively, talking or yelling about things unrelated to classroom instruction	Staying in seat, raising hand, waiting to be called on before responding, keeping body parts to self, using objects appropriately, working quietly

Note. Adapted from Chafouleas (2011).

Academically Engaged Behavior

Academic engagement has consistently been linked to student learning outcomes (Gettinger & Ball, 2008; Gettinger & Walter, 2012). Others have defined engagement more globally, with academic engagement as one facet of a definition of engagement (e.g., Appleton, Christenson, Kim, & Reschly, 2006; Christenson, Reschly, & Wylie, 2012). The definition incorporated in DBR-SIS, however, solely focuses on academically engaged behavior, which includes attention, time on task, and work completion (Gettinger & Ball, 2008; Gettinger & Walter, 2012). Students with high levels of academically engaged behavior are more likely to have the skills and knowledge needed to be successful in school (Briesch et al., 2016; Chafouleas, 2011; Marks, 2000). To begin with, research indicates that engagement with academic material is critical for the cognitive and social development of students (Marks, 2000). Academic engagement also has been shown to predict academic performance across grade levels (Finn & Zimmer, 2012; Reschly & Christenson, 2012; Wang & Holcombe, 2010), along with middle and high school dropout (Fall & Roberts, 2012; Wang & Holcombe, 2010).

Respectful Behavior

Respectful behavior, which includes compliance and polite behaviors, provides students with greater access to positive relationships with the school staff and their peers (Briesch et al., 2016). The importance of teacher–student relationships and student–student relationships has been established for a number of academic, social–emotional, and behavioral outcomes. For example, the quality of peer support and friendships has been shown to be related to academic engagement and engagement in risk behaviors (e.g., substance use, skipping class, and school dropout; Juvonen, Espinoza, & Knifsend, 2012). Positive relationships between teachers and students have been shown to reduce student disruptive behavior and promote a productive learning environment (Koth, Bradshaw, & Leaf, 2008). In addition, teachers have identified "disrespect" as a major challenge in their classrooms (Conley, Marchant, & Caldarella, 2014). Respect has also been identified as a critical component of a positive school climate, particularly for high school students (LaRusso, Romer, & Selman, 2008). Further, when schools promote respect in teacher–student relationships, students are more likely to engage in healthy behaviors and experience increased mental health (LaRusso et al., 2008).

Disruptive Behavior

Disruptive behavior has long been identified by teachers as a primary barrier to successfully teaching the students in their classroom (Conklin, Kamps, & Wills, 2017; Harrison, Vannest, Davis, & Reynolds, 2012). In fact, over 50% of teachers who left the field in 2004 cited student disruptive behavior as the primary factor in their decision to leave teaching (U.S. Department of Education, 2005). Their departure is likely due to the increase in teacher stress and burnout that stems from managing disruptive students (Thompson, 2014). When students engage in disruptive behavior, they interfere not only with their own learning, but also with the learning of their peers (Briesch et al., 2016; Walker, Ramsey, & Gresham,

2004). Students who engage in disruptive behaviors are more likely to be removed from the classroom, which interrupts teacher instruction and limits the student's access to the curriculum (O'Brennan, Bradshaw, & Furlong, 2014; Thompson, 2014). Further, students who have a large number of disruptive peers in their class rate their school climate as less favorable compared to students exposed to fewer disruptive peers (Koth et al., 2008).

Other Behavior Targets

Although the majority of studies to date on DBR have examined these three core behaviors, other studies have begun to look at its application in measuring other constructs. For example, von der Embse and colleagues (2015) explored the use of a self-completed DBR-SIS for progress monitoring academic anxiety among college students. Specifically, students completed a three-item DBR-SIS, scaled from 1 (no anxiety) to 10 (very high anxiety; von der Embse et al., 2015). The items assessed social anxiety (DBR-S), cognitive anxiety (DBR-C), and physiological anxiety (DBR-P; von der Embse et al., 2015). The findings indicated initial evidence to support the use of the DBR-SIS for progress monitoring test anxiety (von der Embse et al., 2015), with recommendations for further research to fully establish its defensibility.

In addition, DBR has been adapted for use in measuring social competence (DBR-SC; Kilgus, Riley-Tillman, Stichter, & Schoemann, 2016; Kilgus, Riley-Tillman, Stichter, Schoemann, & Owens, 2019). Preliminary evidence indicates that the three core behaviors may be more difficult to rate among students with social competence deficits and more significant behavioral concerns (Kilgus et al., 2019). As a result, researchers created behavioral targets specifically designed to measure skills related to social competence and interpersonal relationships with both adults and peers (Kilgus et al., 2016). Specifically, DBR-SC contains two target behaviors: appropriate social interaction with teachers (AT) and appropriate social interaction with peers (AP; Kilgus et al., 2016). Preliminary findings suggest evidence of reliability for DBR-SC ratings and the utility of DBR-SC as a progress monitoring tool (Kilgus et al., 2016).

WHAT ARE APPROPRIATE USES FOR DBR?

In determining the appropriateness of using DBR, we return to our guiding questions:

1. What question am I trying to answer?
2. Which data will best answer the question?
3. What resources are available to collect these data?

In general, DBR offers an effective and efficient option when multiple data points are needed on the same student(s) and/or behavior(s), when resources for data collection are limited, and when a familiar adult is willing to use the method. Given its flexibility, defensibility, and usability, DBR can be an ideal choice within an MTSS framework. DBR can be called upon as an assessment tool for both screening (i.e., identification of a problem) and progress monitoring (i.e., evaluating behavior change in response to intervention). For more detailed descriptions of screening, progress monitoring, and MTSS, refer to Chapter 2. Next we provide some examples of the evidence related to DBR use for screening and progress monitoring student behavior.

DBR in Screening

Several studies point to the utility of DBR as a screening tool (see Chafouleas, Kilgus, & Hernandez, 2009; Chafouleas et al., 2013b; Johnson et al., 2016; Kilgus, Chafouleas, Riley-Tillman, & Welsh, 2012; Kilgus et al., 2014; Miller et al., 2014a; Miller, Patwa, & Chafouleas, 2014b). Most of the available studies on using DBR for screening purposes have focused on the application of DBR-SIS in universal screening (Briesch et al., 2016). DBR-SIS has shown to be effective in identifying those students who need behavioral intervention (Miller et al., 2014b). Screening procedures and cut scores for using DBR-SIS as a universal screener have been established to allow educators to identify students who are at risk in the areas of academically engaged, respectful, and disruptive behaviors (Miller et al., 2014b); we discuss these research-based cut scores and procedures for establishing your own cut scores in the section on summarizing and reporting DBR data.

Briesch and colleagues (2016) outlined nine procedural steps associated with implementing DBR-SIS as a screener for behavioral risk. A summary of those steps is as follows:

1. Establish a decision-making plan that defines how the screening data will be used.
2. Decide who will be responsible for observing and rating the students.
3. Train your raters in the use of DBR-SIS.
4. Establish a data collection plan that specifies which students will be rated and the order in which they will be rated (i.e., first, second, and so on).
5. Determine the DBR-SIS target behaviors for use in screening.
6. Determine when the ratings will take place and the frequency of ratings.
7. Complete the ratings of student behavior using DBR-SIS.
8. Using the decision-making plan from Step 1, determine how you will interpret the collected DBR-SIS data.
9. Compare the student data both globally and within each target area to established cut scores.

As with other DBR procedures, these procedural steps can be adjusted to meet the needs of your classroom, school, or district. Case Examples 5.1 and 5.2 illustrate what these procedures might look like when carried out in screening assessments.

DBR in Progress Monitoring

Given that DBR is repeatable, flexible, and efficient, it offers an ideal tool for progress monitoring student behavior (Fabiano, Pyle, Kelty, & Parham, 2017). In fact, DBR originated as a behavioral progress monitoring tool (Miller & Fabiano, 2017b). As such, there is substantial evidence to support DBR-SIS treatment sensitivity, or its ability to document whether an intervention is effective (Sims, Riley-Tillman, & Cohen, 2017). Specifically, DBR-SIS has successfully detected both significant and insignificant changes in student behavior,

CASE EXAMPLE 5.1

Mr. Wu, the building principal at Great Lake Elementary School, has noticed an increase in student ODRs across grade levels and is interested in establishing opportunities to identify early the students who are at potential risk for behavioral challenges. When he meets with the student support team to discuss the issue, they decide to add a universal screener. Their plan is to have each teacher use DBR-SIS to collect data on students' academically engaged, respectful, and disruptive behaviors in the fall, winter, and spring. All teachers will complete the DBR online training module prior to the first screening period. During each screening period, the teachers will observe and record half of their class in the morning (school start to lunch time) and the other half in the afternoon (after lunch to dismissal) each day for 2 weeks, or until each student has been rated approximately 10 times. At the end of each screening period, the teachers will input the DBR data into an electronic spreadsheet to obtain average ratings and composite scores for each student. The student support team will review the data to identify potentially at-risk students, or those whose average and/or composite scores exceed the DBR's predetermined cut scores. The support team will then discuss the behaviors of these students who are at risk to determine if additional evaluation is needed and/or to identify appropriate strategies or interventions.

CASE EXAMPLE 5.2

Small Pond Elementary School decides to use a screening process in which each teacher nominates 10 students who are potentially at risk for behavior challenges in their classroom. These students will be screened using DBR on the three core behaviors plus an additional behavior indicator taken from their schoolwide positive discipline framework. Screenings will occur three times per year (fall, winter, and spring) for the targeted students, and each target behavior will be reviewed by the student support team. Given their access to and knowledge of the target students, their primary classroom teacher was determined to be the most appropriate rater. As such, the school principal allocated half of the first professional development day to first review the schoolwide behavior support systems and expectations, and then rotate teachers through the computer lab to complete the online DBR training module. The lab was staffed by the school psychologist and counselor, who were available for further questions. The three core behaviors plus the "be responsible" behavior were selected, after a review, for initial teacher nomination. Targeted screening using DBR then occurred, and the evaluation used the single targets for consideration. Throughout the screening period, the teachers rated each target student in the morning (school start to lunch) and afternoon (after lunch to dismissal) each day, amounting to 10 opportunities every week. Ratings were completed immediately following each rating period, and the decision was made to skip completing the ratings if they could not be finished before moving to the next rating period (e.g., morning ratings done before end of lunch period). At the end of the screening period, the student support team compared the resulting summary target scores, based on individual targets, to their corresponding cut scores. Students whose summary scores for academically engaged behavior were equal to or less than their cut scores were considered to be at risk.

which makes it desirable for evaluating intervention effectiveness as part of MTSS (Sims et al., 2017). Further, DBR-SIS has been effectively used for progress monitoring as part of classwide, small group, and individualized behavioral interventions (Miller, Crovello, & Swenson, 2017c).

Miller and colleagues (2017c) offer the following procedures for using DBR-SIS in behavioral progress monitoring. For a more detailed description, please refer to Miller et al. (2017c) or Briesch et al. (2016).

1. Select behavioral targets for progress monitoring.
2. Select a time of day and the length of the observation period(s).
3. Complete the rater training (e.g., the online DBR training module).
4. Collect DBR-SIS data.
5. Evaluate DBR-SIS data.

Case Examples 5.3 and 5.4 illustrate how DBR can be used in progress monitoring. Next we discuss how to prepare the DBR data collection forms for screening and progress monitoring purposes. We also review data collection procedures in more depth, which provides additional context for the steps outlined in this section for using DBR in screening and progress monitoring.

HOW DO I DESIGN THE DBR INSTRUMENT?

There are a few options to choose from when designing the DBR instrument and procedures. First, you can use the core school-based behavior competencies (academically engaged, respectful, and disruptive) as your behavioral targets. Using this option, a trained rater observes student(s) for a predetermined time period and, at the end of the time period, notes

---

CASE EXAMPLE 5.3

Ms. Suarez, a seventh-grade math teacher, is concerned about Franco's behavior in class. He is described as often inattentive, frequently gets up and wanders around the classroom, and has a tendency to bang his fist loudly on his desk. Ms. Suarez decides that DBR would be a good way to assess and monitor Franco's problem behaviors. She decides to use the standard DBR-SIS form to rate Franco's academically engaged, respectful, and disruptive behaviors, but also adds a more specific optional behavior called "out of seat." Since Franco is only in her class three times per week, she decides to rate his behavior during the first half of class and again at the end of class. After 2 weeks of data collection, Ms. Suarez is able to evaluate Franco's behavior to examine patterns (e.g., the second half of class is more problematic than the first half; he most often bangs on his desk during independent seatwork). She decides on an intervention plan: Franco will get a 3-minute break halfway through math class, will self-monitor his behavior during the second half of the class, and will meet with Ms. Suarez when the class ends to compare ratings. She continues to monitor Franco's behavior using DBR to evaluate his response to the support strategies.

CASE EXAMPLE 5.4

The student support team at Mountain Elementary School decided to implement a class-wide intervention with the school's three fourth-grade classes as a result of continued behavioral concerns with the majority of students in this grade. The intervention targeted academically engaged, disruptive, and respectful behaviors, so the team decided to use DBR-SIS (the standard form with three core behaviors) as a progress monitoring tool. Because the classroom teachers were responsible for implementing the intervention, it was determined that three instructional assistants (one per classroom) would complete the ratings. The school principal arranged for professional development for the instructional assistants, during which they completed the online DBR training module. Across a 2-week period, the instructional assistants rated half of the students in the morning (start time to lunch) and the other half in the afternoon (after lunch to dismissal) every day to obtain approximately 10 data points per student. At the end of the 2 weeks, the student support team calculated target and composite summary scores for each fourth-grade class and plotted these scores on a line graph to determine whether the students were responding to the intervention. After reviewing the data, the team modified the intervention to better support students' academically engaged behavior and decided to have the instructional assistants collect DBR data for another 2-week period.

---

their ratings on a scale from 0 to 10 for each core behavior (Miller et al., 2017c). Second, you could forgo using the three core behaviors and determine your own target behavior(s) based on a specified need (e.g., verbal aggression toward peers). Third, you can add target behavior(s) to the three core behaviors—or use any combination of core/noncore target behaviors. Fourth, you can choose between a DBR-SIS and a DBR-MIS scale format. Finally, you can choose the format of your DBR scale when creating a pencil-and-paper rating form.

Creating Your Own Form

First, use the guidelines outlined earlier for selecting an appropriate target behavior. In particular, a precise operational definition of each target behavior is needed to obtain defensible DBR data. Your definitions should include both examples and non-examples of the chosen target behavior(s). If you are using the three core behaviors, this first step has already been done for you—the three core behaviors are defined in Table 5.2. These definitions can also serve as a guide for how to define your own target behaviors.

Next, you need to select the scale format (i.e., DBR-SIS or DBR-MIS). In determining the appropriate format, refer back to your answers to our guiding questions. For example, if Jackson is exhibiting difficulties with multiple disruptive behaviors (e.g., calling out, out of seat, and talking to peers) that you are targeting as part of an individualized intervention, you may wish to rate each of those specific disruptive behaviors. In this case, a DBR-MIS would be an appropriate scale format as it allows you to obtain both a global rating of his disruptive behavior as well as ratings of each specific behavior target. However, if you wish to compare Jackson's disruptive behavior with typically nondisruptive peers, it may make more sense to rate his overall disruptive behavior using a DBR-SIS.

Selecting the scale format can also include designing the scale itself. As noted previously, the standardized form containing the three core behaviors utilizes a scale from 0 to 10, and typically defines the scale so that the ratings estimate the percentage of time that the student engaged in the target behavior. However, you may choose to rate the target behaviors by using a scale from 0 to 5, three emoticons (frown, neutral, and smile), a scale from 1 to 3, and so on. And although the bulk of DBR-SIS research has used a scale that asks the rater to estimate the percentage of time the target behavior occurred, this type of scale is not a requirement since studies have found that different options can produce similar results (e.g., Huber & Rietz, 2015; Miller et al., 2017a). So perhaps the most important consideration is to match your scale format to fit the assessment context. Again, think back to the purpose of the assessment, but also think about who is completing the rating. For example, if you are having a younger student complete their own DBR form, it may be helpful to use emoticons or a scale with fewer numbers to prevent confusion. Refer back to Figure 5.1 for examples of different DBR scale formats.

Finally, you need to actually create the form using, well, paper and pencil (or your choice of word processor if you prefer)! If you are using the three core behaviors, you can find sample forms in Appendix 5.1, on the DBR website (*dbr.education.uconn.edu*), in Briesch et al. (2016), or in Miller et al. (2017c). Intervention Central also offers a Behavior Rating Scales Report Card Maker on their website (*www.interventioncentral.org/teacher-resources/behavior-rating-scales-report-card-maker*), which can be used to create your DBR form. If you are using your own target behaviors, you can also use the sample form in Appendix 5.2 to create your own form. Whether you choose to use the samples as the basis for creating your form or choose to create your own format, we recommend that your DBR form contain the following elements:

1. The date (including day of the week) and observation start and end time.
2. The student and rater names.
3. A brief description of the activity during which the observation is taking place.
4. Clear definitions (including examples and non-examples) of your target behaviors.
5. Directions for completing the ratings (especially if you are not the rater).
6. A separate scale for each of the target behaviors you are rating (be sure to note if any of your scales are "reversed," such that a lower score is more favorable than a higher score).

Rating Student Behavior

After you have established the intended instrumentation and procedures, but prior to the first observation, the rater should:

1. Complete the online DBR training module or an alternative in-person training.
2. Review the definition(s) of behavioral target(s).
3. Gather the materials needed to complete the DBR ratings.

At the beginning of the observation, record the start time on the rating form. Then, observe the target student's behavior for the predetermined length of time. You should specifically look for any noted examples or non-examples of the behavioral targets throughout the observation period. At the end of the observation, record the time and immediately rate the student's behavior.

Anchoring Your DBR Rating

One way to increase the degree to which your ratings represent the observed behavior (e.g., percentage of time engaged in the target behavior) is to create "anchors" on your scale. An anchor is essentially a qualitative descriptor of a numerical rating. In other words, a rating of 5 might correspond with the descriptor "sometimes" or "medium." Figure 5.2 provides an example of how anchors can be used in the standardized 0 to 10 DBR scale. For example, we recommend first thinking about whether the student displayed the target behavior at a Low, Medium, or High level (or rate). Once you have determined whether the observed behavior falls in the Low, Medium, or High range, you can adjust your specific numerical rating within that range to select the best fit for the observation period.

HOW WOULD I SUMMARIZE AND REPORT DATA USING DBR?

The process for summarizing data collected from a DBR is consistent with the process described in Chapter 4 for SDO techniques. That is, DBR data can be quantified, compared, combined, and summarized for summative and formative purposes. For example, the DBR data of Taylor's disruptive behavior over the week can be summarized into a statement of an average daily or weekly rating (6 out of 10 points) or most likely period of high or low disruption (just before lunch) if multiple ratings per day are taken. In contrast to SDO, the options for summarizing data are more limited because DBR data may not be quite as variable (e.g., use a continuous recording). Because DBRs involve a rating on some scale,

Step 2. →	Low			Medium			High		
Step 3. →	0	1	2	3	4	5	6	7	8	9	10
Step 1. →	Never	Occasionally	A little less than half the time	Sometimes	A little more than half the time	Very frequently	Always

Step 1. Think about how often the student engaged in the target behavior.

Step 2. Based on your response to Step 1, determine whether the student engaged in the behavior at a low, medium, or high rate.

Step 3. Adjust your number rating along the scale using your responses to Steps 1 and 2 to select the best fit for the observed behavior.

FIGURE 5.2. DBR anchoring example. Adapted from Volk, Koriakin, Auerbach, Chafouleas, and Riley-Tillman (2018).

the data are summarized relevant to the scale. For example, a simple yes/no checklist can be easily depicted through a bar chart, whereas rating information might be plotted on a line graph, with the intervals on the y axis indicating the DBR scale. See Figure 5.3 for an example of a line graph and Appendix 5.3 for a blank graph with a 10-point scale.

When interpreting and reporting DBR data, it is important to take into account how the scale is presented. For example, DBR-SIS traditionally sets the scale so that the ratings estimate the percentage of time the target student was engaged in the target behavior(s) during the observation period. So, if Zhang Lei receives an average academic engagement rating of 7 across five observations, you would report this result by saying: "On average, Zhang Lei was academically engaged for 70% of the time across all observations." This is an important point to consider when interpreting DBR data, as you can report the data using graphs, a written narrative description, or an oral account. We next present some options for summarizing DBR data; your choice depends on how you wish to report the data.

DBR data can be summarized in a few ways. For instance, you can plot individual ratings for each target behavior on a graph to demonstrate patterns across observations. Figure 5.3 is an example of a line graph created using individual student data on the three core behaviors that were collected over 10 observations. You can also calculate summary single-target scores and combined-scale scores. For single-target scores, you can compute the mean of scores within each DBR-SIS target behavior (e.g., the mean of all academically engaged ratings). For combined-scale scores, compute the mean within each DBR-SIS target, remembering to reverse-score all disruptive behavior scores. Then, sum the means of each target to derive the DBR-SIS combined-scale summary score; we do not recommend using means consisting of fewer than 6 ratings. After you have obtained the summary target and scale scores, you can compare them to their corresponding cut scores. The process and procedures for using cut scores are described next.

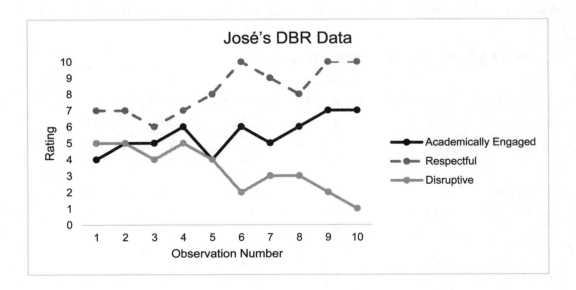

FIGURE 5.3. Sample line graph summarizing DBR student data.

Determining Risk

To identify students who are at risk (i.e., conduct a screening assessment), your assessment tool must be able to differentiate students who are meeting expectations from those who are not. With DBR, a cut score can be used to determine at-risk students. As mentioned in our discussion of using DBR in screening, research-based cut scores have been established across certain grade levels and times of year that allow for the identification of at-risk students (Johnson et al., 2016). Table 5.3 contains the cut scores for lower-elementary, upper-elementary, and middle school students identified during the fall, winter, and spring as reported by Johnson and colleagues (2016). If you choose to establish your own risk scores that pertain to the population of students with whom you work or custom target behavior(s), you should make a priori decisions about your plan, including the comparison score. For example, the criterion could be to select the top 20% of students with more problematic scores as "at risk," indicating a need for further exploration and possible support strategies.

When comparing summary target and scale scores to their corresponding cut scores, be sure that the identified cut scores are appropriate for the target behavior or scale under consideration, as well as for the grades and time of year in which the DBR-SIS was administered. Using the research-based or your own established risk scores, you can generate a list of at-risk students to refer for additional assessment or intervention. Figure 5.4 provides an example of how you can organize DBR data to facilitate a review of risk.

WHAT STRENGTHS ARE ASSOCIATED WITH DBR?

As alluded to throughout this chapter, there are several strengths associated with DBR as an assessment tool. Like SDO, DBR relies on direct observation of student behavior, which generally results in more objective data that are easier to interpret. DBR is also *flexible*, in that there are several available options for creating an instrument, and *repeatable*, in that

TABLE 5.3. Research-Based DBR-SIS Cut Scores

Grade level	Time of year	Academic engagement	Disruptive	Respectful	Composite
Lower elementary	Fall	8.2	1.2	9.1	26.2
	Winter	8.4	1.3	9.1	26.4
	Spring	8.5	1.0	9.2	26.5
Upper elementary	Fall	8.4	0.7	9.5	27.3
	Winter	8.4	0.7	9.4	26.8
	Spring	8.7	0.6	9.7	27.8
Middle	Fall	8.6	0.6	9.7	27.5
	Winter	8.8	0.4	9.7	28.2
	Spring	8.8	0.5	9.7	28.1

Note. Adapted from Johnson et al. (2016). Copyright 2016, with permission from Elsevier.

Student Name	Combined Score	Cut Score	At-risk	Action Taken
			☐ Yes ☐ No	

FIGURE 5.4. Sample format for organizing student DBR data. Adapted from Chafouleas and Miller (2015).

it can be administered on multiple occasions. These strengths make DBR ideal for use in *progress monitoring* student behavior, as we have mentioned. However, unlike SDO, DBR does not share the challenges associated with an event recording or with creating a coding scheme; instead, one rating is completed for each target behavior as in behavior rating scales. In addition, there are *standard procedures* and *evidence-based cut scores* for three core behaviors (academically engaged, respectful, and disruptive) that can serve as general outcome measures for students. Since DBR is generally completed by an individual who is already present in the student's environment, the risk of reactivity is greatly reduced, as are the resources needed to complete the ratings. Finally, DBR is relatively cost free.

WHAT WEAKNESSES ARE ASSOCIATED WITH DBR?

Despite the number of benefits associated with DBR, no assessment method is perfect. It is important to be aware of the tool's limitations in order to limit any threats to the reliability and validity of DBR data. Therefore, we summarize some of the potential threats to the defensibility of DBR and suggest some strategies for minimizing each threat.

Although DBR is a flexible tool, it is important to be aware that its defensibility was established using the standardized DBR form (i.e., the form using the three core behaviors and a 0 to 10 scale). Earlier, we referred to studies that have begun to explore the use of other target behaviors (e.g., Kilgus et al., 2016; von der Embse, 2015), but the evidence for their defensibility is limited to date. Thus, when creating your own scale or defining your own target behavior, the *threat to definition specificity* that can occur in SDO is applicable to DBR.

Since the three core behaviors were chosen for their potential utility as general outcome measures (Chafouleas, 2011), you can reduce this threat to DBR's defensibility by using the three core school-based behavioral competencies as targets, along with your own target behavior(s). If none of the three core behaviors are applicable to the student or situation that you are assessing, you can reduce the threat to definition specificity by using the 0 to 10 scale and closely following the steps for choosing and defining appropriate target behaviors presented in this chapter and in Chapter 4.

One of the positive features of DBR is that the rater can be someone who is naturally present in a student's environment. However, this feature can also threaten the rater's ability to be objective when rating the student's behavior. Further, studies of *rater influence* indicate the potential for variability across raters, meaning that individuals may rate the occurrence of target behaviors differently (Chafouleas et al., 2007a, 2010). Clear operational definitions of target behaviors, along with rater training, can help to reduce the subjectivity of ratings. In addition, increasing the number of observations (and therefore ratings) can increase the reliability of DBR data, particularly for students whose behavior is more variable (Chafouleas et al., 2010). Finally, having one rater complete all the ratings for the target student(s) can help to prevent discrepancies within the data, which can interfere with the ability to assess changes in behavior over time (Chafouleas et al., 2007a, 2010).

CONCLUDING COMMENTS

In summary, DBR is a method that combines features of SDO and rating scales. That is, DBR employs *direct* observation of student *behavior*, summarized in a *rating* that estimates the percentage of time the student was engaged in the behavior. Throughout this chapter, we primarily discussed DBR-SIS and a variety of applications for its use in behavioral assessment. Guidelines for selecting, using, and creating an appropriate, defensible, and usable DBR were also discussed. We also pointed to several resources that provide information about DBR beyond what was covered in this chapter. In the next chapter, we review one of DBR's parent methodologies, behavior rating scales, in greater detail.

Direct Behavior Rating (DBR) Form: Three Standard Behaviors

Date: M T W Th F	Student: Rater:	Activity Description:
Observation Time: Start: _____ End: _____ ☐ Check if no observation today	**Behavior Descriptions:** **Academically engaged** is actively or passively participating in the classroom activity—for example: writing, raising hand, answering a question, talking about a lesson, listening to the teacher, reading silently, looking at instructional materials. **Respectful** is defined as compliant and polite behavior in response to adult direction and/or interactions with peers and adults—for example: follows teacher direction, prosocial interaction with peers, positive response to adult request, verbal or physical disruption without a negative tone/connotation. **Disruptive** is student action that interrupts regular school or classroom activity—for example: out of seat, fidgeting, playing with objects, acting aggressively, talking/yelling about things that are unrelated to classroom instruction.	

Directions: Place a mark along the line that best reflects *the percentage of total time* the student exhibited each target behavior. Note that the percentages do not need to total 100% across behaviors, since some behaviors may co-occur.

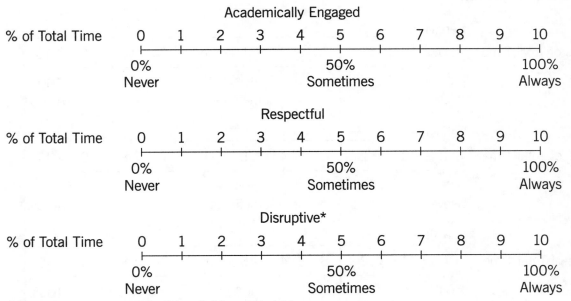

*Remember that a lower score for "Disruptive" is more desirable.

Direct Behavior Rating (DBR) Form: Filled-In Behaviors

Date: M T W Th F	Student: Rater:	Activity Description:
Observation Time: Start: _____ End: _____ ☐ Check if no observation today	Behavior Descriptions:	

Directions: Place a mark along the line that best reflects the *percentage of total time* the student exhibited each target behavior. Note that the percentages do not need to total 100% across behaviors, because some behaviors may covary. If desired, an additional behavior may be defined and rated.

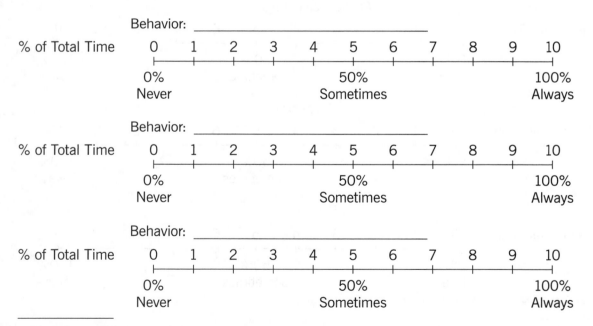

Behavior: _____

| % of Total Time | 0 | 1 | 2 | 3 | 4 | 5 | 6 | 7 | 8 | 9 | 10 |

0%   50%   100%
Never   Sometimes   Always

Behavior: _____

| % of Total Time | 0 | 1 | 2 | 3 | 4 | 5 | 6 | 7 | 8 | 9 | 10 |

0%   50%   100%
Never   Sometimes   Always

Behavior: _____

| % of Total Time | 0 | 1 | 2 | 3 | 4 | 5 | 6 | 7 | 8 | 9 | 10 |

0%   50%   100%
Never   Sometimes   Always

Recording Graph

Student's Name: _____   Teacher: _____

Dates Administered: _____

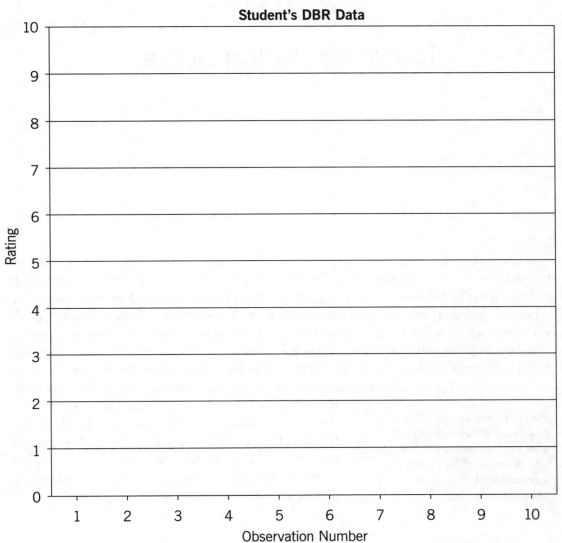

CHAPTER 6

Behavior Rating Scales

Assessment data are often used to understand the global or normative characteristics of student behavior. For example, a school psychologist may want to estimate how a particular student *typically* behaves in a setting. Rather than being interested in out-of-seat and calling-out behavior during instructional time on Tuesdays, information about typical behavior in school related to a broader category of "disruption" may be of interest. Concurrently, we may quantify that behavior and its typicality in another way: by comparing one student's behavior to the behavior that is typically observed in other students of the same age, grade, and/or gender. In this chapter, we review behavior rating scales, which are tools

> **Behavior rating scales are assessment tools that require someone to rate behavior based on what has been encountered during prior observations.**

that allow for the collection of retrospective information that is used to produce data that speak to the broader characteristics of a student's overall behavioral functioning. In this review, we discuss some examples of specific behavior rating scales with an emphasis on making decisions regarding selection and use.

WHAT ARE BEHAVIOR RATING SCALES, AND WHY USE THEM?

Behavior rating scales are assessment tools that require someone to rate behavior based on what has been encountered during prior observations (Kratochwill, Sheridan, Carlson, & Lasecki, 1999). That "someone" is usually referred to as the "rater," and the specific identity of the rater changes depending on the rating scale that's utilized; for instance, the rater could be a teacher rating a student, a parent rating their child, or a student rating themselves. Regardless of the specific rater's identity, it is critical to remember that behavior rating scales are retrospective (i.e., concerned with behavior that occurred in the past), and therefore require that the rater have some level of familiarity with the person who is being rated. However, not all raters are equally equipped to conduct ratings. For example, some raters, like the student themselves, have an entire lifetime of behavior to reflect on, whereas a teacher may have anywhere from a few days to multiple years of behavior to consider. For these reasons, the required degree of familiarity and the specific time period that is being considered when completing the scale is usually, but not always, specified as part of a scale's rating instructions or technical manual. When compared to methods like SDO, retrospective behavior rating scales may be described as "indirect" methods. The data do not reflect observations of behavior that were directly witnessed and immediately recorded, but rather observations that occurred over a period of time when the rater may or may not have been watching out for specific instances of the behavior they are currently being asked to reflect upon. The drawbacks of behavior rating scales reinforce the importance of a multimethod data collection to assist in confirming interpretations of data; to reiterate, we recommend that information derived from a single assessment method not be used as the sole data source, particularly in making high-stakes decisions.

Within this broad definition of behavior rating scales, several additional considerations emerge. First, behavior rating scales can be considered either comprehensive (broadband) or specific (narrowband). *Comprehensive* scales generally comprise a large number of items (often 100+) that cluster together to assess a wide range of behaviors. Comprehensive scales often contain subscales that address more narrow constructs; in other words, broadband behavior rating scales often also contain narrowband subscales. For example, comprehensive measures might assess broadband behaviors, such as externalizing and internalizing problems, as well as narrowband subscales that assess other problems, such as attention, aggression, and adaptive behaviors (Whitcomb, 2017). Whitcomb (2017) used the term "general purpose" to describe this type of behavior rating scale. In contrast, the *specific* type of behavior rating scale is focused on one or two behavioral constructs, such as the behavior that might be included within a narrowband subscale. For example, a scale could be designed to assess symptoms of anxiety, like the Multidimensional Anxiety Scale for Children (March, 2013), or depression, like the Children's Depression Inventory (Kovacs, 2011).

Second, behavior rating scales are most often used to provide a picture of a student's behavior in comparison to a reference group of students. In other words, rating scales are typically *norm referenced,* and this is the type of rating scale that we discuss in this chapter. The standard for comparison is determined by the normative sample of the scale, and generally a range of classification categories are provided with qualitative descriptions (e.g., *significantly below average, below average, average, above average, significantly above average,* or *clinical, borderline [at risk], typical*). In many scales, the raw scores are converted to standard

> **Behavior rating scales are most often used to provide a picture of student behavior in comparison to a reference group of students.**

scores, such as T-scores ($M = 50$, $SD = 10$), to make this comparison, and comparisons may be made according to a variety of characteristics, such as age, grade, gender, or clinical status.

In completing a behavior rating scale, the rater responds to a series of items about a student, like the degree to which a specific student "disrupts other students' learning" on a scale from 1 (*never*) to 4 (*almost always*). Related items are bundled together to reflect the qualities about a given construct (e.g., externalizing behavior), and the ratings on the items are compared to the responses that were found in the normative sample. For example, a scale might include 10 individual items that assess "attentiveness." The ratings from these 10 items would be aggregated and compared to responses from the normative sample to indicate the specific student's attentiveness in relation to what would typically be observed in a student of the same general age and gender. The ultimate score that results from these "attentiveness" items describes how similar or dissimilar the observed responses were to the responses that were most typical for that student's peers. For instance, if the student received a T-score of 50, we would understand that the responses pertaining to this student's attentiveness were very similar to those of an average student.

However, individual scores, like a T-score of 50, only tell us part of the story. This observed T-score is a single (or "point") estimate, and like any estimate, it has error associated with it; for example, if I step on a scale twice, my weight might vary by a couple tenths of a pound each time. As a result, we should not interpret a student's point estimate in isolation; instead, we need to consider the confidence interval surrounding that student's point estimate. The methods used to derive confidence intervals are beyond the scope of this book, although they can be fairly straightforward, in that they incorporate the standard deviation of the normative group alongside the observed reliability of the scores from the measure. For example, after all is said and done, we might measure a student's T-score for social anxiety as 50, with a 95% confidence interval from 45 to 55. In other words, we can be 95% confident that the student's "true" score lies somewhere between 45 and 55, which is still pretty close to typical (Crocker & Algina, 2008). If we instead observed a 95% confidence interval ranging from 30 to 70 for our T-score of 50, we could struggle mightily to provide a meaningful interpretation of the student's score since the "true" score could lie anywhere from far below average to far above average. One final point about confidence intervals: it's important to consider the implications of this uncertainty when we are evaluating students who might be considered "border cases" or who straddle the lines that separate qualitative descriptors like *typical* and *at risk*. Many scales use a T-score of 60 as the line to indicate that an "elevated" status should be considered, and a score of 70 to indicate that "clinically significant" should be considered. If a student has an observed T-score of 68, but the 95% confidence interval for this score ranges from 62 to 74, we need to be very careful in how we interpret this result and describe it to parents, educators, and the student themselves.

Finally, like any behavioral assessment method, the information obtained from behavior rating scales is influenced by rater perception (De Los Reyes & Kazdin, 2005; Smith, 2007). In SDO, the rater may perceive a specific instance of behavior as "disruptive" because of a host of factors, such as negative feelings about the student, a general tendency to rate more negatively, or preexisting biases. In working with behavior rating scales, the "perception" component may be more overt, as the rater responds to the items on the basis of how they retrospectively perceive the student's behavior.

> **Confidence intervals are especially important for students who might be considered "border cases."**

To summarize, the information gleaned from behavior rating scales is based on a rater's retrospective *perception* of a student with regard to a *cluster* of behaviors, and most often in *comparison* to some normative group. Each of these terms (*perception*, *cluster*, and *comparison*) deserves additional attention, as each one influences the appropriateness of selecting behavior rating scales for various purposes in behavioral assessment.

Perception

Behavior rating scales require an individual to rate a student's behavior based on previous observations and interactions over a period of time. We consider two general categories of perception-based issues, *response bias* and *error variance,* and then specifically consider how to think about variance attributable to different raters.

First, remember that when we talk about variance, we are referring to the degree to which numbers within a set are different from one another. Statistics and measurement are really all about variance: if everyone always gets the same score on a rating scale that measures anxious symptomology after every administration, then there isn't really anything to talk about. We could argue about whether the instrument is wacky or whether everyone is really actually the same on this underlying construct, but in the absence of some exceptions that we can examine (or some *variance*), there is no way for us to know for sure. If, on the other hand, we have many different scores for many different people, then we have plenty to discuss. Really though, we have one question with a lot of possible and interesting answers: why are these scores different? Well, first, consider that variance is a property derived from a set of individual scores, and that each of these individual scores consists of a "true" part and an "error" part. For example, my weight almost definitely isn't exactly 170.2 pounds as it says on the scale; as we mentioned earlier, I might weigh myself again immediately and observe a weight of 170.4 pounds, so there is some error associated with this estimate that I need to acknowledge and unpack.

Merrell (2000) and Whitcomb (2017) note that behavior rating scales are vulnerable to error from a number of sources. For example, *response bias* refers to measurement error produced by the rater. This bias can be associated with ratings that are (1) positive or negative based on unrelated characteristics (*halo effect*), (2) overly generous or overly critical (*leniency* or *severity effect*), and/or (3) consistently at the midpoints and avoiding the endpoints of a scale (*central tendency effect*). In other words, response bias refers to how the raters use the scale itself: they might always tend to rate everyone very positively because the rater is a really nice person (*leniency effect*), or they might always use the midpoints of a scale because the rater is really indecisive (*central tendency effect*). In either of these cases, their scores will be different from those of another rater, and not because the underlying construct was actually different. In other words, this variance is not attributable to the behavior we want to measure, but actually something ancillary to the behavior itself. Thus, we feel comfortable calling that difference "error."

Error variance is related to response bias and provides a more general representation of the measurement problems associated with rating scales (Whitcomb, 2017). Four types of error variance are frequently noted: (1) *source variance* (e.g., different raters respond in different ways to the rating format); (2) *setting variance* (e.g., behavior may be present in one but not in all environments); (3) *temporal variance* (e.g., behavior changes over time or the rater changes the approach to rating over time); and (4) *instrument variance* (e.g., a rating difference between two different scales intended to measure similar constructs). With respect to setting variance, Worthen, Borg, and White (1993) suggest that raters tend to remember unusual rather than ordinary behavior. Thus, uneventful behavior (e.g., quietly completing an assigned task) may not be as heavily considered when rating a student. For example, when a teacher is asked to rate John's aggressive behavior over the past month, the teacher may be more likely to rate the more severe behavior at the end of the day after John had just thrown a desk and punched a student.

Let's take a moment to reflect on the issues relating to *source variance,* because it pertains directly to the decisions made by clinicians and educators. The fields of psychology and education (and certainly educational psychology) have not reached a consensus about exactly how to respond when two or more raters use the same measure in assessing the same student and come up with two different scores. However, the evidence suggests that more often than not, raters will not provide the same score; agreement between raters is generally moderate, and certain characteristics of the rating situation, like the student's demographics or the type of behavior being measured, may influence the degree to which two raters agree or disagree (see De Los Reyes & Kazdin, 2005, for a comprehensive review of this literature). Although these discrepancies have been long known and were comprehensively examined by Achenbach and colleagues in the 1980s (e.g., Achenbach, McConaughy, & Howell, 1987), variance between raters "has often been considered something to be erased" (Dirks et al., 2012, p. 559). Unfortunately, erasing rather than embracing variance in scores between raters requires us to suspend our belief that people behave differently in different settings and at different times, and that clinical significance in one setting versus another setting is probably something that should not be ignored. Further, we ultimately have to reach some conclusion based on the assessment data we've collected.

> Variance between raters "has often been considered something to be erased."

To this end, some explicit guidelines have been offered on how to weigh and integrate reports from different informants, such as Smith (2007) who provided a three-dimensional taxonomy for ideal informants based on child age, setting, and behavior type. We endorse the general method described by Frick, Barry, and Kamphaus (2010): first, the assessment results are reviewed, and the clinically significant findings are identified. Convergent and divergent findings across sources are identified, and confidence intervals and "border cases" should be taken into account, rather than exclusively looking at qualitative descriptors. In other words, a *T*-score from one rater may place a student into the clinically significant range, but if the confidence interval around that score includes at-risk ranges as well, then care should be taken before considering two scores with two different qualitative labels as discrepant. When discrepancies are identified, avoid using them as a vehicle for blaming ("Mrs. Aguilar said this was a problem, but mom didn't, so someone is not telling the whole story!") and instead use agreements and disagreements as opportunities to learn more about the student and their behavior. Why might the raters differ? Are the demands across settings different? Do some raters have more or less frequent opportunities to observe specific behaviors than other raters? In short, be critical! It's easy and understandable to lose sight of the big picture when a report just needs to get done, but if we forget the driving questions that these assessment results were meant to answer, then we risk writing a report that does little beyond filling some more space in a student's file.

In summary, the term *perception* actually refers to a myriad of possible sources of error when using behavior rating scales. Thus, we should not assume that all ratings provide accurate pictures of student behavior, nor should we assume that ratings will be consistent across raters, settings, or periods of time. Behavior rating scales should not necessarily be considered unreliable assessment tools; however, we should expect the data obtained from them to vary across raters.

Cluster

Behavior rating scales comprise a series of items that cluster together under one or more scales or subscales. These items are usually measured with Likert-type response options, wherein a series of values are provided alongside anchors for their use. For instance, each presented item could be rated on a continuum of *never, rarely, sometimes,* or *often*; the items featured in Figure 6.1, for example, could be grouped under the general term *attention*. Although just verbally asking a teacher about the typical attentive or inattentive behaviors of the target student would be relatively simple, the inclusion of several items to describe attention has a number of potential advantages. To understand these advantages, let's first ask: "Why don't we just use one item to measure something?" Continuing with the prior example, "Why don't I just ask the teacher to respond to one item on a 5-point scale from *never* to *often* that reads 'Pays attention'?"

Well, you might first say that *attention* consists of more than one specific behavior. Paying attention can look like "orients toward materials during independent work" or "asks questions during class," so just using one overarching item to measure *attention* might not capture all the different ways that *attention* can be manifested by a specific student. In other words, the descriptions of a child's behavior in applied settings often are associated with terms related to a cluster of behaviors rather than one specific behavior. For instance, a student may be described as "hyperactive" rather than "exhibits high rates of fidgeting behavior." Thus, a rating scale provides a common understanding of the specific behaviors that are indicative of a given cluster term. In turn, the term's effectiveness in describing the specific targets of intervention increases.

After discussing the many ways that one general "behavior" can actually be defined and measured, you might also mention that, for whatever reason, the rater might not answer that one item correctly. Maybe the rater wasn't paying attention to that specific item, or maybe they interpreted a word in the item differently from how other raters would. Regardless, a rater's response to that individual item has some error associated with it, and we should try to minimize that error, if possible. Thankfully, we have decades of test theory to

Instructions: Circle the number next to each item that best describes this student's behavior over the past 6 months.

Item	Never	Rarely	Sometimes	Often
1. Is easily distracted	0	1	2	3
2. Does not finish assignments	0	1	2	3
3. Listens carefully	0	1	2	3
4. Daydreams	0	1	2	3

FIGURE 6.1. Hypothetical example of a rating scale for attention.

draw from, which suggests that one simple way to reduce error and increase the amount of "true" variance reflected in an ultimate score is to use a score that is an aggregate across multiple estimates. In other words, instead of just trusting that individual item, trust the aggregate across multiple items instead! In SDO, we might consider aggregating across more raters or across a longer time span, but in retrospective rating scales, we almost always consider aggregating across multiple items. In DBR, we might consider aggregating across any of these dimensions (raters, time, and behaviors), depending on our question of interest and our assumptions about the behavior. A common metric for reliability, Cronbach's alpha, ensures that the score derived from a set of items is more "reliable" to the extent to which it has more items that are more highly related to one another (or intercorrelated).

> If I want to ask questions about change over time, will my selected rating scale be sufficient, or should I consider other methods?

Comparison

An individual student's responses on a behavior rating scale are compared to the responses of other students, most typically described as the students who make up the normative group. Ideally, this normative group includes a representative sample of the population to which we hope to generalize our findings. For most retrospective behavior rating scales used in the United States, this group is representative of students from across the country, and tends to be rather large (e.g., in the thousands) and stratified to ensure that a number of key factors (e.g., socioeconomic status, geography, and gender) are sufficiently represented. Comparison across individuals can be useful in understanding how a student's behavior compares to what typically might be expected. For example, comparing a student's hyperactivity ratings to the ratings of others their age provides a quick indication of the extent to which hyperactivity is a concern. Such information can be useful in assessment purposes involving screening and evaluation. However, comparisons across individuals (interindividual or nomothetic) rather than within an individual (intraindividual or ideographic) may not be as helpful when the goal is to assess incremental behavior change over shorter periods of time (when methods like SDO or Direct Behavior Rating may be more useful). This is a key consideration that should be kept in mind when an assessment question is posed and assessment methods are selected; if I want to ask questions about change over time, will my selected rating scale be sufficient, or should I consider other methods?

WHEN SHOULD A BEHAVIOR RATING SCALE BE USED?

To determine whether to use a behavior rating scale, you have to know the reason that you need the data. For example, if you are evaluating the effects of a yearlong program for teaching social skills to a group of at-risk students, a pretest–posttest administration of behavior rating scales might provide the relevant information to complete the evaluation. However, if the data are needed in order to modify the social skills program as each lesson is conducted, a behavior rating scale may not be the best choice as it may not be sensitive to incremental change. The decision to use a behavior rating scale should relate to whether the obtained information can be practically meaningful for the intended purpose.

Behavior rating scales may be particularly suitable in targeted screening for diagnostic and evaluative assessment purposes. A determining factor in using rating scales is resources: when data on a large number of students are needed, the costs associated with time, materials, and personnel must be considered. For example, when assessing the effects of implementing positive behavior supports throughout the whole school, gathering information on each student using a comprehensive behavior rating scale likely would not be practical, nor would it necessarily be meaningful if the goal is to evaluate systems-level factors. In this example, it might be more efficient to begin universal screening by identifying students at risk for behavioral difficulties through the use of an extant data source (e.g., ODRs) or teacher nominations, and then administer behavior rating scales to that smaller number of students (the targeted group) to confirm the degree and areas of risk.

Although behavior rating scales may often be associated with diagnostic assessment, the assessment data should be linked to efficient and effective intervention. Data gleaned from behavior rating scales can be helpful in explaining terms that describe behavior, which also facilitates making decisions about where to focus intervention efforts. For example, when a teacher describes a student as "highly aggressive," a completed behavior rating scale can further define problem areas and narrow the specificity of intervention efforts. In this student's case, additional information reveals that the student's verbal threats to peers when they don't get their way are more problematic than their physical forms of aggression. In addition, behavior rating scale data may pinpoint appropriate target settings by indicating under what conditions the behavior is more and less likely to be observed. At the level of tertiary (most intensive individual) assessment and intervention, behavior rating scale data can be helpful in generating hypotheses about the behavior that can guide further assessment and/or intervention (see Case Example 6.1).

It is important to be aware that elevated scores on a scale do not necessarily mean that a clinical diagnosis (e.g., ADHD or major depression) is indicated, but higher scores warrant taking a second look at the specific items that suggest a particular diagnosis and collecting other validating forms of data. Additionally, because the terms used to describe a scale (e.g., hyperactivity or aggression) are selected by the authors of a particular scale as a way to define the items falling under that cluster, specific items should be carefully examined rather than assuming that the same term has a similar meaning across different rating scales.

Traditionally, rating scales have not been viewed as amenable for progress monitoring. First, progress monitoring typically involves intraindividual rather than interindividual comparison. When using behavior rating scales, normative comparisons are made about student behavior (interindividual), rather than about pre- and postintervention (intraindividual). Second, information from retrospective behavior rating scales represents a generalized estimate of behavior over a period of time. Such data may not be sensitive to small changes in behavior, which may restrict its use in day-to-day instructional decisions. For example, if a student was initially rated in the 99th percentile on items measuring aggression, even with a significant reduction in aggressive behavior, they might still be rated in the "highly aggressive" range. This situation could lead to the inappropriate conclusion that the intervention was unsuccessful, even though a meaningful reduction in aggressive behavior occurred. Third, although the time (e.g., 15–20 minutes) required to complete a behavior rating scale may be acceptable if the scale is used occasionally, the time needed for repeated administrations of a behavior rating scale is problematic. For example, the administration of a 20-minute behavior rating scale for three students once a week for 6 weeks requires 6 hours of teacher time and is unlikely to be favorably received. Additionally, as described earlier, most rating scales have a specific period of time over which to reflect when responding to items; for instance, raters may be asked to reflect on student behavior over the "last 6 months" or the "last week" and provide their responses accordingly. If the interval between the administrations of the rating scale for progress monitoring purposes is shorter than this window and the instructions for completing the rating scale are therefore modified, then the administration of the rating scale is no longer standardized, and it becomes unclear as to whether the resulting responses would be comparable to those derived from the normative sample.

Many of the issues we have described relate closely to the length and original purpose of traditional rating scales; however, if these rating scales could be condensed and even personalized for an individual student, it is possible that they could serve as a useful tool for progress monitoring. To that end, researchers over the last couple of decades have begun to more critically examine the use of adaptive behavior rating scales (ABRS), also referred to as brief behavior rating scales (BBRS), for the purposes of progress monitoring (e.g., Volpe, Briesch, & Chafouleas, 2010). Numerous methods have been proposed for how to construct an ABRS for progress monitoring, such as selecting those items that have the highest factor loadings or that are most highly endorsed as being problematic for an individual student (Volpe & Gadow, 2010).

HOW SHOULD I CHOOSE A RATING SCALE, AND WHAT ARE MY OPTIONS?

Although assessment is first and foremost an integral part of an overarching problem-solving process, we often fall into the trap of seeing assessment as an end unto itself. Instead of starting with "What questions do we want to answer?," we succumb to routine and time constraints and instead skip straight to asking "What tools are we going to use?" First, this tendency is totally understandable; if you have been asked to step into an IEP team meeting unexpectedly and need to fill out a consent to evaluate form *right now*, you write down the names of some rating scales that you usually use, schedule some student observations, and call it a day.

> **Taking the time to step back, ask good questions, formulate new ones, and select tools to get the information we need *is worth doing*.**

Perhaps this routine response is understandable under the circumstances, but here is the critical thing to remember: *What is all this for?* Is it really just to stay in compliance? Or is it to learn more about this kid so we can support them appropriately? Taking the time to step back, ask good questions, formulate new ones, and select tools to get the information we need *is worth doing*.

CASE EXAMPLE 6.1

Mr. James, a fifth-grade teacher, recently made a referral to his school's prereferral intervention team. He expressed concern about one of the students in his class, Karen, whom he describes as "always off in space." When asked to state his concern more specifically, Mr. James explained that Karen is often doodling or staring out the window when she should be doing schoolwork, and she is often out of her seat. When he has spoken with Karen about these behaviors, she has became "very defensive, sometimes even to the point of anger." The school psychologist volunteered to collect some baseline observational data about Karen's behavior in order to design an appropriate intervention plan. In addition to classroom observations, the school psychologist asked both Mr. James and Karen's mother to complete the BASC-3 Parent and Teacher Rating Forms. The obtained data (both in tabular and graphic forms) are presented below:

Summary of *T*-Scores on BASC-3, Parent and Teacher Scales

	Parent	Teacher
Externalizing problems		
Hyperactivity	49	66*
Aggression	47	57
Conduct problems	52	57
Internalizing problems		
Anxiety	34	48
Depression	45	53
Somatization	35	54
School problems		
Attention problems	**71**	**70**
Learning problems	—	66*
Behavioral Symptoms Index		
Atypicality	58	59
Withdrawal	42	52
Adaptive skills		
Adaptability	36*	39*
Social skills	31*	**22**
Leadership	35*	42
Study skills	43	34*
Functional communication	48	47

Note. **Bold** = clinically significant (70+ on clinical, 30– on adaptive).
* = at risk (60–69 on clinical, 31–40 on adaptive).

(continued)

BASC-3 Clinical Scales

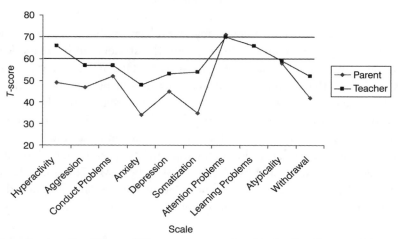

Note. Scores above the upper line (*T*-score of 70 or more) are considered in the clinical range, while scores above the lower line (*T*-score of 60 or more) are considered in the at-risk range.

BASC-3 Adaptive Scales

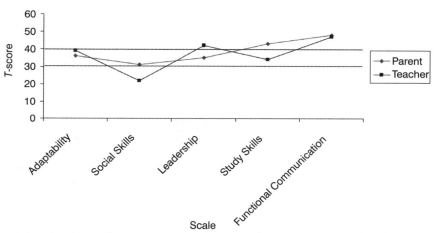

Note. Scores below the lower line (*T*-score of 30 or less) are in the clinical range, while scores below the upper line (*T*-score of 40 or less) are considered in the at-risk range.

Results of the BASC-3 scales indicate that attention is a significant concern for Karen across settings (both in school and at home). In addition, Mr. James rated Karen in the at-risk range for issues of hyperactivity, learning problems, and study skills. In addition, the elevated learning problems and study skills scores suggest that Karen's difficulty is impacting her educational progress. Finally, the Adaptive Scales support this with scores in the clinical range in social skills (parent rater) and in the at-risk range for adaptability, social skills (parent rater), leadership (parent rater), and study skills (teacher rater). Assuming that the school psychologist finds similar patterns during observation sessions, Mr. James's concerns appear warranted in that intervention efforts should focus on improving Karen's attention to task, and perhaps the efforts could be expanded to include both school and home settings. It will be important for this intervention to take into consideration the reported hyperactivity issues as well as the reported adaptive and educational issues.

This conversation is particularly critical to have before we launch into describing the various rating scale options that are out there. It is easy to fall into the habit of using a rating scale because "well, that's just what you do during an evaluation." For some of us, the idea of walking into an IEP team meeting without having a report containing *T*-scores brings up the same feelings as those dreams in which you're naked in public: it's seriously scary. Many times, we do have questions about our rating scales that demand answers; we are just not verbalizing them directly to ourselves and others, nor are we integrating them into an overarching assessment question. So, let's remember what question norm-referenced rating scales answer: "How similar or dissimilar is this student's behavior when compared to other students of the same age/grade/gender?" If this is a question that's worth asking, then rating scales are likely the tool for us.

So, how do you choose one? Ideally, selecting a behavior rating scale involves a consideration of the sampled behaviors, the normed respondent age range and characteristics, the psychometric evidence of the reliability and validity of the resulting scores, its feasibility and ease of use, and the currency of recent versions. We recommend that, when selecting a rating scale, you should begin with the *construct of interest.* Am I interested in learning more about how a wide range of this student's behaviors compares with those of other students of the same age? Or am I specifically interested in their anxious symptomology or their hyperactivity? After identifying the behavior(s) we want to learn more about, we can begin looking for the best tool for the job.

Although a full review of existing behavior rating scales is beyond the scope of this chapter, we describe three examples to illustrate the available options to choose from and the typical considerations to keep in mind: (1) Behavior Assessment System for Children, Third Edition (BASC-3; Reynolds & Kamphaus, 2015); (2) Social Skills Improvement System Rating Scales (SSIS RS; Gresham & Elliott, 2008); and (3) ADHD Rating Scale–5 for Children and Adolescents (ADHD-5; DuPaul, Power, Anastopoulos, & Reid, 2016). The BASC-3 and SSIS RS exemplify comprehensive (or broadband) behavior rating scale systems, whereas the ADHD-5 is an example of a specific-topic (or narrowband) behavior scale.

Behavior Assessment System for Children, Third Edition

The BASC-3 is a general-purpose behavior rating system authored by Reynolds and Kamphaus (2015) and published by Pearson (*www.pearsonclinical.com*). The BASC-3 is a well-established system that features a number of different measures; here, we review the rating scale forms that are completed by parents (Parent Rating Scale; PRS), teachers (Teaching Rating Scales; TRS), and the students themselves (Self-Report of Personality; SRP). The PRS and TRS are available for students ages 2 to 21, whereas the SRP ranges from ages 6 to 25. The three different forms for the PRS, TRS, and SRP are divided into specific age bands. All include a Child (6–11) and Adolescent (12–21) form; the PRS and TRS offer a Preschool-age (2–5) form and the SRP offers a College-age (18–25) form. For children ages 6 and 7, the SRP is administered as an interview, whereas students ages 8 and above complete the form as a self-report.

The TRS and PRS use a 4-point Likert-type scale (N for never, S for sometimes, O for often, and A for almost always), whereas the SRP uses both true/false and the aforementioned 4-point format. The TRS and PRS have considerable overlap with respect to the scales and subscales that they measure. Four composite scores are available for the TRS and PRS: Adaptive Skills, Behavioral Symptoms Index, Externalizing Problems, and Internalizing Problems. A "School Problems" composite is also available for TRS ratings using the Child or Adolescent form. Sixteen clinical and adaptive subscales are also provided in varying degrees throughout the different forms for the TRS and PRS. All ages for both forms have access to 11 of these subscales: Adaptability, Aggression, Anxiety, Attention Problems, Atypicality, Depression, Functional Communication, Hyperactivity, Social Skills, Somatization, and Withdrawal. Seven content scales addressing distinct constructs, such as Resiliency and Bullying, are also available. Finally, there are indices that describe the degree to which student scores are similar to those of students identified with a clinical problem, ADHD, autism, or EBD. A Functional Impairment Index as well as indices aligned with executive functioning are included.

Score reports provide information about raw scores, *T*-scores, associated confidence intervals, and percentile ranks for composites and subscales. Validity indices are used to examine whether the interpretations of scores should be qualified because of unexpected or suspicious patterns in responding. The BASC-3 provides the F index (excessive negativity) for all forms, whereas the L index (extreme positivity) and V index (answering implausible statements) are available for the SRP. Two other indices are also available for digital scoring only.

In terms of feasibility, all versions of the BASC-3 comprehensive rating scales are rather extensive in terms of the total number of items (105–165 items on the TRS, 139–175 items on the PRS, and 137–192 items on the SRP), and thus as one of the longer rating scales, one can expect to spend some time completing a BASC-3. The authors suggest that the TRS takes 10 to 15 minutes to complete, the PRS 10 to 20 minutes, and the SRP 20 to 30 minutes when the rater has prior experience with rating scales. Fortunately, web-based administration scoring is available to facilitate scoring and interpretation. In addition, both English and Spanish translations are available.

In terms of its development and technical characteristics, the updated BASC-3 features a new normative sample updated from the previous version, with 500 to 600 participants completing each individual form, except for the SRP Child form, which has a normative sample of 300. The age band for each form contains 300 students per normed group; the TRS for students ages 2 to 3 contains 200 students. The demographics closely match those of the 2013 U.S. population.

General, clinical, and ADHD normed samples are available, as are combined-gender and separate-gender samples, although the authors generally recommend the use of the combined-gender norms. In other words, individuals using the BASC-3 may ask and answer questions such as "how does this student's behavior compare to that of other male students in the same age range who were identified with a clinical disorder?" However, as more specialized populations are examined, the sample sizes typically grow smaller as well, thus requiring more caution on the part of the interpreter. The clinical norm sample sizes for the BASC-3 were generally fairly large, hovering around 300 students on forms for ages 6–11 and 12–21. However, some ADHD sample sizes are quite small, with a sample of 32 students providing information for students ages 15–18 for the TRS.

Substantial reliability and validity evidence for scores derived from the BASC-3 is documented. Three types of reliability evidence are provided, with high internal consistency estimates and test-retest coefficients. Interrater reliability coefficients are consistent with those typically seen in the field (i.e., moderate agreement among raters). Finally, the authors of the BASC-3 present multiple forms of evidence supporting the validity of the resulting scores (e.g., factor analytic or correlations with other measures of behavior).

Given the extensive effort expended during its development and revision, the BASC-3 likely will remain as a widely used behavior rating scale instrument. Like other comprehensive rating systems, the range of forms makes it useful across many contexts, yet it does require more resources in terms of time (to complete many items) and the relatively high costs involved.

Social Skills Improvement System Rating Scales

The SSIS (Gresham & Elliott, 2008) is a comprehensive set of assessment and intervention tools for supporting positive student social skills, published by Pearson (*www.pearsonclinical.com*). The SSIS includes intervention programs for classwide and individual-level implementation, a screening tool, and a set of rating scales referred to specifically as the SSIS RS. This set of scales has forms for students, parents, and teachers, and one common form used for parent and teacher ratings of students ages 3 to 18. Although the same parent- or teacher-specific form is used for all age groups, the resulting scores are then compared to normed reference groups, which are divided into three age bands: Preschool (3–5 years old), Elementary (6–12), and Secondary (13–18). Two student forms are available, one for students ages 8 to 12 and another for students ages 13 to 18. Spanish-language forms are also available for parents and students. Two core domains, Social Skills and Problem Behaviors, are assessed on every form; a third domain, Academic Competence, is assessed on the teacher form. The Social Skills scale is divided into seven subscales: Communication, Cooperation, Assertion, Responsibility, Empathy, Engagement, and Self-Control. Problem Behaviors are divided into five subscales: Externalizing, Bullying, Hyperactivity/Inattention, Internalizing, and Autism Spectrum.

The BASC-3 and the SSIS RS both utilize similar 4-point Likert-type scales, although the SSIS RS uses different anchors for student responses related to how true a statement is for them. All forms for ages 13 to 18 also include a rating on a 3-point Likert-type scale related to how important a given Social Skills item is to the individual student's success. Finally, Academic Competence, in which teachers are asked to rate a student relative to the other students in the same class on individual learning behaviors, is measured along a 5-point scale. Standard scores ($M = 100$, $SD = 15$), 68% and 95% confidence intervals, percentile ranks, and raw scores are provided for each of these three overarching scales, with five qualitative labels for each range of scores. Only raw scores and qualitative labels, called "Behavior Levels," are included for the subscales. The qualitative labels are derived from the raw score's position relative to the normed group: if a subscale's raw score is more than one standard deviation above the norm's mean, then it is labeled as "Above Average," whereas the raw scores below one standard deviation are labeled "Below Average." Those scores within one standard deviation are labeled as "Average."

Three validity indices are included in the parent, teacher, and student forms. The previously described F index is used, as well as a Response Pattern Index (scoring consecutive items using only one response or a cyclical response) and the Response Consistency Index (scoring items that are similar in similar ways). The SSIS RS technical manual also includes a case study with more detailed feedback on individual scores and interpretation.

As expected for a broadband rating scale, the SSIS RS contains a substantial number of items. The parent forms contain 79 items, 46 of which are related to Social Skills and therefore rated twice, once for frequency and once for importance. The teacher forms contain 82 items, 46 of which are Social Skills items and 7 of which rate Academic Competence. Finally, both student forms contain 75 items, 46 of which are related to Social Skills and thus rated twice by 13- to 18-year-old students.

The normative sample for the SSIS RS was collected in 2006 and 2007 and closely matches the national demographics derived from the 2006 census. The cases in the normative sample for each age band and form varies from 200 cases for the teacher forms for the 3–5 and 13–18 age bands, to 2,000 cases for the parent form for the 5–12 age band. The median number of cases across all eight combinations of forms and age bands is 400. An equal number of forms for male and female students were represented in the normed sample. Scores derived from the SSIS can be compared to combined-gender and separate-gender samples for all age groups. The cases drawn from clinical populations are included in the overall normed sample; no separate clinical normed sample is provided.

Substantial evidence for the reliability and validity of scores derived from the SSIS RS is presented in the technical manual. Three types of reliability evidence are provided (internal consistency, test–retest reliability, and interrater reliability), with expected and positive results for all the forms and age bands. Numerous forms of evidence support the validity of the scores derived from the SSIS RS, including within- and between-measure interitem correlations; item-total correlations; and patterns based on gender, age, and special populations.

The SSIS RS is a widely used broadband set of rating scales; it has an explicit focus on social skills and problem behaviors, covers a broad range of age bands with between 75 and 82 items per form, and demonstrates substantial evidence for its reliability and validity. Again, similar to other comprehensive rating systems, use does require more resources in terms of time and costs involved for use.

ADHD Rating Scale–5

The ADHD-5 is an 18-item set of ADHD-specific short rating scales authored by DuPaul et al. (2016) and published by The Guilford Press (*www.guilford.com*). Forms for two settings, one for parents (Home Version) and one for teachers (School Version), are provided. Two versions of each form are included for two general age groups: Child and Adolescent, and each of these forms is available in both English and Spanish. Unlike most normed rating scales, which require ongoing purchases of materials or online administrations after the initial purchase of rating scale materials, the ADHD Rating Scale-5 requires only a one-time purchase of the manual. The rating scales are included as appendices, and photocopying them for individual use is permitted.

In contrast to the large number of constructs measured by the BASC-3 and the SSIS RS, the ADHD-5 was designed for a specific purpose, the identification of behaviors that are associated with a diagnosis of ADHD. Although it is more limited in scope than a broadband rating scale, the specific focus of the ADHD-5 offers a significant advantage in terms of feasibility. Simply put, the ADHD-5 is brief enough to be quickly and efficiently administered, and reviewers have noted that the brevity of the form *may* make it a feasible tool for progress monitoring (Angello et al., 2003). Questions on the ADHD-5 use a 4-point scale ranging from 0 (never or rarely) to 3 (very often) and comprise two subscales (Inattention and Hyperactivity-Impulsivity) that are aligned with the two dimensions of ADHD in the *Diagnostic and Statistical Manual of Mental Disorders, 5th edition* (DSM-5; American Psychiatric Association, 2013).

Normed samples are provided by gender and age bands (5–7, 8–10, 11–13, and 14–17 years old). Norms for the Home Version are based on ratings from 2,079 parents and guardians who each rated one child, and norms for the School Version are derived from 1,070 teachers who each rated two children. Demographic characteristics of the sample are generally aligned with 2013 U.S. population benchmarks with respect to race/ethnicity, region, income level, and age/gender.

The manual for the revised ADHD-5 presents evidence supporting the structural validity of the scores from the instrument using confirmatory factor analyses for both versions of the measure. Reliability evidence in the form of internal consistency estimates, test-retest reliability, and interrater agreement is presented and is in line with professional expectations. Validity evidence is presented in the form of correlations between the subscales and the total scores on the ADHD-5 and similar and distinct measures, such as the Conners 3 and the BOSS.

> **Critical skills include not only how to give and interpret scales but also how to match tools to specific assessment needs.**

With the BASC-3 and SSIS RS on one end representing comprehensive broadband scales and the ADHD-5 on the other end representing a specific narrowband scale, we have presented the full range of different rating scale options. As we stated earlier, as long as your assessment question is solidly anchored in "how similar or dissimilar is this student's behavior when compared to other students of the same age/grade/gender?," then a norm-referenced rating scale is likely to be one of your best sources of information. Having identified this general method, the next step is to identify which data will best answer this question: Do I need a comprehensive assessment of multiple behaviors, and am I able to ask my raters to complete a lengthy instrument? If so, the BASC-3 or SSIS RS could fit the bill. Do I need specific information about ADHD-related symptomology? If so, the ADHD-5 could be a great fit. Publishers will continue to release both updated and brand new scales, so the critical skills for any practitioner lie in evaluating these tools and in the ability to match them to specific assessment needs, rather than in just knowing how to administer and interpret one or two specific scales.

HOW DO YOU SUMMARIZE DATA COLLECTED FROM BEHAVIOR RATING SCALES?

Options for summarizing data collected from behavior rating scales are restricted by the type of data obtained. As previously noted, the raw scores on most behavior rating scales are converted to standard scores, such as *T*-scores, based on age and/or gender comparisons. This standardized information is then used to interpret behavior. Typically, data are presented in tabular or graphic form, in which a student's *T*-scores across each scale are compared. Case Example 6.2 highlights the general utility of this type of tool and how the outcome data might be presented.

CASE EXAMPLE 6.2

In January, Ms. Wilson decided to implement a classwide behavior management system with her fourth-grade class. In addition to looking for change at the classwide level, she is interested in determining the impact of the system on the behavior of one particular student, Chris. In this situation, behavior rating scales could be used as one tool for gathering outcome data. The options for summarizing the data, however, will depend on which scales are utilized and whether these scales have been administered in the past. In Chris's case, both his classroom teacher and his parents completed the Conners 3rd Edition (Conners 3) early in the previous school year because of concerns about inattention and hyperactivity. Thus, Ms. Wilson could use this information to derive a general estimate of Chris's functioning at the beginning of the school year (see the table below). Then, completion of the scales again at the end of the classwide intervention can provide information for use in evaluation.

Results of the Conners 3 for Chris—Beginning of Fall Semester

Subscale/index	Teacher version		Parent version	
	T-score	Level	T-score	Level
Inattention	65	Elevated	60	High Average
Hyperactivity/Impulsivity	60	High Average	64	High Average
Learning Problems	52	Average	58	Average
Executive Functioning	61	High Average	64	High Average
Aggression	44	Average	42	Average
Peer Relations	45	Average	45	Average

Results of the Conners 3 for Chris—Spring Semester, Following Classwide Intervention

Subscale/index	Teacher version		Parent version	
	T-score	Level	T-score	Level
Inattention	60	High Average	55	Average
Hyperactivity/Impulsivity	55	Average	60	High Average
Learning Problems	48	Average	53	Average
Executive Functioning	59	Average	58	Average
Aggression	44	Average	42	Average
Peer Relations	45	Average	45	Average

Note. Scores are reported as T-scores, which have a mean of 50, and a standard deviation of 10. In general, higher T-scores are associated with more problems or a higher frequency of problems. T-scores above 70 indicate clinically significant problems.

Although Chris's behavior was not highly problematic (i.e., clinically significant) according to the behavior rating scale results obtained in the fall, some concerns regarding inattentive and hyperactive behavior and executive functioning were confirmed—but a decision was made not to develop an individualized intervention at that time. Following the implementation of a classwide intervention designed to increase attention and executive

(continued)

functioning skills, the results of the behavior rating scales suggested that Chris's behavior fell in the more typical range in comparison to peers. However, before drawing any final conclusions, it is important to note exactly what these scores do and do not suggest. The scores suggest that, according to the raters, Chris's behavior became more typical in relation to what is expected over the course of the year. Although one explanation for the change could be the classwide intervention, it is not possible to definitively confirm this outcome with these data. Regardless of the specific cause(s), this source of data does tell us that we may no longer need to be concerned about his behavior. Assuming that the findings from other data sources are consistent (e.g., teacher/parent reports and extant data), Chris's case could be set aside to focus on students with more challenging behaviors that require intensive intervention.

WHAT ARE THE STRENGTHS ASSOCIATED WITH BEHAVIOR RATING SCALES?

Reliable Estimates of Multiple Behaviors

Many behavior rating scales show evidence of good technical properties. Thus, the scales can be valuable in identifying the prevalence and severity of clusters of behavior. Reliable global information about an individual's behavior can be useful in determining the next steps in assessment and/or intervention.

Use for Targeted Screening, Diagnostic, and Evaluative Purposes

An important strength of behavior rating scales is the capacity for interindividual comparison when the concern is on current progress compared to what would be expected. Such information can be useful when deciding whether an intervention is needed, where intervention efforts might best be focused, and whether the desired outcomes are being achieved. Information obtained from behavior rating scales can provide a structured overview of raters' perceptions of a student's behavior, which, in turn, may be useful in the development of behavioral interventions (Nelson, Benner, Reid, Epstein, & Currin, 2002). However, this information may be more useful for preintervention exploration of a student's behavior (Sandoval & Echandia, 1994) than for the creation of specific intervention strategies.

Feasibility with Infrequent Administration

The commitment involved in using behavior rating scales is generally minimal when they are administered infrequently, and thus, a great deal of information can be captured in a relatively short period. Although little training is needed for a rater to complete the scale, the person interpreting the information must have prior training and experience. Although completion of a comprehensive scale may take 20 minutes or more, this time involved is relatively short in comparison to other measures that obtain a similar volume of information (e.g., semistructured interview). If the rater were asked to complete a comprehensive behavior rating scale on a frequent basis, time efficiency could be an issue; however, traditional behavior rating scales tend not to be used in a formative manner. In addition, although the indirect nature of the scales increases the degree of inference needed in interpretation, intrusiveness within the school environment is limited. Overall, when selecting a scale, feasibility must be considered with regard to the burden placed on existing resources (e.g., time or cost).

Assistance with Assessment of Low-Frequency Behaviors

When a problem behavior occurs infrequently, direct assessment tools that require the presence of an individual to observe the behavior can be challenging. If a behavior occurs only a few times a week, an observer is unlikely to "catch" the behavior unless some information is available about when it is predicted to occur. Because the rater is asked to consider a larger time period (e.g., 1 month) when completing a behavior rating scale, the occurrence of low-frequency behaviors may be more easily documented.

WHAT ARE THE WEAKNESSES ASSOCIATED WITH BEHAVIOR RATING SCALES?

Limited Evidence of Use in Progress Monitoring

As previously noted, the evidence supporting the use of comprehensive behavior rating scales in short-term progress monitoring is limited, and current recommendations are generally based on practical suggestions rather than on empirical support. However, the ongoing development of ABRS may provide an option for adapting behavior rating scales for progress monitoring purposes. Most full-length behavior rating scales are not designed to be sensitive to incremental change in behavior. Thus, their use is limited to long-term monitoring, such as in an evaluative assessment capacity. However, when they are used in a pretest–posttest fashion, the effects of the intervention are not monitored directly, so linking behavior change to the intervention becomes difficult. Any number of factors could influence behavioral change, including other interventions, changes in outside conditions (e.g., related to medications or family matters), different social relationships, or changes in the instructional curriculum. Additionally, the data obtained in a summative rather than a formative manner reduces the opportunity to alter the intervention in a timely way if it is not found to be effective.

Limited Use in Intraindividual Comparison

Behavior rating scale information is based on interindividual comparisons, that is, with a normative sample representing a larger population of students (usually national). Although the information is useful for some purposes, it limits our ability to understand the immediate context and behavior of an individual student and the specific effects of an intervention on behavior change. From one setting to the next, different expectations affect what is perceived as constituting appropriate behavior within different environments (e.g., classroom vs. playground, elementary vs. high school, and rural vs. urban). Thus, comparing a student's behavior to their own past behavior and/or the behavior of local peers may be more relevant and informative.

Influence of the Rater

Perhaps the most significant weakness of this method is that the data are influenced by rater perceptions of behavior that occurred in an extended period of time. Therefore, any noted change in ratings must be considered as a possible change in the perception of the rater. Although a change in the student's behavior would be one reason for a change in rater perception, other possibilities should be considered (e.g., familiar vs. unfamiliar rater, good or bad previous experiences, or limited fluency with the scale). In the end, if the need is to directly and objectively measure a student's behavior, behavior rating scales should be set aside in favor of other more direct assessment methods. This is not, of course, to say that the perception of an adult is a categorically bad source of information; rather, this information source does not easily determine whether an intervention has actually changed a student's behavior.

Potential Cost

In contrast to methods requiring only paper and pencil, published norm-referenced behavior rating scales have costs associated with their use. Although the individual protocols are not excessively expensive, the expense rises when they are used with a large number of students or when systems become more complex (e.g., necessitate electronic access). In addition, the initial expenses associated with obtaining scoring sheets, training, manuals, and so forth can be high.

Focus on Problems Rather Than Strengths

Although comprehensive scales often include an assessment of adaptive behavior, most behavior rating scales are focused on maladaptive behaviors and clinical problems. This can lead to an excessive emphasis on what is "wrong" with the student rather than what the student does well, and can also potentially draw attention away from what can be done within a given context to support prosocial behavior.

Applicability to Diverse Populations

Normative samples are typically sampled and weighted in order to approximate a nationally representative sample of students as reflected by gender, race/ethnicity, geographical area, and other variables. As such, when we derive and interpret a *T*-score for a student on a rating scale, we're inferring the extent to which this student's behavior is similar or dissimilar to that of the average student (or average score) in that normative sample. There are a couple of points to consider regarding this comparison. First, if a student is a member of a group that makes up a relatively small portion of the population, then we are comparing that student to a normative sample that represents very few people who are also members of that group. In other words, if I am assessing a Native American student, the normative sample may be nationally representative, but there were still only 20 Native American students who contributed scores to the normative sample. Thus, it is critical to remember that a nationally representative sample doesn't necessarily confer meaningful comparability for all variables of interest. It is also critical to note that the demographic characteristics of the United States' population are changing rapidly, but particularly with respect to children; according to the United States Census, in 2020, less than half of the children in the United States will be identified as non-Hispanic White (Vespa, Armstrong, & Medina, 2018). Thus, it is important to attend to the specific reference year for a rating scale's normative sample.

CONCLUDING COMMENTS

To summarize, traditional behavior rating scales should be considered indirect behavioral assessment tools. They involve rater perceptions about behavior, usually after the behavior has occurred. The obtained information should be considered a general estimate of behavior over time in comparison to a normative sample. Given these characteristics, comprehensive behavior rating scales are best suited for diagnostic and evaluative assessments that provide information about a broad range of behavioral constructs. Behavior rating scales are useful when progress can be assessed over a limited number of administrations or when the emphasis is on interindividual rather than on intraindividual comparison. An increasing number of shorter behavior rating scales are being developed that focus on a specific range of behaviors for use in targeted screening or progress monitoring. Fundamentally, if your assessment question is "How similar or dissimilar is this student's behavior when compared to other students of the same age/grade/gender?," then norm-referenced rating scales are likely one of the most defensible methods you could choose.

CHAPTER 7

Using Behavioral Assessment Data to Make Decisions

Up to this chapter, we have primarily focused on methods of assessment with an eye toward the collection of psychometrically defensible and usable data. Although the assessment method used when measuring an outcome variable is critical, it seems that far too often, the use of such data ends after the information has been collected. Over the past 30 years, we have witnessed the increasing collection of all types of data in schools. The end-of-year standardized tests, screenings for children who are "at risk" for a variety of concerns, comprehensive diagnostic tests, and progress monitoring of key academic and behavioral outcomes are now commonplace. Although this trend is generally encouraging in comparison to past trends in which schools collected far less data, it would be a mistake to assume that, as a result of increased data collection, schools are actually engaging in more data-driven decision making. Indeed, going "all in" on assessment can sometimes result in decision making that makes little to no practical sense (e.g., VanDerHeyden & Burns, 2017). We have watched as school personnel amass relevant and potentially useful outcome data only to then not fully use the data when decisions are made, or instead to sit down with the resulting spreadsheets and ask, "Well, now that we have these data, what actually are we going to use them for?" As drivers of educational assessment practices, we own partial responsibility for this inability to follow through; if we don't clearly and effectively communicate the "why" and the "how" of data-based decision making along with "what" assessments should be used, then we are responsible for wasted resources that result in a loss of educator time without any resulting improvement in student outcomes.

Our observations about the lack of actual data "use" even when potentially actionable data are gathered are not new, and have led many researchers to push for a shift in the focus of assessment development away from documenting the reliability, validity, and sensitivity to change toward actually examining whether and how the resulting data can serve to accomplish a desired goal (Messick, 1995). Of course, such uses aren't necessarily always beneficial for children and adults (e.g., when discipline referral data perpetuate exclusionary practices). This concern has been discussed earlier in the book, but here we focus on one critical way of converting psychometrically defensible outcome data into a format that promotes its intended use and results in behavior change in schools.

In order to be usable, data typically go through some analytic process and are then presented in a standard format. In a research journal, that might involve the presentation of descriptive statistics followed by some analyses that are based on the reporting standards of organizations such as the American Psychological Association or the American Educational Research Association. The standard presentation of data allows for the journal reader to know what to expect in the presentation, such as being able to understand the relationship between the research questions and the outcome data. These standards have been developed after decades of work by research methodologists and academic researchers, who have shaped what is considered best practice. Ideally, the American educational system also would have a similar common approach to the presentation of data. A standard model would allow for the efficient analysis and presentation of data in order to drive effective educational decisions. Recently, such models have been proposed for graphical data presentation in research contexts (Dart & Radley, 2017), but sadly, *data use* has typically received far less attention than *data collection* in U.S. schools. In fact, exploratory work has uncovered some concerns about teachers' data literacy skills— that is, the comprehension, interpretation, and use of student assessment data (U.S. Department of Education, Office of Planning, Evaluation and Policy Development, 2011). Given the lack of agreement regarding data presentation in U.S. schools, in this chapter, we provide guidelines for summarizing and presenting outcome data.

GUIDELINES FOR SUMMARIZING AND INTERPRETING BEHAVIORAL DATA

Next, we provide suggested guidelines that aid in summarizing and interpreting assessment data, with an emphasis on formative assessment data that are used to monitor and evaluate the effects of intervention implementation. This approach is consistent with two goals: progress monitoring and documenting the impact of an intervention. We use line graphs (for progress monitoring), which illustrate simple A-B intervention designs (baseline data [A] followed by an intervention [B]), given the fact that they can be easily created and therefore are more likely to be used in school settings.

Summarizing Data through Visual Presentation: Creating the Line Graph

Although data may be summarized in many ways, visual formats like charts and graphs are generally considered to be more effective and efficient at facilitating the interpretation of the underlying data than nonvisual formats like simple lists of numbers. Visual displays of information, when formatted well, can provide us with key insights into how the data are behaving and how we should respond. We should, of course, also point out that poor visual displays of information can do the opposite, and may cause more harm than good, sometimes in a catastrophic manner (e.g., see Tufte, 1997, for a discussion of the visual display of information and its relationship to the Space Shuttle *Challenger* explosion). It is therefore critical that, when we display data, we aim for a clear understanding of what the data are saying through a consistent presentation.

Much of our conversation in this book has surrounded formative data, or data that are collected repeatedly over time regarding a specific individual, because these data are fundamental to making meaningful decisions about the effectiveness of interventions and our corresponding responses to their effects. As a result, this chapter focuses on one specific type of graph—the line graph—because it provides a simple and intuitive way to review data collected over time, especially for progress monitoring. The steps involved for summarizing data with line graphs are as follows:

1. Label the *y* (vertical)-axis with the behavior of interest (e.g., the percentage of time on task or number of times a student calls out).
2. Select the scale for the *y*-axis based on the data collected (e.g., 0–100% for the percentage of time on task, the percentage of intervals out of seat, the number of words per minute, the number of aggressive acts per day, or the average daily DBR).
3. Select the scale for and label the *x* (horizontal)-axis with the observation intervals (e.g., days, weeks, or other time periods).
4. Separate the preintervention (baseline) and the intervention phase data with a vertical dashed line (e.g., 5 days of baseline data followed by 15 days of intervention).
5. Connect the consecutive data points within phases to show progress. To highlight a summary of the data within phases, do not connect the lines across the phases (i.e., preintervention to intervention) or across the missing data. Represent the missing data points by a break in the lines and the changes in the intervention conditions with a vertical line.

In Figure 7.1, "calling-out" behavior (the *y*-axis) was recorded once a day for a total of 20 days (the *x*-axis). A visual analysis reveals that the maximum number of calling-out behaviors reported in a day is 16 (with the scale set at 0–18). Note that the same scale must

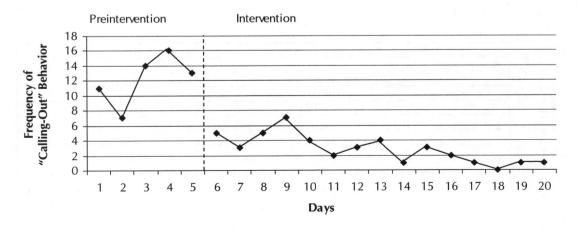

FIGURE 7.1. Example of an intervention graph.

be used when comparing information across graphs in order to avoid an inaccurate interpretation due to a distorted presentation. The vertical dotted line separates the preintervention (baseline) period from the intervention phase and enables an evaluation of the effectiveness of an intervention. Consecutive data points within phases are connected.

Goal lines are useful for interpreting intervention effectiveness (see Figure 7.2), and are based on a determination of what the desired level of the behavior should be at the end of a specified period of time. This behavior goal is expressed on the graph using the following steps:

1. Find the median (the middle value) of the last three baseline data points on the y-axis.
2. Place a point on the graph where x = the last day of the baseline data and y = the median value identified in Step 1.
3. Determine the desired level for the behavior at the end of the intervention period as well as the length of the period.
4. Extend the x-axis out over the entire intervention period.
5. Place a point on the graph where x = the last day of the intervention period and y = the level at which the behavior is expected to be if the goal is met.
6. Draw the goal line between the baseline median and the goal point.

A-B Design

Once the data are converted into a line graph, it becomes easier to evaluate the intervention. This simple approach to monitoring intervention effectiveness is called an A-B design. As we have discussed, the focus of any intervention is to "change" something. Throughout this book, there has been an explicit assumption that we monitor behavior for the purpose of identifying when children present at-risk behavior, and then use an evidence-based intervention with the goal of changing the behavior. For example, a behavior intervention focused on decreasing problem behavior is initiated only when there is a reason to have some concern about the level of problem behavior for a specific student. Given that an intervention is designed to result in a change in a target outcome variable (e.g., disruptive

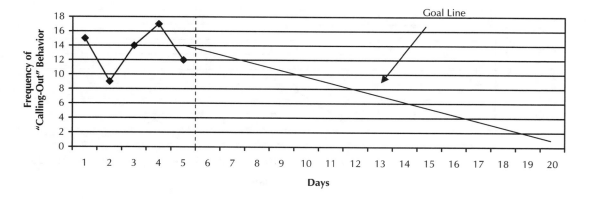

FIGURE 7.2. Adding a goal line to the intervention phase.

behavior), it is important to both document the level of the behavior prior to the intervention (baseline phase) and after the intervention is in place (intervention phase). As such, an A-B design depicts the results of both the preintervention and subsequent intervention data to allow for this analysis of potential change.

Technically, an A-B design is a *quasi-experimental* method of single-case design (Tawney & Gast, 1984) since, unlike "experimental" methods, it does not include any random assignment of cases to conditions. In the baseline stage, the data are attempting to address the question of "What would happen if nothing was done?" In a sense, behaviors that are considered important (e.g., disruptive behavior or on-task behavior) are measured to estimate the current level (amount) and trend (stability of direction), and it is critical that enough data be collected to be confident that current behaviors are adequately measured. It is reasonable to ask, "How many data are enough for each phase?" Practically speaking, there is no hard and fast answer. If a target behavior is stable, and the assessment method is reliable, then three to five data points will be sufficient to establish the baseline level. On the other hand, if the target behavior is highly variable, or the method of assessment has lower levels of reliability, more observations will be necessary. So in other words, there is no required set number of observations, and with time, educators who acquire experience with A-B designs will realize when more observations are necessary before a baseline is considered defensible.

After the baseline has been established, the effectiveness of an intervention can be observed by implementing it in the same setting as the baseline observations. Any change in the outcome data observed in the line graph can, to some degree, be attributed to the intervention. In the next section, we review the methods of analysis related to this change (or lack thereof).

Although an A-B design allows for a change of behavior to be documented concurrently with the implementation of an intervention, the relationship between them should not be overstated. Technically, it is well documented that A-B designs suffer from significant threats to internal and external validity (Campbell & Stanley, 1966; Kratochwill, 1978; Tawney & Gast, 1984). In other words, one can't be sure that there were no other concurrent changes that caused an observed change in the outcome data. As such, although it is defensible to indicate that a change in the target behavior occurred or did not occur when an intervention was introduced, it is not defensible to state that the intervention caused the change. In order to suggest that an intervention caused an observed change, more complex versions of single-case design are required. Although a comprehensive review of other single-case designs is beyond the scope of this book, refer to Table 7.1 for a brief overview. For a full overview of the use of single-case design for monitoring the response to interventions, see Riley-Tillman, Burns, and Kilgus (2020).

STRATEGIES FOR SUMMARIZATION AND ANALYSIS OF BEHAVIORAL DATA

Visual Analysis

Now that the data have been graphed, the next step is to conduct a visual analysis. Pragmatically, a visual analysis can be conducted in a formal or an informal manner. Anyone who looks at a graph will have some impression of what it means, but without a structured

TABLE 7.1. Summary of Possible Intervention Designs

Name of design	Description	When you might want to use this design	Limitations to consider
AB	A baseline (no treatment phase) is followed by the introduction of an intervention. This is the most basic of all of the single-subject designs.	• When you are more concerned with simply finding a treatment that works rather than demonstrating experimental control	• Weak demonstration of experimental control (does not account for other possible factors influencing the dependent variable)
ABAB	After the intervention has been introduced, it is withdrawn to see whether the behavior reverses to baseline levels and then reintroduced to see if the effect of the intervention is replicated.	• When the behavior is reversible (and it is ethical to reverse it) • When the effects of the treatment on the behavior will significantly decrease (or disappear) once the treatment is removed	• Returning the behavior to baseline may be difficult or undesirable • Takes more time than a simple AB design
Multiple baseline	The basic AB design is replicated within the same investigation across at least three people, behaviors, or settings. Although all three baselines begin at the same time, introduction of the intervention is staggered across individuals, behaviors, or settings.	• When withdrawing the intervention, or reversing the effects of an intervention, is impossible or unethical • When intervention is needed for more than one individual, behavior, or setting	• Time and resources necessary • Must control for cross-baseline factors • Must ensure independence across baselines (they do not covary) • All individuals, behaviors, or settings must be expected to react in a similar way to one intervention
Alternating treatments	The relative effectiveness of different treatments is determined by rapidly alternating the introduction of counterbalanced treatments over time.	• When you want to compare multiple treatments quickly and efficiently • When the treatments are sufficiently different from one another • When behavior is severe enough to warrant skipping a baseline phase, *or* baseline data are unavailable or highly unstable (it is not necessary to collect baseline data in an alternating treatments design)	• The learner must be able to discriminate among treatments/conditions • Possible multiple treatment interference (treatments might interact) • Possible difficulty reversing effects • Ensuring implementation fidelity more difficult (counterbalancing interventions and ensuring they are introduced an equal number of times) • Not useful if treatment produces slow behavioral change
Changing criterion	A variation on the basic AB design in which the baseline phase (A) is followed by an intervention phase (B), which is divided into subphases. Within each subphase, the implementer establishes a response criterion level, waits for the behavior to reach the criterion level, and then establishes a new criterion (either increases or decreases).	• When the target behavior is likely to be responsive to contingency changes (and change gradually in a stepwise fashion) • When the student has demonstrated that he or she can perform the target behavior, but the behavior needs to be increased or decreased • When withdrawing the treatment is not appropriate or possible	• Time • Should be used only when the intervention is contingency-based (reinforcement/punishment) • Can be difficult to determine/set the criterion levels

approach, the impression can be erroneous. For example, there is an assumption that when a line goes up on a graph, it is "good"— but in some cases the graphed behavior is negative. We recommend that, in practice, the data be presented in a manner to avoid such errors and that a formal model of visual analysis be concurrently conducted. Visual analysis includes examining (1) a change in level, (2) the latency of change, (3) a change in variability, and (4) a change in trend.

Change in Level

A visual analysis typically begins with an examination of the data immediately after an intervention is initiated, referred to as level or step changes. Given that an intervention is being used to change behavior, the level or rate of behavior observed after the intervention phase is a logical place to start. In Figure 7.3, the arrow indicates the point at which there is a large change in the level of the behavior. A large and immediate change in the level between the baseline and intervention phases is desirable, as is mentioned in the next section discussing the latency of change. If no change in the level is observed between phases, possible changes in trend at the time of the intervention should be examined. Level changes that occur after some time has passed postintervention might indicate the influence of a factor (either facilitating or interfering) external to the intervention or instruction.

Another simple way to interpret the data is to compare the mean or median of the data during the baseline phase with the mean or median of the data in the intervention phase. In Figure 7.1, the mean number of observed "calling-out" behaviors in the baseline phase was 12.2 times per day, compared to 2.8 times per day during the intervention phase. Although an analysis of means suggests a dramatic decrease, examining the intervention effectiveness using only the mean provides an incomplete interpretation. In the example figure, not only is there a decrease in the rate of call-outs between phases, but during the intervention phase the rate of call-outs demonstrates a decreasing trend. Another concern is the impact that a single deviant data point may have upon the mean. In the example, if the data for days 14 and 15 were actually 15 and 16, instead of 1 and 3, respectively, the intervention mean would increase from 2.8 to 4.5. Thus, mean scores should be considered in the context of whether they occur within and between phase trends. When outliers may be influencing the mean in a way that hinders interpretation, one might consider also interpreting the

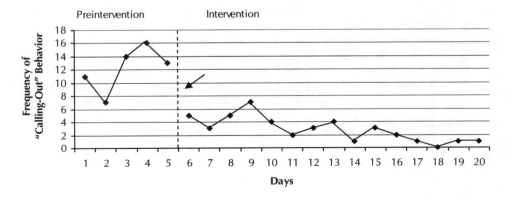

FIGURE 7.3. Examination of change in level from baseline to intervention.

median data point, which is the middle-most ranked point within a data set and is therefore not influenced by the relative size of very small or very large data points.

Latency of Change

Latency of change refers to the amount of time that it took for an intervention to have an impact on the behavior. Intervention effects can be immediate or delayed; thus an examination of behavior trends should be included in the analysis of latency of change: that is, the closer in time the observed change is to the initiation of the intervention, the greater the confidence one might have that the behavior change is related to the intervention. An analysis of the baseline and intervention data represented in Figure 7.4 suggests that the impact of the intervention is immediate.

Change in Variability

Variability refers to the amount of variation in the range and/or the degree of consistency in a set of data. In Figure 7.5, a classwide intervention was implemented to decrease "out-of-seat" behavior. In the baseline phase, considerable variability can be observed. (Remember, mean scores are not representative of variability.) However, during the intervention phase, the overall level and variability of the problem behavior are decreased.

Change in Trend

Change in trend is another important consideration in visual analysis. The trend, which refers to the rate of change generally observed within a series of data, may be increasing or decreasing, or be zero. An increasing trend indicates that the data are generally moving from lower values to higher values as time increases, whereas a decreasing trend indicates that the data are generally moving from higher values to lower values as time increases. A zero trend indicates that the data are not increasing or decreasing, but rather staying the same as time increases. It is critical to note that measures of trend, like a simple correlation coefficient, are very easily manipulated such that the data that visually appear very differ-

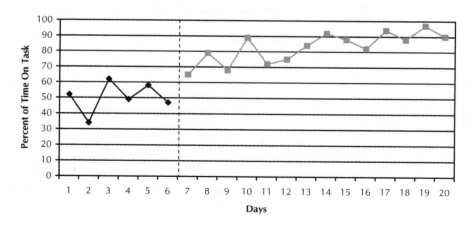

FIGURE 7.4. Examination of latency of change across the baseline and intervention phases.

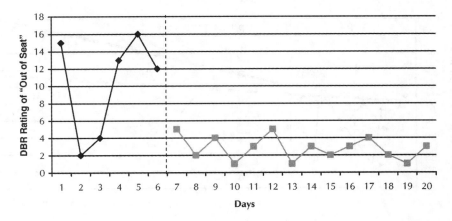

FIGURE 7.5. Example of an intervention graph demonstrating a high variability in the baseline phase with a decreased variability during intervention.

ent demonstrate the same summary statistics. For example, the *datasaurus dozen* is a set of 12 data sets with information on two variables: *x* and *y* (Matejka & Fitzmaurice, 2017). In each of these data sets, the mean for *x* is 54.26, and the mean for *y* is 47.83. All data sets also share the same standard deviations for *x* (16.76) and *y* (26.93) and the same correlation coefficients (–.06). However, when these data sets are plotted on *x*- and *y*-axes, the patterns they depict look very different. Some patterns are circles, some are lines, and one pattern is even in the shape of a dinosaur. Thus, be forewarned to not strictly rely on summary statistics when interpreting the behavior of a data set. Be critical and think hard about what's in the data set that you're looking at.

A simple method for determining the change in trend is the split-middle technique (White, as cited in Kazdin, 1982), which is applied to datasets within phases. The steps for determining a split-middle trend line for each phase are as follows (and are shown in Figure 7.6):

1. Split the data within a phase in half. In the example, the baseline data are split into two groups of 3 points, and the intervention phase data are split into two groups of 7 points. If working with an odd number of data points, make the split at the middle data point (i.e., point 3 of 5), and do not include this point in the remaining steps.
2. Within each half of each phase, identify the point at which the middle value on the *x*-axis meets the middle value on the *y*-axis. On the *x*-axis, the median value will always be the middle day or session. On the *y*-axis, the median value is identified. For example, in Figure 7.6, the middle day in the first half of the baseline data is the second day (the median of 1, 2, and 3) on the *x*-axis (days) and the third data point (which is 50, or the median of 35, 50, and 54) on the *y*-axis (percentage of time on task). One vertical line is drawn through the *x*-axis median, and another horizontal line is drawn through the *y* axis median point to indicate an intersection.
3. Connect the two points formed by the median values for each half to form the trend line for the data in that phase. The same procedure is applied to the intervention data to determine a second trend line.
4. Describe the trend lines within and between phases with respect to their direction and change.

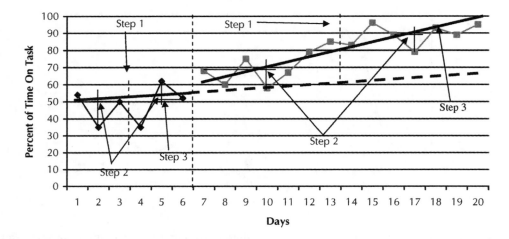

FIGURE 7.6. Step-by-step procedures for using the split-middle technique.

By extending the trend line beyond the data used to draw the initial line, a tentative prediction of future behavior is indicated and can be used to analyze current behavior patterns (e.g., intervention effects vs. predicted performance if the baseline data had been continued).

The data in Figure 7.6 might be described as follows: During the baseline phase, a slightly accelerating trend was indicated with moderate variability. After the intervention was initiated on Day 6, a small initial upward level change was observed and a slight increase in accelerating trend was indicated, with no change in variability. By comparing the intervention trend line to a projected baseline trend, the effect of the intervention is determined to be positive because the on-task behavior increased or accelerated once the intervention was implemented.

Goal celeration lines can be used to visualize goal development and decision making by illustrating what the ideal data could look like if the goal were being met. A celeration line is defined as the best fit line through liner data. In this case, we are developing a theoretical celeration line that illustrates what the ideal outcome data would be if the goal is being met. To develop a goal celeration line, follow these steps:

1. Identify the points on the celeration line corresponding to the first and last day of the phase (e.g., Days 1 and 6 in the baseline phase) and determine the *y* values (percentage of time on task). On Day 1 in the example, the celeration line is at 50% of time on task. On Day 5, the celeration line is at 52% of time on task. In the intervention phase, on Day 14 the celeration line is at 83% of time on task, and at 93% 4 days later (Day 18).

2. Divide the larger value by the smaller value. In this case, 52/50 results in 1.04, which means that during the baseline phase, the percentage of time on task increased 0.04% over the course of 5 days, which would be a long time before substantial change might be realized. In the intervention phase, on the other hand, 93/83 results in 1.12, indicating an increase of 12% over the same period of 5 days.

Computing behavioral change and stating it in numerical terms can be helpful in determining the length of time before a goal will be reached. In the current example, to achieve the goal of a 40% gain in on-task behavior, 100 school weeks with no intervention in place would have been required. With the intervention in place, that goal was obtained in less than 3 weeks. This type of information is critical given that school resources are limited. The information can help educators decide whether an intervention approach is a reasonable one, based on a consideration of whether the need to reach a particular goal within a certain period of time justifies the resources needed to get there.

MOVING FROM SUMMARIZATION AND ANALYSIS TO DECISION MAKING

After the data are summarized and described, decisions about what to do next can be formulated by answering first "Is the intervention working?" If it is working, then a decision about whether to continue the intervention as is, to modify it (i.e., change the goal), or to terminate it (i.e., goal met) needs to be made. If the intervention is not working as expected, then we suggest analyzing why it is not by asking first if there are concerns about the way it was implemented (i.e., was the plan put in place as expected), which suggests that a discussion about the need for retraining or for modifying the procedures is called for. If the implementation is appropriate, however, then decisions about the intervention itself might focus on whether it should be modified or whether another intervention might be tried instead.

Before directly answering these questions about intervention effectiveness, a first step is to determine whether the data are adequate to answer the questions. Adequacy is determined by asking questions about what data should be and have been collected, about what method was used to collect the data, and about whether the method was used appropriately. Additional questions to ask regarding your data are listed in Table 7.2 (adapted from Merrell, 2003).

If the collected data can appropriately answer the intended questions, an interpretation of the data patterns can occur at two levels. First, the chosen intervention should be one in which effective decisions can be made. Figure 7.7 outlines a suggested step-by-step process for making intervention decisions.

Effective monitoring of intervention effects also requires more specific decisions. In Table 7.3, the types of decisions that can be made on the basis of data analysis are pre-

---

TABLE 7.2. Questions to Ask When Interpreting Your Data

- Do the data confirm the identified problem?
- What additional information do the data provide?
- How can we use the data to answer the referral questions?
- Are there other factors that appear to be contributing to the problem?
- Are any data missing (and if so, how will I collect those data)?

Note. Based on Merrell (2003).

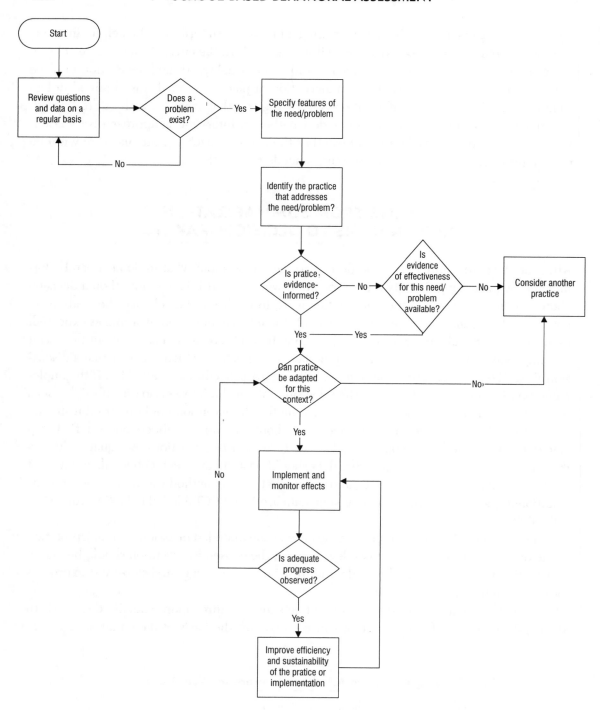

FIGURE 7.7. Suggested process for intervention decision making.

TABLE 7.3. Possible Intervention Decisions Based on Collected Data

If . . .	Then . . .	Description
The student is making sufficient progress toward a goal, and the intervention is being implemented with fidelity.	Make no change.	Make no changes to the current intervention program, but continue to monitor progress and fidelity.
The student is making sufficient progress toward a goal, but the intervention is not being implemented with fidelity.	Evaluate the intervention.	Consider whether all components of the intervention are necessary to continue progress. If adaptations to the intervention have been made by the implementer, learn more about the changes to evaluate whether other parts of the intervention remain necessary.
It does not look like the student will achieve their goal in the allotted amount of time, but the intervention appears appropriate, is having positive effects, and is being implemented with fidelity.	Change the goal date.	Push back the date by which you expect the student to achieve the goal.
The student has been successful with changing some part of the behavior and/or skill and the intervention is being implemented with fidelity, but the student is not making progress overall.	Scale back.	Scale back the behavior/skill change to a more manageable level. For academic behaviors, perhaps focus on only one type of problem at a time. For social behaviors, perhaps reduce the behavioral goal (e.g., aim for 60% rather than 80% on task).
The current work is simply too difficult for the student to be successful.	Step back.	Step back to teach and review an earlier skill in order to ensure that the student possesses the prerequisite skills.
The goal is appropriate and the intervention is being implemented with fidelity, but the student is not making sufficient progress.	Try a different instructional procedure.	Make a change to either the antecedent conditions (e.g., try a different method of teaching a skill) or consequent conditions (e.g., ignore problem behaviors rather than reprimanding the student).
The student's progress has reached a sufficient plateau (started off progressing at an adequate rate, but then has flattened out or dropped off at 80%).	Investigate whether the intervention is still being implemented with fidelity. If not, respond. If so, move on to a new phase of learning.	Although the student is performing the behavior with accuracy, they may now need to work on building fluency. It may be necessary to provide more time to practice the skill or additional incentives for improving fluency.
The student has met the goal more quickly than expected (and the behavior is observed across settings to be both accurate and fluent).	Move on to a new skill.	Establish a new goal, which could be accomplished by either setting a higher goal for the same behavior or moving on to an entirely new skill/behavior.
The goal is appropriate for the student, the student is already receiving adequate assistance to meet the goal, and the intervention is being implemented with fidelity, but the student is not making progress.	Begin compliance training.	It may be necessary to work on improving the student's responsiveness to teacher directives.
The student is not making sufficient progress toward the goal, and the intervention is not being implemented with fidelity.	Improve implementation.	Consider action planning, coping planning, and response strategies in order to improve implementation.

Note. Adapted from Wolery, Bailey, and Sugai (1988) and Collier-Meek, Fallon, Sanetti, and Maggin (2013).

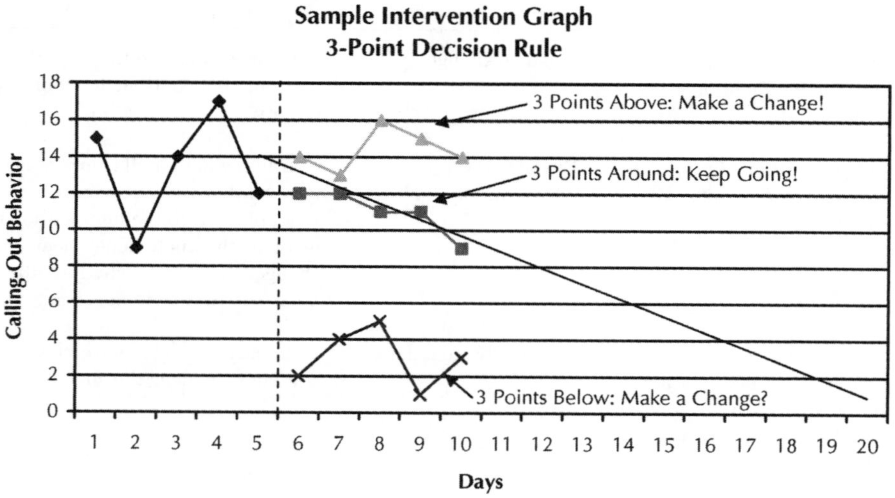

Sample Intervention Graph
3-Point Decision Rule

FIGURE 7.8. Using the 3-point decision rule to make intervention decisions.

sented, and data interpretation ("If . . ." column) corresponds to the intervention action plan ("Then . . ." column). In the example shown in Figure 7.5 involving "out-of-seat" behavior, an analysis of the data suggests a decrease in that behavior. If an agreement is reached that the goal has been met, a decision can be made to (1) continue the intervention as is, (2) discontinue the intervention outright, or (3) institute procedures to fade the use of the intervention. In this case, the decision could involve continuing the intervention but changing the target behavior to another behavior of interest. If this decision was reached, a phase line would be drawn, a new goal or goal date would be established, and data collection and monitoring would continue. If improvements to implementation are necessary, we recommend referring to Sanetti and Collier-Meek (2019) for more detailed guidance.

The *3-point decision rule* can also be applied to guide decision making. Using the 3-point decision rule, the last three intervention data points are examined to determine if they fall (1) well below (deceleration target) or above (acceleration target) the goal line (good progress) or (2) around the goal line (adequate progress toward goal). If good progress is documented, a decision might be made to modify the intervention for efficiency and the maintenance of effects. In Figure 7.8, examples of the use of the 3-point decision rule are presented. The solid line represents the goal, which is a decrease in calling-out behavior. The pattern in the top line of the intervention data does not suggest that the goal will be attained in the time allotted; thus, a change to the intervention should be considered. The middle line of the data appears to fall around the goal line, which suggests that the goal is likely to be met in the time allotted, and that the intervention should continue as planned. Finally, the bottom line of the intervention data suggests that the goal will be attained more quickly than expected, and that perhaps some changes to the intervention could be considered.

CONCLUDING COMMENTS

In summary, many options for the summarization and analysis of behavioral data exist, and typically the options are used in combination. Given the critical importance of progress monitoring and of documenting the outcomes of an intervention, we recommend using line graphs, which allow for the comparison of behavior in both the baseline and intervention phases. The combination of this graphing approach with strategies for visual analysis has a long history, is widely accepted, and is easy to use. Using this approach helps ensure that the most accurate and appropriate decisions can be made using behavioral assessment and related interventions.

CHAPTER 8

Practical Applications of Behavioral Assessment

By now you should have a solid understanding of *when, why,* and *how* you can use behavioral assessments in schools. You learned how to ask the right questions to drive the assessment process in Chapter 2. You became acquainted with the ins and outs of using extant data, SDO, DBR, and rating scales to screen and progress monitor behavior in Chapters 3 through 6. In Chapter 7, you gained insight into how you can continue using behavioral assessment data after the data have been collected and how to use data to make meaningful decisions. In this final chapter, we pull it all together into a school-based behavioral assessment framework that can help you organize and conceptualize your own cases. This framework summarizes the general steps outlined in this book, expanding on the conversation about behavioral assessment we began in Chapter 2. Since we know that effective instruction includes opportunities to practice new skills, this chapter offers sample cases at different grade levels with which you can practice before attending your next data team meeting, new framework in hand. The case studies illustrate how assessments can be used for both screening and progress monitoring, not only within different grade-level contexts, but also for varied student social, emotional, and behavioral concerns.

USING OUR FRAMEWORK TO WORK THROUGH CASES

We start with a description of the framework presented in Figure 8.1. This figure will help guide you through the case studies presented next, and hopefully through future cases in your own practice. A blank version of the figure, with space for taking notes, is available in Appendix 8.1. The first few steps of the figure were introduced in Chapter 2 and should look familiar. But if you need a refresher, we suggest skimming Chapter 2 prior to working through the case studies presented here.

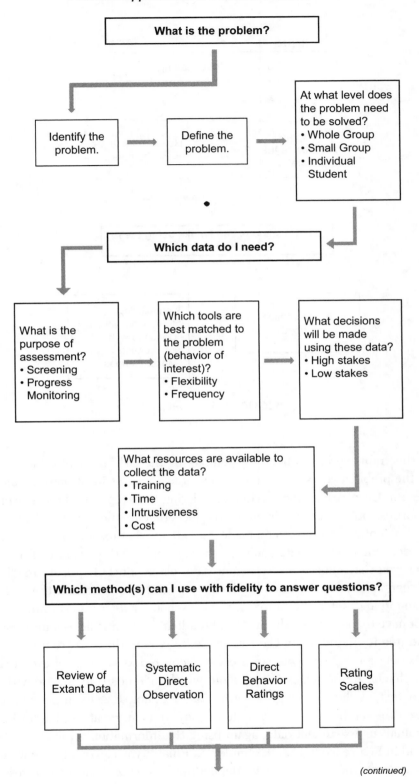

FIGURE 8.1. Framework for use in selecting a behavioral assessment tool.

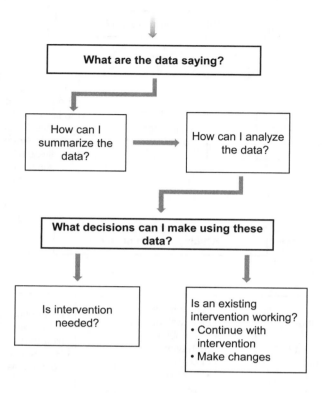

FIGURE 8.1. *(continued)*

Using this framework, you begin by completing the tasks of identifying, defining, and redefining the problem you seek to solve using assessment, as illustrated in Chapter 2 and in Figure 8.2 in Case Example 8.1. After completing this step, you then answer questions about the purpose of the assessment, about the tools that are most appropriate to use, about the stakes of potential decisions to be made, and about what resources are at your disposal to help you determine which data you need. For example, if the purpose of the assessment is screening, you may choose to use extant data, classwide DBR, or a broadband rating scale. If higher-stakes decisions are involved, you want to ensure that the tool is psychometrically sound and defensible. Finally, if your school or district has minimal resources, you may not have the ability to administer a broadband rating scale as a universal screener (as demonstrated in Figure 8.3 in Case Example 8.1, where the data are used to help make lower-stakes decisions). Next, you can use your acquired knowledge of extant data, SDO, DBR, and behavior rating scales to figure out which methods you can use with fidelity in the given context, as shown in Figure 8.4 in Case Example 8.2. Even prior to data collection, based on the method(s) you choose to employ, you can create a plan for how to summarize and analyze assessment data, again using the information available in the relevant chapter(s) and in Figure 8.5 in Case Example 8.2. Finally, you can determine what decisions you can make using the collected data, depending on the context of the assessment (e.g., screening or progress monitoring), and how to continue using the data after the collection period ends. Refer to Figure 8.6 in Case Example 8.3 and revisit Chapter 7 to assist with completing this step.

CASE EXAMPLE 8.1. ELEMENTARY WHOLE-CLASS SETTING

One month into the new school year, Mrs. Newman, a third-grade teacher at Glacier Elementary School, feels that she has exhausted all options for dealing with a student's disruptive behavior. Frustrated, Mrs. Newman reaches out to the school psychologist, Mr. Pacheco, and asks him to evaluate the student, Cory. Upon receiving the referral for Cory, Mr. Pacheco sits down with Mrs. Newman for an interview and asks her for information regarding the disruptive behavior. Mrs. Newman indicates that Cory's disruptive behavior has been an ongoing concern, and it seems as if he misbehaves throughout the entire school day. She says that Cory shouts out during class, jumps on his chair, knocks over various objects in the classroom, yells at his peers, and sings songs aloud quite frequently. According to Mrs. Newman, Cory is disruptive during all activities and lessons, and trying to identify situations in which his behavior is more likely to occur is pretty much impossible. She explains that Cory is "very disruptive," and notes how such behavior affects the other students in the classroom.

Following the interview with Mrs. Newman, Mr. Pacheco decides that his initial assessments should be geared toward understanding the frequency with which Cory displays disruptive behavior. To measure the frequency and duration of the disruptive behavior, Mr. Pacheco creates a simple form that he can use during observations. This form allows him to record the start and stop time for each observed occurrence of disruptive behavior as well as information about what else is happening in the classroom while Cory engages in this behavior.

Mr. Pacheco visits Mrs. Newman's classroom to observe on a Tuesday morning during whole-group math instruction. Cory is seated near the teacher's desk and is singing aloud. Mr. Pacheco sits in the back of the room and begins collecting data, while Mrs. Newman is at the front of the room teaching the students multiplication. After a few minutes, Mr. Pacheco notices that many of the students are engaging in disruptive and off-task behaviors: they are talking among themselves, throwing paper across the room, and yelling loudly. Mr. Pacheco decides to continue with collecting data on Cory as originally planned but chooses to create an impromptu momentary time sampling form 15 minutes later. To complete the observation form, Mr. Pacheco records the behavior of five random students who can be observed from his seat. He takes note of the frequency and duration with which the five students engaged in disruptive behaviors, such as running around the classroom and playing loud music from their phones. Mr. Pacheco stays in the classroom for an hour during this initial observation and conducts similar observations on 2 additional days.

After the observations are completed, Mr. Pacheco reviews the data and determines that Cory displays disruptive behavior as frequently as the other students in the classroom. Furthermore, he notices that the duration of Cory's behavior is the same as that of his peers. With this information in hand, Mr. Pacheco holds a meeting with Mrs. Newman. He shows Mrs. Newman the graphs he has created that depict the daily frequency and duration of Cory's disruptive behavior and his peers' disruptive behaviors. By comparing the graphs, Mrs. Newman notices that Cory's behavior is not much different from that of her other students. She reflects on the last month and talks about how "rowdy" her class has been. She asks what she could do better to improve the overall behavior in her classroom, and Mr. Pacheco describes a few management strategies she could try. They discuss directly teaching behavioral expectations, posting them on the classroom wall, giving praise for appropriate student behavior, and implementing a token system so the students can work toward a highly preferred "dance party."

After the meeting, Mr. Pacheco begins to think about the classroom management strategies he proposed and realizes that he needs to assess whether these strategies are effective in improving the students' behavior in Mrs. Newman's classroom. He wants to use the data to determine if these strategies influence the amount of disruptive classroom behaviors. He knows that frequent data collection would allow him to continuously monitor the impact of the strategies and make adjustments as needed. Now that he has a clear purpose, Mr. Pacheco decides that he wants to collect progress monitoring data.

Mr. Pacheco recalls a previous conversation with Mrs. Newman and thinks that she would be willing to help with collecting the data. Even with the teacher's help, however, he reasons that the tool he chooses will need to allow for the data to be collected frequently and quickly. Since they will need data about the behavior of the entire class, Mr. Pacheco believes the tool needs to be efficient and easy to use. The stakes in this situation are relatively low because the whole-class data will not be used to make a high-stakes decision (e.g., special education eligibility decisions); rather, the data will be used to make adjustments within a classroom.

In considering the options for data collection, Mr. Pacheco considers the available resources. Time is tight for both him and Mrs. Newman. Mr. Pacheco must conduct numerous assessments this month, attend many student support meetings, and prepare for a conference he is attending soon. Mrs. Newman manages 30 students in her classroom, coaches the basketball team, sponsors the science club, and serves on various committees. Since time is precious, the data collection method must not only be quick, but also not require

1. What is the problem?		
1a. Identify the problem	1b. Define the problem	1c. At what level does the problem need to be solved?
Disruptive behavior	**Definition:** Student behavior that interrupts regular school or classroom activity. **Examples:** Shouting out during class, jumping or running around the room, knocking over or throwing objects, yelling at peers, singing or vocalizing loudly. **Non-Examples:** Choral response to teacher directive/question/request, running or moving during an approved motor break, talking to peers during group work.	Whole group—Mrs. Newman's third-grade class

FIGURE 8.2. Completed Example Step 1 of the Data-Based Decision-Making Worksheet for Behavioral Assessment.

2. Which data do I need?			
2a. What is the purpose of assessment?	2b. Which tools are best matched to the problem?	2c. What decisions will be made using these data?	2d. What resources are available to collect the data?
Progress monitoring the effectiveness of new classroom management strategies	*Flexible, quick to complete, appropriate for the whole group*	Low stakes	*School psychologist, classroom teacher*

FIGURE 8.3. Completed Example Step 2 of the Data-Based Decision-Making Worksheet for Behavioral Assessment.

too much training. Even though Mrs. Newman is willing to participate in the training, Mr. Pacheco wants to choose a tool that is understandable and easy to navigate, allowing him to easily teach her how to use it. Mr. Pacheco understands that the data collection method should not interrupt the flow of the classroom, so as to not distract students and cause more disruptive behavior. He also notes that the ideal tool should be able to be completed during noninstructional times and should be cost free since the budget is limited for this academic year.

Having a firm grasp of the resources available and the goals of the data collection, Mr. Pacheco considers the methods he could use to accurately gain insight into whether the classroom management strategies are working. He has already conducted a review of the extant data, particularly the referrals from Mrs. Newman's classroom. The referrals indicated that disruptive behavior was a concern for Mrs. Newman, as she frequently sent Cory and a few other students to the principal's office.

Although the SDO method allowed Mr. Pacheco to gather the necessary information and to understand the problem, he reasons that the method would not be very feasible to continue using during progress monitoring. SDOs would need to be completed several times a week—a time-consuming task. Given his heavy workload and Mrs. Newman's other responsibilities within the classroom, Mr. Pacheco decides that he needs to choose a different data collection method.

Mr. Pacheco considers using rating scales but realizes that such tools usually ask for ratings of behavior over a long period and may require substantial time to complete. Although rating scales would likely provide useful information, the gaps between reporting periods would not allow for routine progress monitoring. Instead, Mr. Pacheco begins to think about DBR. He has used DBR in the past, and has received favorable reports from teachers, who found this tool easy to complete. Furthermore, he knows that DBR can be used to collect and track data for the three core behaviors often seen in school settings, including disruptive behavior. Mr. Pacheco decides to ask Mrs. Newman for a meeting so he can explain the scale to her and find out if she is willing to use this method.

Later that week, Mr. Pacheco and Mrs. Newman meet to discuss DBR. Mr. Pacheco explains how the tool allows for repeated, frequent measurement of a specific behavior, making it ideal for progress monitoring and tracking the effectiveness of her classroom management strategies. He notes that he would like Mrs. Newman to collect data daily on the disruptive behaviors in her class. Mrs. Newman nods along, stating how she likes the sim- plicity of the forms. However, she raises some skepticism about how she will be expected to complete the scales for each of her students every single day. Mr. Pacheco acknowledges her concern and explains that he would like her to complete a rating of the whole class to measure classwide behavior on average. Relieved, Mrs. Newman indicates that she under- stands and agrees to try DBR.

Mr. Pacheco proceeds to teach Mrs. Newman how to use the DBR form, which has single-item scales and addresses the core behaviors. She says that she likes how each behav- ior is defined at the top of the page. For each behavior, she is instructed to indicate the percentage of total time the randomly chosen student exhibited each target behavior, with "0" corresponding to "0%/Never" and "10" representing "100%/Always."

They both agree that she can begin to collect data during the following week, as Mr. Pacheco prepares the materials for the classroom management strategies and after Mrs. Newman completes the freely available online DBR training module. After baseline data has been collected for 1 week, Mr. Pacheco will help Mrs. Newman in implementing the classroom management strategies. The two colleagues decide that they will meet again 2 weeks after the intervention implementation to review the data and discuss outcomes.

Mr. Pacheco visits Mrs. Newman's classroom during lunchtime 2 weeks after she began using the classroom management strategies to collect the DBR forms. To compare the level of behaviors occurring in the classroom before and during strategy implementation, Mr. Pacheco averages the data by week. The students in Mrs. Newman's class engaged in high levels of disruptive behavior during the baseline week (an average of 80% of the time). During the first week in which Mrs. Newman used the classroom management strategies, the class engaged in disruptive behavior 70% of the time. The average level of disruptive behavior decreased to 50% in the second week of implementation. To show Mrs. Newman that the classroom management strategies were having an effect on the students' disruptive behavior, Mr. Pacheco creates a graph of the DBR data and displays the level of disruptive behavior recorded for each day across the 3 weeks.

When Mr. Pacheco and Mrs. Newman meet the next day after school, Mrs. Newman asserts that the behavior in her classroom has improved some. She also says that she has been able to implement the classroom strategies as planned, and that the students seem to like the changes. She also reports that collecting data using the DBR method was fairly easy to do on a daily basis. Happy to hear this news from Mrs. Newman, Mr. Pacheco shares the DBR data graph showing that the strategies are making a positive difference. However, since the students are still engaging in high levels of disruptive behavior, Mr. Pacheco suggests that they continue with implementation and data collection to support further improvements in class behavior. Mrs. Newman agrees, and says that she will con- tinue implementing the strategies she has been using for the past 2 weeks.

CASE EXAMPLE 8.2. MIDDLE SCHOOL SMALL GROUP

It's the second Wednesday of the month, and it's time for Martin Luther King Jr. Middle School's biweekly Student Support Team (SST) meeting. After a few minutes of informal conversation, the team gets going with the agenda. First up on the list is the quarterly deep dive into the referral data that have been collected so far this year, led by the school psychologist, Ms. Esparza. Ms. Esparza pulls up the bar graphs that she exported from her web-based student information system. Each of these graphs displays the frequency of referrals on the *y*-axis and a different variable on the *x*-axis, like student, teacher, grade, or setting (e.g., lunch, hallway, or classroom).

Ms. Esparza starts with the student-specific referral chart, and folks on the team briefly discuss the students who have a high number of referrals, recognizing that each of them are already on their radar for support. They notice that there are more students with two to three referrals than they saw at this time last year and a few more students with an even higher number than usual. As Ms. Esparza clicks over to the graph depicting referrals by grade, the team in the room lets out a big "wow." They knew that the seventh graders were having trouble meeting behavior expectations, but in the busyness of the last few months, they had not quite realized to what extent. The seventh-grade students had over three times the number of referrals than the sixth and eighth graders combined!

As Ms. Esparza presents the graph of referrals by teacher, the SST realizes why. Although a few teachers tend to write referrals more than others, Mr. Galen has referred a much higher number of students than most other teachers. Everyone in the meeting is pretty surprised by these data; Mr. Galen has been at MLK Middle School for about 6 years, and he has a reputation as a very solid language arts teacher, who has good classroom management skills and a great rapport with students. Ms. Esparza navigates through her student information system and notices that almost all of Mr. Galen's referrals are from his seventh-period language arts block, and that they appear to be focused on three specific students. When she pulls up what behaviors these referrals were written for, she sees that they were mostly for disruptive behavior, inappropriate language, and defiance. Ms. Esparza offers to meet with Mr. Galen to discuss the issue the next day and then follow up with the SST by email.

On Thursday morning, Ms. Esparza asks Mr. Galen what's been going on. Mr. Galen exhales and says that it has been a really tough class this year, especially with a group of three students who seem to be vying for his attention. They used to sit in a group and ask him for help repeatedly during class, so he has instituted assigned seating and separated them. However, this strategy has not been successful, because now he ends up spending more time with each student individually. Over the past few weeks, the students have escalated to using inappropriate language if he doesn't immediately provide attention, so he's been writing them up for inappropriate language. He has noticed that on the days when he has a rotating aide or paraprofessional in the room, the swearing happens a lot less, so he is convinced that the behavior is related to attention.

Mr. Galen invites Ms. Esparza to visit the classroom to observe the behavior firsthand, so Ms. Esparza sets up a time to come by Mr. Galen's class the next day. She heads back to her office and jots down the definitions of the behaviors that Mr. Galen described— "requesting help" and "inappropriate language." She adds some examples and non-examples to her operational definitions based on Mr. Galen's feedback, and sends him a quick email to confirm that she'll be coming in for an observation during seventh period tomorrow. Finally, with her observation scheduled and her operational definitions identified, Ms. Esparza determines how these data are going to be collected. She has identified and defined the problem with Mr. Galen, and it sounds like it could be an individual-student or a small-group issue; it could be the case that one student is responsible for most of the behaviors during class, although Mr. Galen perceives that multiple students are responsible, or that the behaviors are generally engaged in by this specific trio of students. It could also be that this is an issue experienced by lots of students in the classroom, and if that's the case, then Ms. Esparza might consider some whole-group classroom management support for Mr. Galen, rather than focusing on a more individual-student or small-group intervention.

Ms. Esparza has set out a few goals for her data collection. One, she wants to confirm at what level (individual, small group, whole group) the problem is located. Two, she wants to get a sense of why the students might be engaging in these behaviors, so she can identify an appropriate intervention strategy. She knows that the paraprofessional, Mrs. Khatri, generally rotates in and out of classes during seventh period, but she hasn't been able to connect with Mrs. Khatri to find out when she expects to be in Mr. Galen's class tomorrow. Ms. Esparza knows that her data sheet will need to be flexible enough to accommodate changes during the observation (like Mrs. Khatri entering or exiting the class), and allow for the opportunity to collect data on a few specific students as well as the rest of the class in order to tease out at what level the problem is located.

Now it's time for Ms. Esparza to decide on a method or methods for her data collection. She decides that SDO seems like the way to go for this situation. Both of her target behaviors are amenable to frequency counts; they have a discrete start and end, they don't really vary in terms of length, and it generally makes sense to ask "How many times did this happen?" rather than "How long did this happen for?" for each of the two behaviors. The stakes for this decision making are moderate: not as high as an eligibility decision, nor as low as just making some simple modifications to a classroom. They are behaviors that are really disrupting Mr. Galen's class and that are showing up in a significant way in the form of discipline referrals. Ms. Esparza is very comfortable with using SDO in the form of frequency counts, so no training will be necessary for her. She is able to commit the initial 30 minutes to conduct the observation, and because many adults float in and out of classrooms in this middle school, she doesn't expect her presence to be particularly intrusive. Finally,

3. Which methods can I use with fidelity to answer questions?			
Review of extant data	Systematic Direct Observation	Direct Behavior Ratings	Rating scales
Yes—schoolwide, class, and individual student extant data can be collected via the web-based student information system.	Yes— specific problem behaviors have been defined, are observable, and can be measured using objective frequency counts.	No—although specific, observable problem behaviors have been defined with examples and non-examples, classroom teachers may be too biased to complete accurate ratings of the target students.	No— classroom teachers may be too biased to complete accurate ratings of the target students.

FIGURE 8.4. Completed Example Step 3 of the Data-Based Decision-Making Worksheet for Behavioral Assessment.

there are no costs involved beyond Ms. Esparza's time and the sheet of paper she'll need to print out to complete the observation.

To allow for flexibility in her data collection form, she creates a sheet that enables her to collect frequency count data for both multiple kids and the whole class; each group is given a separate row, with 5-minute intervals marked along the width of the form to include more details about when the behaviors were occurring. She'll draw a vertical line through the sheet when Mrs. Khatri comes in and draw another vertical line to indicate when she's left. Simple and informative!

Ms. Esparza has used quite a few different data sources so far to solve this problem, and thus far it has been manageable. She used extant data in the form of discipline referrals to identify the problem, interviews with a staff member to further define the problem and context, and now she has designed an SDO method to drill down into the meaningful next steps. She reflects upon the work she's done so far, and asks herself, "After I do this in-class observation tomorrow, am I likely to have the information I need to move toward intervention?" She might notice that, even if she has the information about which students are engaged in the behaviors and about whether the behaviors lessen when Mrs. Khatri is in the room, she still might not have convincing evidence to suggest whether the behavior change when the paraprofessional is present is due to a skill or a performance deficit. In other words, even if these students do exhibit concerning levels of behavior during the observation, why might the behavior be occurring? Maybe they are asking for help because they genuinely don't understand how to do the work; in other words, they might not have the skills necessary to complete it (skill deficit). Ms. Esparza quickly checks the grades and benchmark scores using her district's digital student information platform. She drills down to Mr. Galen's seventh-period class, and sees a reasonable distribution of benchmark scores and grades. Although there are some students struggling in language arts, they are not the students noted as having the concerning behaviors. Nonetheless, Ms. Esparza sends a quick email to Mr. Galen asking him to confirm that he has not observed significant academic concerns from these students.

The next morning, Ms. Esparza checks her email; Mr. Galen has replied, confirming that these students are among the best performers academically. Knowing that a skill deficit is unlikely, Ms. Esparza heads on over to Mr. Galen's seventh-period class to conduct the observation.

Two minutes have passed since the class started, and Ms. Esparza already realizes that her intended data collection method has flaws. The frequency of "requesting help" and "inappropriate language" behaviors from this trio of students is higher than she had anticipated, and she simply can't accurately record each event, because each one is engaging in these behaviors rapidly and at the same time as the other students. So, Ms. Esparza takes a breath, turns her data sheet over to the blank side, and draws out a new sheet to use. On this literally-just-created form, she makes three rows, one for each student. She writes "inappropriate help requests" at the top, because it's apparent that these requests are one and the same for each of these students. She pulls out her phone and starts her stopwatch; in minute-long intervals, Ms. Esparza plans to rotate around to each student and count the number of inappropriate help requests from each one. She starts with Student 1, counting four inappropriate help requests from him for that minute. When her stopwatch shows

4. What are the data saying?	
4a. How can I summarize the data?	4b. How can I analyze the data?
Frequency counts can be summarized into a statement of total occurrences per day, per period, or per student, and may then be presented in a bar or line graph.	Over multiple days or weeks, frequency counts can be analyzed to determine the average daily occurrence of problem behavior, the most likely time of occurrence, and whether occurrences are increasing or decreasing.

FIGURE 8.5. Completed Example Step 4 of the Data-Based Decision-Making Worksheet for Behavioral Assessment.

"1:00," she switches over to the row for Student 2, counting six help requests from her. At "2:00," she moves to Student 3, marking five inappropriate help requests from this student. Ten minutes into the observation, Mrs. Khatri arrives, so Ms. Esparza draws a big vertical line through her rows and starts tallying on the other side of the sheet. After 10 minutes of working in the classroom, Mrs. Khatri leaves; Ms. Esparza draws another vertical line, and finishes up another 10 minutes of data collection before heading out.

The data are compelling; the students are much less disruptive when Mrs. Khatri is in the classroom. Anecdotally, Ms. Esparza noticed that Mrs. Khatri spent almost all of her time with the trio of students while she was in the room. Ms. Esparza decides that, since this behavior is likely about obtaining adult attention, these students would be great candidates for the school's Check-In, Check-Out (CICO) program. The scores on the students' CICO forms will provide some data to indicate whether they are responding to the intervention, but to confirm this, Ms. Esparza will pop into Mr. Galen's class once a week for 30 minutes to conduct observations using the same method she did previously. If a decrease in disruptive behavior during those observations is aligned with similar outcomes on the CICO forms, she will have some robust evidence to suggest that the targeted intervention strategy was a success.

CASE EXAMPLE 8.3. HIGH SCHOOL INDIVIDUAL STUDENT

In the beginning of November at Eastport High School, Mr. Hall asks to consult with the school psychologist, Dr. Lee, about a student, Marissa, whose grade in his sophomore English class has dropped significantly since the beginning of the year. Mr. Hall reports that the drop is largely due to a lack of participation in class presentations and an inability to complete tests and quizzes. He has noticed that Marissa frequently asks to go to the nurse or is absent from class on the days when she is expected to give a presentation or complete a test or quiz. When Mr. Hall attempted to address his concerns with Marissa individually, she avoids eye contact, speaks very quietly, and begins picking at her fingernails. He has been in contact with Marissa's parents over email to inform them about her grades.

Dr. Lee refers to Eastport's schoolwide sources of behavioral data used to identify students at risk for social, emotional, or behavioral problems. She reviews Marissa's attendance data, her trips to the nurse's office, and the school climate survey response data, along with the list of flagged students to be discussed at the November data team meeting. Students who are absent and/or tardy at least 10 times are flagged to be considered for more intensive supports. Five or more trips to the nurse's office in a 30-day period trigger a parent meeting to discuss potential health concerns, including somatization. Items on the school climate survey related to risk behavior, isolation from adults and/or peers, and symptoms of depression or anxiety are flagged, and students who describe moderate to high levels of these indicators are placed on an at-risk list. Placement on this list triggers an SST meeting to review additional sources of extant data (e.g., attendance, grades, standardized test performance, or ODRs) and to determine whether the student requires small-group or individualized intervention.

Dr. Lee learns that Marissa was flagged across all data sources at the end of October. Although she did attend school most days, Marissa was absent from each of her classes at least 10 times between September and October. The school nurse indicated that Marissa came to her office at least twice per week, most frequently as a result of a headache or stomachache. Finally, Marissa endorsed responses on target items in the fall school climate survey that indicated social, emotional, or behavioral risk. Specifically, Marissa indicated that she feels sad in school and worries about many things, that she doesn't feel like she belongs, that she doesn't have someone at school with whom she can talk about personal problems or a teacher/other adult whom she can trust, and that she doesn't believe she can do well in school.

Based on these data alone and on district and school policies regarding student behavioral risk, Dr. Lee believes that she has enough information to determine that Marissa needs support beyond what is provided at the whole-school level. Dr. Lee schedules an SST meeting and invites Marissa's parents to inform them and the team of her findings and to discuss conducting additional screening methods. Marissa's general education teachers, guidance counselor, and assistant principal are also invited to attend as part of Marissa's SST during this process. After the school staff and Marissa's parents have a chance to discuss their concerns, Eastport High School's procedures require the student to be invited into the SST meeting so that they can share information, gain experience in self-advocacy, and contribute to the intervention plan.

During the meeting, Marissa's parents also express concerns that her grades have dropped, despite prior evidence indicating that she is capable of achieving excellent marks in advanced-level courses. They also note that she often appears tired, frequently bites her nails, is afraid of being alone, and often worries about bad things happening (e.g., someone breaking into their home). When asked about the duration of these symptoms, Marissa's parents note that they have become worse over the last 6 weeks but could not identify a reason why this might be the case. Mr. Hall reiterates his concerns to the team, which are validated by Marissa's other teachers who have observed similar behavior. Mrs. Okoye, Marissa's guidance counselor, notes that Marissa had not come to see her voluntarily and did not report any challenges during their check-in meeting at the end of September.

At this point, Marissa is invited into the meeting, is given a summary of the team discussion and is asked to work with the team to develop next steps. Although it is clear that she needs additional supports and is exhibiting signs related to internalizing problems, the team needs more information to develop an effective intervention plan. Before sharing her thoughts with the team, Dr. Lee considers the available options for collecting the additional data to determine the appropriate direction for the intervention. She recognizes that the assessment tools must be flexible, while maintaining fidelity, given Marissa's variable attendance. The screening data will be used to determine the intensity of the intervention Marissa needs, as well as whether the existing tiered behavioral supports are appropriate. The methods to collect these data should be reliable and valid since they will help identify if existing supports are the right match for her needs or what other evidence-informed supports and subsequent resources (e.g., additional time, staff, and materials) are most appropriate.

Although extant data are flexible and don't require Marissa to be present, Dr. Lee has already analyzed and summarized the available extant data and obtained the degree of possible significant and/or useful information. Even though direct observation methods such as SDO or DBR may be useful, again given Marissa's variable attendance coupled with a lack of behavior challenges that are clearly observable, they likely are not the most efficient ways to obtain data on the problem. Dr. Lee realizes that, given the nature of the problem, behavior rating scales offer the most effective and efficient means for getting the necessary information. Since Marissa is in high school, she is able to complete self-report rating scales that will reveal information about her perception of the problem(s). Rating scales also offer an efficient method for obtaining data on the perceptions of Marissa's parents and teachers. A broadband rating scale can be used to identify more specific internalizing concerns, perhaps followed by a narrowband rating scale, which can provide more information about these specific concerns.

Next, Dr. Lee schedules an individual meeting with Marissa to conduct an informal student interview, as well as to have her complete a broadband behavior rating scale, the BASC-3 Self-Report of Personality for Adolescents (SRP), that provides comprehensive screening across several areas, including internalizing concerns. Dr. Lee also sends the teacher and parent versions of these scales to Marissa's teachers and parents to obtain information about their perceptions. In order to analyze and summarize the data from this initial rating scale, Dr. Lee scores each form to obtain standardized T-scores for each rater and then compares them for similarities and differences. Across raters, Marissa's scores were elevated on the Internalizing Problems composite of the BASC-3, which includes scales related to anxiety, depression, and somatization. All three scales within the composite were elevated, but the anxiety scale was elevated to a level that is clinically significant, meaning that the T-score is above 70.

Given the picture painted by these data, Dr. Lee asks Marissa and her parents to complete a narrowband rating scale, the Multidimensional Anxiety Scale for Children, Second Edition (MASC-2), to gain more specific information about the nature of her symptoms of anxiety. This rating scale provides an overall score that indicates anxiety probability, with scales assessing separation anxiety and phobias, social anxiety, generalized anxiety, obsessions and compulsions, physical symptoms, and harm avoidance. Furthermore, the social anxiety scale has two subscales related to humiliation/rejection and performance fears, and the physical symptoms scale also has two subscales that measure panic and tension/restlessness. On the narrowband rating scale, Marissa's self-report and her parents' T-scores for anxiety probability were again elevated. However, both raters' scores were specifically elevated on the social anxiety scale and subscales related to humiliation/rejection and performance fears.

5. What decisions can I make using these data?	
5a. Is an intervention needed?	5b. Is the intervention working?
Yes—compared to norm/reference groups, Marissa demonstrated elevated levels of internalizing concerns.	*N/A*

FIGURE 8.6. Completed Example Step 5 of the Data-Based Decision-Making Worksheet for Behavioral Assessment.

At this point, Dr. Lee and the SST meet to review the screening results. Because the team used reliable methods to conduct additional screening, these data enable them to make valid decisions regarding the appropriateness and focus of the intervention. The SST determines that the small-group interventions available at Eastport High School are not well matched to the needs of students struggling with social or performance anxiety. As a result, the team decides that Eastport's cognitive-behavioral therapy-based intervention at the individualized level offers the best fit for Marissa's needs. In order to effectively monitor Marissa's progress as she receives this individualized intervention, Dr. Lee suggests that Marissa be trained to self-complete a DBR-SIS (single-item scale) for anxiety. The team will also use extant data to monitor her progress in attendance, her visits to the school nurse, and her academic performance.

CONCLUDING COMMENTS

In this chapter, we introduced a framework for conducting behavioral assessment across contexts. We explained how to use this framework in your practice to identify the problem, select the best assessment tool to analyze the problem, and use data to make decisions about further assessment and intervention. To illustrate how to use the assessment decision-making tool, we presented case studies that employ behavioral assessment methods at the elementary, middle, and high school levels. Further, each case example demonstrates a practical example of engaging in behavioral assessment for various student social, emotional, and behavioral concerns. We hope that this book has given you a foundational understanding of behavioral assessment methods, the tools to help you conduct behavioral assessment within your school or district, and resources that provide additional information about each method.

Data-Based Decision-Making Worksheet
for Behavioral Assessment

1. What is the problem?		
1a. Identify the problem.	1b. Define the problem.	1c. At what level does the problem need to be solved?

2. Which data do I need?			
2a. What is the purpose of assessment?	2b. Which tools are best matched to the problem?	2c. What decisions will be made using these data?	2d. What resources are available to collect the data?

3. Which methods can I use with fidelity to answer questions?			
Review of extant data	Systematic Direct Observation	Direct Behavior Ratings	Rating scales

4. What are the data saying?	
4a. How can I summarize the data?	4b. How can I analyze the data?

5. What decisions can I make using these data?	
5a. Is intervention needed?	5b. Is the intervention working?

References

Achenbach, T. M., McConaughy, S. H., & Howell, C. T. (1987). Child/adolescent behavioral and emotional problems: Implications of cross-informant correlations for situational specificity. *Psychological Bulletin, 101,* 213–232.

American Psychiatric Association. (2013). *Diagnostic and statistical manual of mental disorders* (5th ed.). Arlington, VA: Author.

Angello, L. M., Volpe, R. J., Gureasko-Moore, S. P., Gureasko-Moore, D. P., Nebrig, M. R., Ota, K., et al. (2003). Assessment of attention deficit hyperactivity disorder: An evaluation of six published rating scales. *School Psychology Review, 32,* 241–262.

Appleton, J. J., Christenson, S. L., Kim, D., & Reschly, A. L. (2006). Measuring cognitive and psychological engagement: Validation of the Student Engagement Instrument. *Journal of School Psychology, 44,* 427–445.

Ashdown, D. M., & Bernard, M. E. (2012). Can explicit instruction in social and emotional learning skills benefit the social-emotional development, well-being, and academic achievement of young children? *Early Childhood Education Journal, 39,* 397–405.

Bambara, L. M., & Kern, L. (Eds.). (2005). *Individualized supports for students with problem behaviors: Designing positive behavior plans.* New York: Guilford Press.

Barton, C. J., & Ascione, F. R. (1984). Direct observation. In T. H. Ollendick & M. Hersen (Eds.), *Child behavior assessment* (pp. 166–194). New York: Pergamon Press.

Bear, G. G., Yang, C., & Pasipanodya, E. (2015). Assessing school climate: Validation of a brief measure of the perceptions of parents. *Journal of Psychoeducational Assessment, 33,* 115–129.

Blood, E., Johnson, J. W., Ridenour, L., Simmons, K., & Crouch, S. (2011). Using an iPod Touch to teach social and self-management skills to an elementary student with emotional/behavioral disorders. *Education and Treatment of Children, 34,* 299–322.

Bottiani, J. H., Bradshaw, C. P., & Mendelson, T. (2017). A multilevel examination of racial disparities in high school discipline: Black and white adolescents' perceived equity, school belonging, and adjustment problems. *Journal of Educational Psychology, 109,* 532–545.

Bradshaw, C. P., Waasdorp, T. E., Debnam, K. J., & Johnson, S. L. (2014). Measuring school climate in high schools: A focus on safety, engagement, and the environment. *Journal of School Health, 84,* 593–604.

Bramlett, R. K. (1993). *The preschool observation code.* Unpublished manuscript, University of Central Arkansas, Conway, AR.

Bransford, J., & Stein, B. (1984). *The ideal problem solver: A guide for improving thinking, learning, and creativity.* New York: Freeman.

Briesch, A. M., & Briesch, J. M. (2016). Meta-analysis of behavioral self-management interventions in single-case research. *School Psychology Review, 45,* 3–18.

Briesch, A. M., Briesch, J. M., & Mahoney, C. (2014). Reported use and acceptability of self-management interventions to target behavioral outcomes. *Contemporary School Psychology, 18,* 222–231.

Briesch, A. M., & Chafouleas, S. M. (2009). Review and analysis of literature on self-management interventions to promote appropriate classroom behaviors (1988–2008). *School Psychology Quarterly, 24,* 106–118.

Briesch, A. M., Chafouleas, S. M., Neugebauer, S. R., & Riley-Tillman, T. C. (2013). Assessing influences on intervention use: Revision of the Usage Rating Profile-Intervention. *Journal of School Psychology, 51,* 81–96.

Briesch, A. M., Chafouleas, S. M., & Riley-Tillman, T. C. (2010). Generalizability and dependability of behavior assessment methods to estimate academic engagement: A comparison of systematic direct observation and direct behavior rating. *School Psychology Review, 39,* 408–421.

Briesch, A. M., Chafouleas, S. M., & Riley-Tillman, T. C. (2016). *Direct Behavior Rating: Linking assessment, communication, and intervention.* New York: Guilford Press.

Briesch, A. M., Volpe, R. J., & Floyd, R. G. (2018). *School-based observation: A practical guide to assessing student behavior.* New York: Guilford Press.

Burns, M. K., & Gibbons, K. (2012). *Implementing response-to-intervention in elementary and secondary schools.* New York: Taylor & Francis.

Campbell, D. T., & Stanley, J. C. (1966). *Experimental and quasi-experimental designs for research.* Skokie, IL: Rand McNally.

Cavanaugh, B. (2016). A preliminary investigation examining the use of minor discipline referral data to identify students at risk for behavioral difficulties: Observations within systems of schoolwide positive behavior interventions and supports. *Journal of Applied School Psychology, 32,* 354–366.

Chafouleas, S. M. (2011). Direct Behavior Rating: A review of the issues and research in its development. *Education and Treatment of Children, 34,* 575–591.

Chafouleas, S. M., Briesch, A. M., Riley-Tillman, T. C., Christ, T. J., Black, A. C., & Kilgus, S. P. (2010). An investigation of the generalizability and dependability of Direct Behavior Rating Single Item Scales (DBR-SIS) to measure academic engagement and disruptive behavior of middle school students. *Journal of School Psychology, 48,* 219–246.

Chafouleas, S. M., Christ, T. J., Riley-Tillman, T. C., Briesch, A. M., & Chanese, J. A. (2007a). Generalizability and dependability of Direct Behavior Ratings (DBRs) to assess social behavior of preschoolers. *School Psychology Review, 36,* 63–79.

Chafouleas, S. M., Jaffery, R., Riley-Tillman, T. C., Christ, T. J., & Sen, R. (2013a). The impact of target, wording, and duration on rating accuracy for Direct Behavior Rating. *Assessment for Effective Intervention, 39,* 39–53.

Chafouleas, S. M., Kilgus, S. P., & Hernandez, P. (2009). Using Direct Behavior Rating (DBR) to screen for school social risk. *Assessment for Effective Intervention, 34,* 214–223.

Chafouleas, S. M., Kilgus, S. P., Jaffery, R., Riley-Tillman, T. C., Welsh, M., & Christ, T. J. (2013b). Direct Behavior Rating as a school-based screener for elementary and middle grades. *Journal of School Psychology, 51,* 367–385.

Chafouleas, S. M., Kilgus, S. P., Riley-Tillman, T. C., Jaffery, R., & Harrison, S. (2012). Preliminary evaluation of various training components on accuracy of Direct Behavior Ratings. *Journal of School Psychology, 50,* 317–334.

Chafouleas, S. M., & Miller, F. G. (2015, February). *Direct Behavior Rating: Use in targeted screening of student behavior.* Presented at the annual convention of the National Association of School Psychologists, Orlando, FL.

Chafouleas, S. M., Riley-Tillman, T. C., Jaffery, R., Miller, F. G., & Harrison, S. E. (2015). Preliminary investigation of the impact of a web-based module on Direct Behavior Rating accuracy. *School Mental Health, 7,* 92–104.

Chafouleas, S. M., Riley-Tillman, T. C., & McDougal, J. (2002). Good, bad, or in-between: How does the daily behavior report card rate? *Psychology in the Schools, 39,* 157–169.

Chafouleas, S. M., Riley-Tillman, T. C., Sassu, K. A., LaFrance, M. J., & Patwa, S. S. (2007b). Daily behavior report cards (DBRCs): An investigation of consistency of on-task data across raters and method. *Journal of Positive Behavior Interventions, 9,* 30–37.

Christ, T. J., Riley-Tillman, T. C., & Chafouleas, S. M. (2009). Foundation for the development and use of Direct Behavior Rating (DBR) to assess and evaluate student behavior. *Assessment for Effective Intervention, 34,* 201–213.

Christ, T. J., Riley-Tillman, T. C., Chafouleas, S. M., & Boice, C. H. (2010). Direct Behavior Rating (DBR): Generalizability and dependability across raters and observations. *Educational and Psychological Measurement, 70,* 825–843.

Christenson, S. L., Reschly, A. L., & Wylie, C. (2012). *Handbook of research on student engagement.* New York: Springer.

Cohen, J., McCabe, E. M., Michelli, N. M., & Pickeral, T. (2009). School climate: Research, policy, practice, and teacher education. *Teachers College Record, 111,* 180–213.

Cole, C. L., & Bambara, L. M. (1992). Issues surrounding the use of self-management interventions in the schools. *School Psychology Review, 21,* 193–201.

Collier-Meek, M. A., Fallon, L. M., Sanetti, L. M., & Maggin, D. M. (2013). Focus on implementation: Assessing and promoting treatment fidelity. *Teaching Exceptional Children, 45,* 52–59.

Cone, J. D. (1978). The behavioral assessment grid (BAG): A conceptual framework and a taxonomy. *Behavior Therapy, 9,* 882–888.

Conklin, C. G., Kamps, D., & Wills, H. (2017). The effects of class-wide function-related intervention teams (CW-FIT) on students' prosocial classroom behaviors. *Journal of Behavioral Education, 26,* 75–100.

Conley, L., Marchant, M., & Caldarella, P. (2014). A comparison of teacher perceptions and research-based categories of student behavior difficulties. *Education, 134,* 439–451.

Cooper, J. O., Heron, T. E., & Heward, W. L. (2007). *Applied behavior analysis* (2nd ed.). Upper Saddle River, NJ: Pearson.

Crabtree, T., Alber-Morgan, S. R., & Konrad, M. (2010). The effects of self-monitoring of story elements on the reading comprehension of high school seniors with learning disabilities. *Education and Treatment of Children, 33,* 187–203.

Crocker, L., & Algina, J. (2008). *Introduction to classical and modern test theory.* Mason, OH: Cengage.

Dart, E. H., & Radley, K. C. (2017). The impact of ordinate scaling on the visual analysis of single-case data. *Journal of School Psychology, 63,* 105–118.

De Los Reyes, A., & Kazdin, A. E. (2005). Informant discrepancies in the assessment of childhood psychopathology: A critical review, theoretical framework, and recommendations for further study. *Psychological Bulletin, 131,* 483–509.

Dirks, M. A., De Los Reyes, A., Briggs-Gowan, M., Cella, D., & Wakschlag, L. S. (2012). Annual Research Review: Embracing not erasing contextual variability in children's behavior: Theory and utility in the selection and use of methods and informants in developmental psychopathology. *Journal of Child Psychology and Psychiatry, 53,* 558–574.

DuPaul, G. J., Power, T. J., Anastopoulos, A. D., & Reid, R. (2016). *ADHD Rating Scale—5 for children and adolescents: Checklist, norms, and clinical interpretation.* New York: Guilford Press.

Erchul, W. P., & Martens, B. K. (2010). *School consultation: Conceptual and empirical bases of practice* (3rd ed.). New York: Springer.

Fabiano, G. A., Pyle, K., Kelty, M. B., & Parham, B. R. (2017). Progress monitoring using Direct Behavior Rating Single Item Scales in a multiple-baseline design study of the Daily Report Card intervention. *Assessment for Effective Intervention, 43,* 21–33.

Fall, A., & Roberts, G. (2012). High school dropouts: Interactions between social context, self-perceptions, school engagement, and school dropout. *Journal of Adolescence, 35,* 787–798.

Ferguson, T. D., Briesch, A. M., Volpe, R. J., & Daniels, B. (2012). The influence of observation length on the dependability of data. *School Psychology Quarterly, 27,* 187–197.

Finn, J. D., & Zimmer, K. S. (2012). Student engagement: Why does it matter? In S. L. Christenson, A. L. Reschly, & C. Wylie (Eds.), *Handbook of research on student engagement* (pp. 97–131). New York: Springer.

Flannery, K. B., Fenning, P., Kato, M. M., & McIntosh, K. (2014). Effects of school-wide positive behavioral interventions and supports and fidelity of implementation on problem behavior in high schools. *School Psychology Quarterly, 29,* 111–124.

Frick, P. J., Barry, C. T., & Kamphaus, R. W. (2010). *Clinical assessment of child and adolescent personality and behavior* (3rd ed.). New York: Springer.

Fuchs, D., & Fuchs, L. S. (2017). Critique of the national evaluation of response to intervention: A case for simpler frameworks. *Exceptional Children, 83,* 255–268.

Gadow, K. D., Sprafkin, J., & Nolan, E. E. (1996). *ADHD School Observation Code.* Stony Brook, NY: Checkmate Plus.

Ganz, J. B. (2008). Self-monitoring across age and ability levels: Teaching students to implement their own positive behavioral interventions. *Preventing School Failure, 53,* 39–48.

Gettinger, M., & Ball, C. (2008). Best practices in increasing academic engaged time. In A. Thomas & J. Grimes (Eds.), *Best practices in school psychology V* (pp. 1043–1058). Bethesda, MD: National Association of School Psychologists.

Gettinger, M., & Walter, M. J. (2012). Classroom strategies to enhance academic engaged time. In S. L. Christenson, A. L. Reschly, & C. Wylie (Eds.), *Handbook of research on student engagement* (pp. 653–673). New York: Springer.

Gilliam, W. S. (2005). *Prekindergarteners left behind: Expulsion rates in state prekindergarten programs.* New York: Foundation for Child Development.

Gion, C., McIntosh, K., & Smolkowski, K. (2018). Examination of American Indian/Alaska Native school discipline disproportionality using the vulnerable decision points approach. *Behavioral Disorders, 44,* 40–52.

Girvan, E. J., Gion, C., McIntosh, K., & Smolkowski, K. (2017). The relative contribution of subjective office referrals to racial disproportionality in school discipline. *School Psychology Quarterly, 32,* 392–404.

Glover, T. A., & Albers, C. A. (2007). Considerations for evaluating universal screening assessments. *Journal of School Psychology, 45,* 117–135.

Gresham, F. M., & Elliott, S. N. (2008). *Social skills improvement system rating scales.* Minneapolis, MN: Pearson.

Gulchak, D. J. (2008). Using a mobile handheld computer to teach a student with an emotional and behavioral disorder to self-monitor attention. *Education and Treatment of Children, 31,* 567–581.

Harrison, J. R., Vannest, K., Davis, J., & Reynolds, C. (2012). Common problem behaviors of children and adolescents in general education classrooms in the United States. *Journal of Emotional and Behavioral Disorders, 20,* 55–64.

Harrison, S. E., Riley-Tillman, T. C., & Chafouleas, S. M. (2014). Direct Behavior Rating: Considerations for rater accuracy. *Canadian Journal of School Psychology, 29,* 3–20.

Hawken, L. S., Crone, D. A., Bundock, K., & Horner, R. H. (2020). *Responding to problem behavior in schools: The check-in, check-out intervention* (3rd ed.). New York: Guilford Press.

Hintze, J. M., Christ, T. J., & Methe, S. A. (2006). Curriculum-based assessment. *Psychology in the Schools, 43,* 45–56.

Hintze, J. M., Volpe, R. J., & Shapiro, E. S. (2002). Best practices in the systematic direct observation of student behavior. In A. Thomas & J. Grimes (Eds.), *Best practices in school psychology* (4th ed., pp. 993–1006). Bethesda, MD: National Association of School Psychologists.

Hoff, K. E., & Sawka-Miller, K. D. (2010). Self-management interventions. In G. Gimpel Peacock, R. A. Ervin, E. J. Daly, & K. W. Merrell (Eds.), *Practical handbook of school psychology: Effective practices for the 21st century* (pp. 337–352). New York: Guilford Press.

Hosp, M. K., Hosp, J. L., & Howell, K. W. (2016). *The ABCs of CBM: A practical guide to curriculum-based measurement* (2nd ed.). New York: Guilford Press.

Howell, K. W., Hosp, M. K., Hosp, J. L., & Morehead, M. K. (2007). *Multilevel Academic Skills Inventory—Revised.* Bellingham, WA: Western Washington University, Applied Research and Development Center.

Howell, K. W., & Nolet, V. (2000). *Curriculum-based evaluation: Teaching and decision making* (3rd ed.). Belmont, CA: Wadsworth.

Huang, F. L., Cornell, D. G., Konold, T., Meyer, J. P., Lacey, A., Nekvash, E. K., et al. (2015). Multi-level factor structure and concurrent validity of the teacher version of the authoritative school climate survey. *Journal of School Health, 85,* 843–851.

Huber, C., & Rietz, C. (2015). Behavior assessment using Direct Behavior Rating (DBR): A study on the criterion validity of DBR single-item-scales. *Insights into Learning Disabilities, 12,* 73–90.

Hulac, D. M., & Briesch, A. M. (2017). *Evidence-based strategies for effective classroom management.* New York: Guilford Press.

Institute of Medicine. (2012). Best care at lower cost: The path to continuously learning health care in America. Retrieved July 20, 2019, from *https://nam.edu/wp-content/uploads/2017/12/Briefing-Book_Combined.pdf.*

Jenson, W. R., Rhode, G., & Reavis, H. K. (2009). *The tough kid tool box.* Eugene, OR: Ancora.

Johnson, A. H., Chafouleas, S. M., & Briesch, A. M. (2017). Dependability of data derived from time sampling methods with multiple observation targets. *School Psychology Quarterly, 32,* 22–34.

Johnson, A. H., Goldberg, T. S., Hinant, R. L., & Couch, L. K. (2019). Trends and practices in functional behavior assessments completed by school psychologists. *Psychology in the Schools, 56,* 360–377.

Johnson, A. H., Miller, F. G., Chafouleas, S. M., Welsh, M. E., Riley-Tillman, T. C., & Fabiano, G. A. (2016). Evaluating the technical adequacy of DBR-SIS in triannual behavioral screening: A multisite investigation. *Journal of School Psychology, 54,* 39–57.

Joseph, L. M., & Eveleigh, E. L. (2011). A review of the effects of self-monitoring on reading performance of students with disabilities. *Journal of Special Education, 45,* 43–53.

Juvonen, J., Espinoza, G., & Knifsend, C. (2012). The role of peer relationships in student academic and extracurricular engagement. In S. L. Christenson, A. L. Reschly, & C. Wylie (Eds.), *Handbook of research on student engagement* (pp. 387–401). New York: Springer.

Kanfer, F. H., & Gaelick-Buys, L. (1991). Self-management methods. In F. H. Kanfer & A. P. Goldstein (Eds.), *Pergamon general psychology series: Vol. 52. Helping people change: A textbook of methods* (p. 305–360). New York: Pergamon Press.

Kazdin, A. E. (1982). *Single-case research designs: Methods for clinical and applied settings.* New York: Oxford University Press.

Kehle, T. J., Clark, E., & Jenson, W. R. (1986). Effectiveness of self-observation with disordered elementary school children. *School Psychology Review, 15,* 289–295.

Kilgus, S. P., Chafouleas, S. M., Riley-Tillman, T. C., & Welsh, M. E. (2012). Direct Behavior Rating scales as screeners: A preliminary investigation of diagnostic accuracy in elementary school. *School Psychology Quarterly, 27,* 41–50.

Kilgus, S. P., Riley-Tillman, T. C., Chafouleas, S. M., Christ, T. J., & Welsh, M. E. (2014). Direct Behavior Rating as a school-based universal screener: Replication across sites. *Journal of School Psychology, 52,* 63–82.

Kilgus, S. P., Riley-Tillman, T. C., Stichter, J. P., & Schoemann, A. M. (2016). Reliability of Direct Behavior Ratings—Social Competence (DBR-SC) data: How many ratings are necessary? *School Psychology Quarterly, 31,* 431–442.

Kilgus, S. P., Riley-Tillman, T. C., Stichter, J. P., Schoemann, A. M., & Owens, S. (2019). Examining the concurrent criterion-related validity of Direct Behavior Rating: Single Item Scales with students with social competence deficits. *Assessment for Effective Intervention, 44*(2), 123–134.

Konrad, M., Fowler, C. H., Walker, A. R., Test, D. W., & Wood, W. M. (2007). Effects of self-determination interventions on the academic skills of students with learning disabilities. *Learning Disability Quarterly, 30,* 89–113.

Kosterman, R., Hawkins, J. D., Mason, W. A., Herrenkohl, T. I., Lengua, L. J., & McCauley, E. (2010). Assessment of behavior problems in childhood and adolescence as predictors of early adult depression. *Journal of Psychopathology and Behavioral Assessment, 32,* 118–127.

Koth, C. W., Bradshaw, C. P., & Leaf, P. J. (2008). A multilevel study of predictors of student perceptions of school climate: The effect of classroom-level factors. *Journal of Educational Psychology, 100,* 96–104.

Kovacs, M. (2011). *Children's Depression Inventory* (2nd ed.). North Tonawanda, NY: Multi-Health Systems.

Kratochwill, T. R. (1978). Foundations of time-series research. In T. R. Kratochwill (Ed.), *Single-subject research: Strategies for evaluating change.* New York: Academic Press.

Kratochwill, T. R., & Bergan, J. R. (1990). *Behavioral consultation in applied settings: An individual guide.* New York: Springer.

Kratochwill, T. R., Hitchcock, J., Horner, R. H., Levin, J. R., Odom, S. L., Rindskopf, D. M., et al. (2010). Single case designs technical documentation. Retrieved from *http://ies.ed.gov/ncee/wwc/pdf/wwc_scd.pdf.*

Kratochwill, T. R., Sheridan, S. M., Carlson, J. S., & Lasecki, K. L. (1999). Advances in behavioral assessment. In C. Reynolds & T. Gutkin (Eds.), *The handbook of school psychology* (3rd ed., pp. 350–382). New York: Wiley.

Lane, K. L., Oakes, W. P., Carter, E. W., & Messenger, M. (2014). Examining behavioral risk and academic performance for students transitioning from elementary to middle school. *Journal of Positive Behavior Interventions, 17,* 39–49.

La Salle, T., Peshak George, H., McCoach, D. B., Polk, T., & Evanovich, L. L. (2018). An examination of school climate, victimization, and mental health problems among middle school students self-identifying with emotional and behavioral disorders. *Behavioral Disorders, 43,* 383–392.

LaRusso, M. D., Romer, D., & Selman, R. L. (2008). Teachers as builders of respectful school climates: Implications for adolescent drug use norms and depressive symptoms in high school. *Journal of Youth and Adolescence, 37,* 386–398.

LeBel, T. J., Kilgus, S. P., Briesch, A. M., & Chafouleas, S. M. (2010). The impact of training on the accuracy of teacher-completed Direct Behavior Ratings (DBRs). *Journal of Positive Behavior Interventions, 12,* 55–63.

Maggin, D. M., & Bruhn, A. (2018). Evidence-based assessment and single-case research: A commentary for the special issue on Direct Behavior Ratings. *Assessment for Effective Intervention, 43,* 71–78.

Mandinach, E. B. (2012). A perfect time for data use: Using data-driven decision making to inform practice. *Educational Psychologist, 47,* 71–85.

March, J. S. (2013). *Multidimensional Anxiety Scale for Children* (2nd ed.). Toronto, ON, Canada: Multi-Health Systems.

Marks, H. M. (2000). Student engagement in instructional activity: Patterns in the elementary, middle, and high school years. *American Educational Research Journal, 37*, 153–184.

Martinez, A., McMahon, S. D., & Treger, S. (2016). Individual- and school-level predictors of student office disciplinary referrals. *Journal of Emotional and Behavioral Disorders, 24*, 30–41.

Masten, A. S., Roisman, G. I., Long, J. D., Burt, K. B., Obradovic, J., Riley, J. R., et al. (2005). Developmental cascades: Linking academic achievement and externalizing and internalizing symptoms over 20 years. *Developmental Psychology, 41*, 733–746.

Matejka, J., & Fitzmaurice, G. (2017). The datasaurus dozen—same stats, different graphs: Generating datasets with varied appearance and identical statistics through simulated annealing. Retrieved from *www.autodeskresearch.com/publications/samestats*.

McIntosh, K., Campbell, A. K., Russell Carter, D., & Zumbo, B. D. (2009). Concurrent validity of office discipline referrals and cut points used in schoolwide positive behavior support. *Behavioral Disorders, 34*, 100–113.

McIntosh, K., Girvan, E. J., Horner, R. H., & Smolkowski, K. (2014). Education not incarceration: A conceptual model for reducing racial and ethnic disproportionality in school discipline. *Journal of Applied Research on Children, 5*, 1–22.

Merrell, K. W. (2000). Informant reports: Theory and research in using child behavior rating scales in school settings. In E. S. Shapiro & T. R. Kratochwill (Eds.), *Behavioral assessment in schools: Theory, research, and clinical foundations* (pp. 233–256). New York: Guilford Press.

Merrell, K. W. (2003). *Behavioral, social, and emotional assessment of children and adolescents* (2nd ed.). Mahwah, NJ: Erlbaum.

Messick, S. (1995). Validity of psychological assessment: Validation of inferences from persons' responses and performances as scientific inquiry into score meaning. *American Psychologist, 50*, 741–749.

Miller, F. G., Chafouleas, S. M., Riley-Tillman, T. C., & Fabiano, G. A. (2014a). Teacher perceptions of the usability of school-based behavior assessments. *Behavioral Disorders, 39*, 201–210.

Miller, F. G., Cohen, D., Chafouleas, S. M., Riley-Tillman, T. C., Welsh, M. E., & Fabiano, G. A. (2015). A comparison of measures to screen for social, emotional, and behavioral risk. *School Psychology Quarterly, 30*, 184–196.

Miller, F. G., Crovello, N., & Swenson, N. (2017c). Bridging the gap: Direct Behavior Rating–Single Item Scales. *Assessment for Effective Intervention, 43*, 60–63.

Miller, F. G., & Fabiano, G. A. (2017b). Direct Behavior Ratings: A feasible and effective progress monitoring approach for social and behavioral interventions. *Assessment for Effective Intervention, 43*, 3–5.

Miller, F. G., Patwa, S. S., & Chafouleas, S. M. (2014b). Using Direct Behavior Rating-Single Item Scales to assess student behavior within multi-tiered systems of support. *Journal of Special Education Leadership, 27*, 76–85.

Miller, F. G., Riley-Tillman, T. C., Chafouleas, S. M., & Schardt, A. A. (2017a). Direct Behavior Rating instrumentation: Evaluating the impact of scale formats. *Assessment for Effective Intervention, 42*, 119–126.

Molloy, L. E., Moore, J. E., Trail, J., Van Epps, J. J., & Hopfer, S. (2014). Understanding real-world implementation quality and "active ingredients" of PBIS. *Prevention Science, 14*, 593–605.

Nelson, J. R., Benner, G. J., Reid, R., Epstein, M. H., & Currin, D. (2002). An investigation of the convergent validity of office referrals with the Child Behavior Checklist Teacher Report Form. *Journal of Emotional and Behavioral Disorders, 10*, 181–189.

O'Brennan, L. M., Bradshaw, C. P., & Furlong, M. J. (2014). Influence of classroom and school climate on teacher perceptions of student problem behavior. *School Mental Health, 6*, 125–136.

Office of Civil Rights. (2017). *Civil rights data collection 2013–14* [Data file]. Retrieved from *https://ocrdata.ed.gov/downloads/projections/2013-14/Corporal-Punishment.xlsx.*

Oliver, R. M., & Reschly, D. J. (2010). Special education teacher preparation in classroom management: Implications for students with emotional and behavioral disorders. *Behavioral Disorders, 35,* 188–199.

O'Neill, R. E., Albin, R. W., Storey, K., Horner, R. H., & Sprague, J. R. (2014). *Functional assessment and program development for problem behavior: A practical handbook* (3rd ed.). Stamford, CT: Cengage Learning.

Pas, E. T., Bradshaw, C. P., & Mitchell, M. M. (2011). Examining the validity of office discipline referrals as an indicator of student behavior problems. *Psychology in the Schools, 48,* 541–555.

Patterson, G. R., Forgatch, M. S., Yoerger, K. L., & Stoolmiller, M. (1998). Variables that initiate and maintain an early-onset trajectory for juvenile offending. *Development and Psychopathology, 10,* 531–547.

Predy, L., McIntosh, K., & Frank, J. L. (2014). Utility of number and type of office discipline referrals in predicting chronic problem behavior in middle schools. *School Psychology Review, 43,* 472–489.

Pustejovsky, J. E., & Swan, D. M. (2015). Four methods for analyzing partial interval recording data, with application to single-case research. *Multivariate Behavioral Research, 50,* 365–380.

Reaves, S., McMahon, S. D., Duffy, S. N., & Ruiz, L. (2018). The test of time: A meta-analytic review of the relation between school climate and problem behavior. *Aggression and Violent Behavior, 39,* 100–108.

Reschly, A. L., & Christenson, S. L. (2012). Jingle, jangle, and conceptual haziness: Evolution and future directions of the engagement construct. In S. L. Christenson, A. L. Reschly, & C. Wylie (Eds.), *Handbook of research on student engagement* (pp. 3–19). New York: Springer.

Reynolds, C., & Kamphaus, R. W. (1992). *Behavior Assessment System for Children.* Circle Pines, MN: American Guidance Service.

Reynolds, C., & Kamphaus, R. W. (2015). *Behavior Assessment System for Children—Third Edition.* San Antonio, TX: Pearson.

Richards, S. B. (2018). *Single-subject research: Application in educational and clinical settings* (3rd ed.). Boston: Cengage Learning.

Riley-Tillman, T. C., Burns, M. K., & Kilgus, S. P. (2020). *Evaluating educational interventions: Single-case design for measuring response to intervention* (2nd ed.). New York: Guilford Press.

Riley-Tillman, T. C., Christ, T. J., Chafouleas, S. M., Boice, C. H., & Briesch, A. M. (2010). The impact of observation duration on the accuracy of data obtained from Direct Behavior Rating (DBR). *Journal of Positive Behavior Interventions, 13,* 119–129.

Riley-Tillman, T. C., Kalberer, S. M., & Chafouleas, S. M. (2005). Selecting the right tool for the job: A review of behavior monitoring tools used to assess student response to intervention. *California School Psychologist, 10,* 81–92.

Rock, M. L. (2005). Use of strategic self-monitoring to enhance academic engagement, productivity, and accuracy of students with and without exceptionalities. *Journal of Positive Behavior Interventions, 7,* 3–17.

Rogosa, D., & Ghandour, G. (1991). Statistical models for behavioral observations. *Journal of Educational Statistics, 16,* 157–252.

Salvia, J., Ysseldyke, J., & Witmer, S. (2017). *Assessment in special and inclusive education* (13th ed.). Boston: Cengage Learning.

Sandoval, J., & Echandia, A. (1994). Behavior Assessment System for Children. *Journal of School Psychology, 32,* 419–425.

Sanetti, L. M. H., & Collier-Meek, M. A. (2019). *Supporting successful interventions in schools: Tools to plan, evaluate, and sustain effective implementation.* New York: Guilford Press.

Saudargas, R. A. (1997). *State–Event Classroom Observation System (SECOS)*. Unpublished manuscript, University of Tennessee–Knoxville, Knoxville, TN.

Saudargas, R. A., & Lentz, F. E. (1986). Estimating percent of time and rate via direct observation: A suggested observational procedure and format. *School Psychology Review, 15*, 36–48.

Sayal, K., Washbrook, E., & Propper, C. (2015). Childhood behavior problems and academic outcomes in adolescence: Longitudinal population-based study. *Journal of the American Academy of Child and Adolescent Psychiatry, 5*, 360–368.

Schlientz, M. D., Riley-Tillman, T. C., Briesch, A. M., Walcott, C. M., & Chafouleas, S. M. (2009). The impact of training on the accuracy of Direct Behavior Ratings (DBR). *School Psychology Quarterly, 24*, 73–83.

Severson, H. H., Walker, H. M., Hope-Doolittle, J., Kratochwill, T. R., & Gresham, F. M. (2007). Proactive, early screening to detect behaviorally at-risk students: Issues, approaches, emerging innovations, and professional practices. *Journal of School Psychology, 45*, 193–223.

Shapiro, E. S. (2011). *Academic skills problems—fourth edition workbook*. New York: Guilford Press.

Sheridan, S. M., Swanger-Gagne, M., Welch, G. W., Kwon, K., & Garbacz, S. A. (2009). Fidelity measurement in consultation: Psychometric issues and preliminary examination. *School Psychology Review, 38*, 476–495.

Silva, F. (1993). *Psychometric foundations and behavioral assessment*. Newbury Park, CA: SAGE.

Sims, W. A., Riley-Tillman, C., & Cohen, D. R. (2017). Formative assessment using Direct Behavior Ratings: Evaluating intervention effects of Daily Behavior Report Cards. *Assessment for Effective Intervention, 43*, 6–20.

Smith, R. L., Eklund, K., & Kilgus, S. P. (2018). Concurrent validity and sensitivity to change of Direct Behavior Rating Single-Item Scales (DBR-SIS) within an elementary sample. *School Psychology Quarterly, 33*, 83–93.

Smith, S. R. (2007). Making sense of multiple informants in child and adolescent psychopathology: A guide for clinicians. *Journal of Psychoeducational Assessment, 25*, 139–149.

Splett, J. W., George, M. W., Zaheer, I., Weist, M. D., Evans, S. W., & Kern, L. (2018). Symptom profiles and mental health services received among referred adolescents. *School Mental Health, 10*, 96–110.

Steege, M. W., Davin, T., & Hathaway, M. (2001). Reliability and accuracy of a performance-based behavioral recording procedure. *School Psychology Review, 30*, 252–261.

Suen, H. K., & Ary, D. (1989). *Analyzing quantitative behavioral observation data*. Hillsdale, NJ: Erlbaum.

Tawney, J., & Gast, D. (1984). *Single subject research in special education*. Columbus, OH: Merrill.

Thapa, A., Cohen, J., Guffey, S., & Higgins-D'Alessandro, A. (2013). A review of school climate research. *Review of Educational Research, 83*, 357–385.

Thompson, A. M. (2014). A randomized trial of the Self-Management Training and Regulation Strategy for disruptive students. *Research on Social Work Practice, 24*, 414–427.

Tufte, E. R. (1997). *Visual and statistical thinking: Displays of evidence for making decisions* (Vol. 12). Cheshire, CT: Graphics Press.

U.S. Department of Education. (2005). Special analysis 2005—mobility in the teacher workforce. Retrieved from *https://nces.ed.gov/pubs2005/2005094_Analysis.pdf*.

U.S. Department of Education, Office of Planning, Evaluation and Policy Development. (2011). *Teachers' ability to use data to inform instruction: Challenges and supports*. Washington, DC: Author.

U.S. Department of Health and Human Services, New Freedom Commission on Mental Health. (2003). Achieving the promise: Transforming mental health care in America: Final report (DHHS Pub. No. SMA-03-3832). Retrieved from *https://govinfo.library.unt.edu/mentalhealth-commission/reports/FinalReport/downloads/downloads.html*.

U.S. Government Accountability Office. (2018). Discipline disparities for Black students, boys, and students with disabilities (GAO-18-258). Retrieved from *www.gao.gov/products/GAO-18-258*.

Van der Kleij, F. M., Vermeulen, J. A., Schildkamp, K., & Eggen, T. J. H. M. (2015). Integrating data-based decision making, assessment for learning and diagnostic testing in formative assessment. *Assessment in Education: Principles, Policy, and Practice, 23*, 324–343.

VanDerHeyden, A. M., & Burns, M. K. (2017). Four dyslexia screening myths that cause more harm than good in preventing reading failure and what you can do instead. *Communique, 45*(7), 1–26.

Vespa, J., Armstrong, D. M., & Medina, L. (2018). *Demographic turning points for the United States: Population projections for 2020 to 2060* (Current population reports, P25-1144). Washington, DC: U.S. Census Bureau.

Volk, D. T., Koriakin, T. A., Auerbach, E., Chafouleas, S. M., & Riley-Tillman, C. (2018, February). *DBR Connect: Using technology to enhance screening and progress monitoring.* Presented at the annual conference of the National Association of School Psychologists, Chicago, IL.

Volpe, R. J., & Briesch, A. M. (2012). Generalizability and dependability of single-item and multi-item direct behavior rating scales for engagement and disruptive behavior. *School Psychology Review, 31*, 246–261.

Volpe, R. J., Briesch, A. M., & Chafouleas, S. M. (2010). Linking screening for emotional and behavioral problems to problem-solving efforts: An adaptive model of behavioral assessment. *Assessment for Effective Intervention, 35*, 240–244.

Volpe, R. J., & Gadow, K. D. (2010). Creating abbreviated rating scales to monitor classroom inattention-overactivity, aggression, and peer conflict: Reliability, validity, and treatment sensitivity. *School Psychology Review, 39*, 350–363.

von der Embse, N. P., Scott, E., & Kilgus, S. P. (2015). Sensitivity to change and concurrent validity of Direct Behavior Ratings for academic anxiety. *School Psychology Quarterly, 30*, 244–259.

Wagner, M., Friend, M., Bursuck, W. D., Kutash, K., Duchnowski, A. J., Sumi, W. C., et al. (2006). Educating students with emotional disturbances: A national perspective on school programs and services. *Journal of Emotional and Behavioral Disorders, 14*(1), 12–30.

Wagner, M., Newman, L., Cameto, R., Garza, N., & Levine, P. (2005). *After high school: A first look at the post-school experiences of youth with disabilities* [A report from the National Longitudinal Transition Study-2 (NLTS2)]. Menlo Park: SRI International.

Walker, H. M., Horner, R. H., Sugai, G., Bullis, M., Sprague, J. R., Bricker, D., et al. (1996). Integrated approaches to preventing antisocial behavior patterns among school-age children and youth. *Journal of Emotional and Behavioral Disorders, 4*, 193–256.

Walker, H. M., Ramsey, E., & Gresham, F. M. (2004). *Antisocial behavior in school: Evidence-based practices.* Belmont, CA: Wadsworth/Thomson Learning.

Walker, H. M., Severson, H. H., & Feil, E. G. (2014). *Systematic screening for behavior disorders* (2nd ed.). Eugene, OR: Pacific Northwest.

Wang, M., & Degol, J. L. (2016). School climate: A review of the construct, measurement, and impact on student outcomes. *Educational Psychology Review, 26*, 315–352.

Wang, M., & Fredricks, J. (2014). The reciprocal links between school engagement, youth problem behaviors, and school dropout during adolescence. *Child Development, 85*, 722–737.

Wang, M., & Holcombe, R. (2010). Adolescents' perceptions of school environment, engagement, and academic achievement in middle school. *American Educational Research Journal, 47*, 633–662.

Watkins, M. W., & Pacheco, M. (2000). Interobserver agreement in behavioral research: Importance and calculation. *Journal of Behavioral Education, 10*, 205–212.

Wei, R. C., Darling-Hammond, L., Andree, A., Richardson, N., & Orphanos, S. (2009). *Professional learning in the learning profession: A status report on teacher development in the United States and abroad.* Dallas, TX: National Staff Development Council.

Whitcomb, S. A. (2017). *Behavioral, social, and emotional assessment of children and adolescents.* London: Routledge.

White, N., La Salle, T., Ashby, J. S., & Meyers, J. (2014). A brief measure of adolescent perceptions of school climate. *School Psychology Quarterly, 29,* 349–359.

Wolery, M., Bailey, D. B., & Sugai, G. M. (1988). *Effective teaching: Principles and procedures of applied behavior analysis with exceptional students.* Boston: Allyn & Bacon.

Worthen, B. R., Borg, W. R., & White, K. R. (1993). *Measurement and evaluation in the schools: A practical guide.* White Plains, NY: Longman.

Zirkel, P. A. (2011). RTI confusion in the case laws and the legal commentary. *Learning Disability Quarterly, 34,* 242–247.

Zirkel, P. A. (2017). RTI and other approaches to SLD identification under the IDEA: A legal update. *Learning Disability Quarterly, 40,* 165–173.

Zirkel, P. A. (2018). Response to intervention: Lore v. law. *Learning Disability Quarterly, 41,* 113–118.

Zullig, K. J., Koopman, T. M., Patton, J. M., & Ubbes, V. A. (2010). School climate: Historical review, instrument development, and school assessment. *Journal of Psychoeducational Assessment, 28,* 139–152.

Index

Note. *f* or *t* following a page number indicates a figure or a table.